SO-AAK-757

Passionately Human, No Less Divine

"The task of
the ghetto is
to
destroy you, and
it does that
very rule

"The exception of the
rule", does not
exclude the
loss of so many."

Passionately Human, No Less Divine

RELIGION AND CULTURE IN BLACK CHICAGO, 1915–1952

Wallace D. Best

PRINCETON UNIVERSITY PRESS

PRINCETON AND OXFORD

Copyright © 2005 by Princeton University Press

Published by Princeton University Press, 41 William Street, Princeton,
New Jersey 08540

In the United Kingdom: Princeton University Press, 3 Market Place, Woodstock,
Oxfordshire OX20 1SY

All Rights Reserved

Second printing, and first paperback printing, 2008
Paperback ISBN: 978-0-691-13375-1

The Library of Congress has cataloged the cloth edition of this book as follows

Best, Wallace D. (Wallace DeNino)
  Passionately human, no less divine : religion and culture in Black Chicago, 1915–1952 /
Wallace D. Best.
  p. cm.
  Includes bibliographical references and index.
  ISBN 0-691-11578-8 (cloth: alk. paper)
  1. African Americans—Religion—Illinois—Chicago. 2. Chicago (Illinois)—Church
history—20th century. I. Title.

BR563.N4B47 2004
277.3'11'08208996073—dc22   2004053357

British Library Cataloging-in-Publication Data is available

This book has been composed in 10/12 Janson

Printed on acid-free paper. ∞

press.princeton.edu

Printed in the United States of America

10 9 8 7 6 5 4 3 2

Roger Lee Best
March 12, 1939–August 12, 1996

Audrey Katrina Best
September 28, 1940–August 31, 1998

Contents

Abbreviations

ABC	Associated Business Club
AME	African Methodist Episcopal
AMEZ	African Methodist Episcopal Zion
CME	Christian (Colored) Methodist Episcopal
COGIC	Church of God in Christ
FSA	Farm Security Administration
FWP	Federal Writers' Project
NBC	National Baptist Conference, U.S.A., Inc.
PCH	Parkway Community House
WPA	Works Progress Administration

Figures

Tables

Preface

IN GEOGRAPHIC TERMS, Washington, D.C. is a long way from Chicago. But for me this project about the religious culture of black Chicago actually began years ago in a little church that sat just outside the D.C. line. Faith Temple No. 2 Free Will Baptist Church, my home church, was a place of infinite fascination to me in my initial years there. My pastor, who also became "Godfather" to many members of the congregation, possessed great presence and charisma. His absence at any church event rendered it funereal; his attendance lifted even the most banal business meeting to a level of grand importance. Working from the black sermonic tradition and bedecked in clerical garb of regal colors, his preaching was narrative and performative. Very often he drew his text from the Old Testament, telling stories of men in the bellies of fishes and Hebrew children thrown into fires and surviving unharmed. But he always brought those ancient stories to bear upon the lives of the people in the congregation, who, as his fiery delivery suggested, didn't always "live right." Typically, as he neared the end of his sermon, he would punctuate every chanted sentence with a rapid inhale of breath and a thunderous slap of his palm on the pulpit Bible.

The congregation comprised some of the most memorable people I have ever encountered. Because they dressed in what appeared to be the finest clothes and often drove the latest model cars, I thought they were all rich. Sunday was a fashion extravaganza, with men in suits of Italian design accented by silk ties and gold or silver tie clips. The women's hats with plumes of feathers reaching toward the ceiling would, quite literally, take your breath away. Sequins and pearls speckled their dresses of taffeta, silk, cotton and suede. The march to the offering plate was nothing short of a parade. But my understanding of the congregants's daily lives increased the night I saw one of the women of the church "shouting" (holy dancing) in what appeared to be diamond-studded shoes. With her arms uplifted and those shoes catching and refracting the light, she appeared angelic or, at least, very prosperous. After accompanying my cousin, who offered this "sister" a ride home that evening however, I realized that I had gotten some things very wrong. The woman lived in a house in obvious, great disrepair in a neighborhood that bore the signs of years of poverty, neglect, and commercial divestment. Neither the woman with the "diamond shoes," nor anyone else in that congregation was rich in a material sense. Indeed, many of them were very poor. Most were workers of various sorts. They drove cabs, cleaned houses, and clerked in retail shops. They were janitors and bus drivers and factory workers. Many worked for the federal government, profiting from that post–World War II opening of civil service jobs to blacks.[1]

This was not a community tied together by status or wealth. The lack of status or wealth served, in part, to explain the inventive spiritual and organizational hierarchies within the church. Their frequent testimonials followed a pattern that acknowledged these hierarchies. The testimonies always gave "honor to God" first. Then they honored the bishop, other ministers, missionaries and evangelists and finally the "deacons, mothers, saints, and friends." ("Friends" comprised that catchall category that included invited guests or those "sinners" in the congregation, whom it was not proper to directly acknowledge during testimony.) These titles gave a sense of one's relationship to God on the one hand, and one's relationship to the rest of the congregation on the other. The titles and, to some degree, the fashionable clothes indicated that these ordinary working-class people were "somebodies" before God and "somebodies" within the context of a specific sacred space, despite the lack of wealth and position outside that space.

What tied this community together was a region in North Carolina specifically and the American South more broadly. Many of the core group who joined the Pastor when he established the church in the early 1960s had come from within a twenty-mile radius in Wayne, Wilson, and Johnson counties. They knew each other well, having come from the same working, familial, and church communities. The three women who met with the pastor of Faith Temple the night he established the church had known him since childhood. They knew him as the boy preacher who would preach to anyone willing to listen and who was so committed to gathering a congregation that he often held funerals for deceased chickens, dogs, and cats.[2] They, like him, had recently migrated north to build new lives in a strange, unfamiliar place.

Many others followed. The pattern of migration out of North Carolina and other areas in the South repeated itself so often that by the mid-1970s, when my family joined the congregation, Faith Temple was a church of migrants, a transplanted or "regathered" community. Eventually the church comprised whole families and intricate webs of extended family recently migrated from the South. High school friends and former coworkers found each other again. Even those who had lost touch over long periods of time reconnected in the congregation. Many sent word south of their new church affiliation, ensuring that any friends or relations making their way to D.C. would at least visit the church. Very often they, too, would make Faith Temple their church home if they decided to remain in the area. This informal communication network increased the membership rolls by the hundreds.

Although the increase in the church's membership suggested to me a large depopulation in southern churches, I was struck by how in emotional and cultural terms many of the members never really left the South. In the first place, there was a fair amount of mobility back and forth. On annual special days—"men's day," "women's day," or pastor's anniversary—whole congregations would come up to "render services," and, of course, that favor was always returned. The occasion of someone's death usually meant that the bulk of the congregation would be "going home" for the "going-home services." Few, if any, members were buried in the North, especially in the early history of the congregation. Typically, vacations were taken in the south in addition to the regular family visits. Perhaps because of these strong physical bonds, the emotional and cultural bonds with the South were palpable and inextricable. For the most part, people saw themselves as southerners and identified the South as their home. This was the case even for those who had been in the D.C. area for the majority of their lives. They expressed this southern identity in nearly every way, from their food to their speech patterns and worldview. They took pride in their southern identity and in the connections they maintained to "home." The church as well as the lives of the congregants assumed decidedly southern flavors, as the members attempted to translate their southern selves to a new place and a new institution.

This translation, however, was not exact. The lives of these poor and working-class southern migrants were inexorably changed by the process of migration. Although they conscientiously identified as southerners, they no longer lived in the rural South. They lived in the urban North, or what technically is the urban "Upper South." This relocation changed them to the same degree that they changed the new social and spatial context in which they found themselves. The translation of a southern self to the North is best understood as transformation. Their lives were transformed by migration and urbanization, and so was the church to which they all belonged, Faith Temple.

It has taken me years to grapple with the full implications of the phenomenon of migration and its impact on individual lives and on religious culture and institutions. But my investigation began years ago in that little church that sat just outside the Washington, D.C., line, a church like countless others that played a small role in a much larger, national story of which Chicago was the vital and iconographic center.

Acknowledgments

EXPERIENCE HAS TAUGHT me that books are most often the work of a collection of individuals rather than the production of a single person. One person may do the writing, but numerous others have a hand in the book's conception and the various stages of revision on its journey toward publication. That is certainly the case here, and I want to acknowledge that collection of individuals, as well as a number of groups and organizations that have been sources of institutional support over the past several years.

The institutional support began early in my career with a fellowship from the Illinois Consortium for Educational Opportunity Program (ICEOP). Four years of funding released me from teaching responsibilities, allowing me to devote even more time than usual to my research. The King V. Hostic Award from the Illinois State Historical Library in Springfield provided funds for research in the library's rich archives. I found there what I still consider to be a largely untapped wealth of material on black religious life in Chicago. A generous fellowship from the Louisville Institute supported an entire year of writing, and Northwestern's history department provided funding for additional research at a critical juncture. I received three summer research fellowships from the University of Virginia that helped me begin the revision phase in earnest. For the generosity of the university and the Religious Studies Department in particular, I am enormously grateful.

A veritable host of librarians and archivists have assisted me in my research over the years. I want to give special thanks to the many fine men and women at the Library of Congress, particularly in the main reading room and the manuscripts division. Thanks to Betty Layton at the American Baptist Historical Society. Thanks also to the staffs at the Schomburg Center for Research in Black Culture, special collections at the Harold Washington Library in Chicago, special collections at Howard University, Regenstein Library at the University of Chicago, Firestone Library at Princeton University, and Widener Library at Harvard. Lois Walker, the librarian at the Chicago Defender Archives allowed me into that treasure trove at a time when so few scholars had done so before. For her graciousness and for the graciousness of the *Defender's* Earl Calloway, I will always be grateful. I spent many hours at the Newberry Library working with James Grossman, Janice Reiff, Ann Keating, and Carol Summerfield on the *Encyclopedia of Chicago History*. During that time I took great advantage of the library's genealogical resources and special collections. The late

Archie Motley, who for much of his life was archivist in the manuscripts division of the Chicago Historical Society, believed strongly in this project and was always ready to show me some new material. His vast knowledge of Chicago history was and remains a source of inspiration. I spent perhaps the most time with Michael Flug, archivist at the Vivian G. Harsh Collection of Afro-American History and Literature, Carter G. Woodson Regional Branch of the Chicago Public library. Michael's consummate skill, high enthusiasm, and encouragement were a boon to me and the research at several crucial moments.

I was fortunate to have worked with four talented scholars working in the field of United States history. Adam Green, Henry Binford, Nancy MacLean, and James T. Campbell all contributed to the project in different and important ways. Adam and Henry were central to a large group who all had a hand in my intellectual development, including Sarah Maza, Mike Sherry, Robert Lerner, T. W. Hycke, John Bushnell, and the late Robert Weibe. Quite simply, I would never have finished the book without the expertise and care of Nancy MacLean. She worked tirelessly on my behalf, reading every chapter and offering her keen critique and wise direction. For all that she has done to push me to be a better researcher and writer, I owe her a great debt. James T. Campbell is the reason I am a historian. He inspired me to pursue this project with his infectious enthusiasm for American and African religious history, time after time transcending the boundaries of what someone should reasonably expect from an adviser. He gave patient readings to every chapter, responding at length to each one. More than that, he modeled for me a balanced way to do American history with his brilliance, skill, and dignity.

My fortunes for the completion of the book brightened with successive yearlong fellowships from the Center for the Study of Religion at Princeton University and the W. E. B. Du Bois Institute at Harvard University. The Center for the Study of Religion, under the direction of Robert Wuthnow and the acting codirectorship of Wendy Cadge, welcomed me into discussions that stretched me in many ways and honed my own analysis of religion. I met a group of very fine scholars who shared with me their great insight, intellect, and friendship. They include Tracey Hucks, Jonathan Sheehan, Gustav Niebuhr, Carolyn Chen, Cleo Kearns, Eugene Rogers, Thomas A. (Tal) Lewis, Timothy Jackson, and Daniel Zelinski. I am grateful to Robert Wuthnow and R. Marie Griffith for inviting me to that table. I am also grateful to my editor, Fred Appel, whom I met during my year at Princeton. His enthusiasm, support, and encouragement remained constant over many months. The fellowship at the Du Bois Institute introduced me to a new group of scholars and a different set of conversations about the project. I want to especially thank Rebeccah Welch, June Pym, David Kim, and Robert Korstad for their careful and sensitive readings. They comprised the core of a wonderful community of colleagues and friends. My assistant, Benesha Bobo, helped me maintain order in times of great busyness. I owe many thanks to Henry Louis Gates, Jr., acting director Lawrence Bobo, and the faculty and administration of the African and African American Studies Department at Harvard, especially Evelyn Brooks Higginbotham.

I want also to acknowledge a wider community of scholars and Chicago residents who helped to shape the project. Mark Noll, James Grossman, James Oakes, Colleen McDannell, Carolyn DeSwart Gifford, Dennis Dickerson, and R. Marie Griffith all provided help and useful comments at different times. Nancy MacLean's advisee group, which included David Johnson, Charlotte Brooks, Karen LeRoux, Steve Reich, Michelle Mitchell, Leslie Dunlap, Brett Gadsden, and Marisa Chappell gave invaluable feedback early in the writing process. David Johnson, who possesses good insight and a remarkable talent for writing well, was particularly helpful. University of Virginia's Charles Marsh, Heather Warren, and Reginald Butler also lent their talents and insights. Al Raboteau, Kimberley L. Phillips, Clarence Walker, and Nick Salvatore read the work with such care and knew what needed to be said for clarification or to push the analysis further. A number of Chicagoans allowed me into their homes and lives to tell me what they know about the city's African American religious culture. I want to particularly thank Caroll Hibler, Bishop Otto Houston, Timuel Black, and "Little Lucy" Collier.

An assortment of terrific friends, in and outside the academy, made it all worthwhile. I will always cherish the intellectual and emotional support I received from Dario Gaggio (Il Mio Amico), David Johnson, Sarah Fenton, Chad Heap, Amanda Seligman, Dylan Penningroth, Alexander Rehding, Anne Monius, Mark Peco, Ton Wintels, Scott VandenBerg, Christophe Lomon, Kathryn L. Dawson, José Valezco, Thomas and Lorraine Cochran, and Marc Brunninga. My family has shown such patience, even if they didn't always understand the academic life I chose. I thank last, but not least, Queen Esther Best, the late Leviticus Best, Bishop Limmie Nathaniel Forbes, and all my loving sisters and brothers: Barbara Morrison, Dorothy Holmes, Maxine James, Pervilla Best, Rosetta Martin, Vanessa Best, Versity Wallace, Cornell, Donnell, Jimmie, Tony, and Vic Best.

It is clear that the study of Negro religion is not only a vital part of the history of the Negro in America, but no uninteresting part of American history.

—W. E. B. Du Bois, "Of the Faith of Our Fathers"

THE HISTORY of African Americans is in large part a religious history. It is a story deeply anchored in themes of captivity, exile, enslavement, and deliverance.[1] It is an account of a diasporic people that closely follows the historical narrative of the Hebrews of Old Testament scripture. Indeed, the affinity of the slave experience to that of the Hebrews of the Old Testament is a major reason many slaves in the United States embraced the Exodus story. The captivity and subsequent deliverance of the Children of Israel seemed an ancient account of the slave's lived experience and cherished hopes. Many of the most revered Negro spirituals, such as "Go Down, Moses," bear this out.

> Go down, Moses
> Way down in Egypt's land.
> Tell old Pharaoh
> To let my people go![2]

One can even say that, above all, the dual themes of captivity and deliverance, or captivities and deliverances, have comprised the very core of the black experience in the United Stats since the slave era. They are the most intimate and enduring aspects of black life.

This book is about the transformations that took place among the black Protestant churches and in the religious culture of black Chicago during one of those deliverances, the period known as the Great Migration. Beginning in 1915 at the time of the First World War, the Great Migration, or the "second exodus," was the signal event of the early twentieth century, when large numbers of blacks relocated from the rural South to the urban North, "leaving the land," in the words of Richard Wright, "for the streets of the city."[3] As an integral part of the deliverance motif in black American life, migration itself has been a lasting theme. Blacks have long connected their freedom to the ability to move, to change place or spatial direction, recognizing that, as Ralph Ellison put it, "geography is fate."[4] In the often chaotic and disruptive process of migration, all aspects of African American life underwent incredible transformation. Since the beginning of the mass social and demographic movement, scholars from various disciplines have attempted to chronicle the full range of those changes in dozens of books, documentaries, and articles.[5] Only a few of these analyses, however, have given adequate attention to black churches or to African-American religion more broadly. Thorough investigations of the religious transformations intrinsic to the migration era have not been a central concern, nor has religion factored prominently in the narrative. This book intends to fill a large gap in the historiography of the Great Migration to Chicago and in our understanding of the relationship between the migration of southern blacks, urbanization, and religious change. It shows that the Great Migration stimulated new urban religious practices and traditions among the black Protestant churches of Chicago that reflected aspects of both black southern religion and the exigencies of city life. These practices and traditions may have been rooted in the folk culture of the rural South, but their expression developed from southern migrants' confrontation with the urban North.[6]

The book illustrates how the migration of black southerners to Chicago launched a new sacred order in the city. It was new because so much of this order's ritual and institutional expression differed from previously established patterns. The notion of the sacred also differed in important ways from some interpretations of the concept. It did not involve a juxtaposition of sacred and profane in the strictest sense, as demonstrated by history of religions scholar and philosopher Mircea Eliade.[7] African American religion has historically defied this polarity. In the simplest terms, the sacred component to black Chicago's new order was that which was set apart yet attributable fundamentally to human action in the tradition of French philosopher Emil Durkheim.[8] The sacredness of things (objects, relics, symbols) or moral communities (churches) is not inherent; it comes by social agreement, or as Karen Fields has asserted, it is "made so by doing."[9] It was a process of setting apart by human action that was at work in the construction of black Chicago's new sacred order.

The new sacred order did not so much topple an old religious establishment as it rendered that establishment's long-held institutional priorities ineffective in a rapidly changing religious climate. In contrast to the old religious establishment that was run by a coterie of well-educated, middle-class male ministers, the new sacred order was largely a female order, as black women constituted more than 70 percent of the membership in many churches. The new order was also fundamentally Protestant and explicitly Christian, which refutes notions that black religion during the first decades of the twentieth century was overrun by "cults and sects."[10] While black urban religion was most certainly represented by many non-Christian and quasi-Christian groups, black mainstream Protestant churches were the truest indicators of change to the religious culture in Chicago. Black southerners imbued these churches with a "folk" religious sensibility, and in doing so ironically recast conceptions of modern African American religion in terms that reflected the rural past. In the same way that working-class cultural idioms such as jazz and blues ascended in the secular arena as vehicles to represent black modernity, African American religion in Chicago—with its negotiation between the past and the present, rural and urban, old and new—exhibited African American religion in modern form.[11] At the broadest level of argument, the book reveals how an African American religious diaspora from the rural South, which some Chicago sociologists and writers deemed "premodern" because of migrants' inexperience with urban culture, ushered in the modern era of black religion in Chicago.

The central questions that drive the book emerge from anthropological understandings of culture, and to some degree, religion. Given that culture, as Lawrence Levine has reminded us, is not static but is a process, what impact did the demographic shift have on Chicago's African American religious culture and historic conceptions of "the black church"?[12] How did African-American Protestant congregations respond (or not respond) to migrants, and what role did these migrants play in the shaping of a new religious environment? If the African American sociologist St. Clair Drake was correct when he asserted, "the city is a world of rapid change," affecting "religious behavior profoundly," in what specific ways did it influence the religious behavior and theological understandings of black congregants?[13] This book answers these questions, identifying southern migrants' agency, adaptation, and collectivity in the construction of black religion in Chicago.

The notion of construction is important here, and one could even employ the terms "deliberate" construction and "active" construction to further emphasize human agency. Historically we have been more accustomed to think of religion as spontaneous and supernatural. Religion is something that just happens—outside of human control and irrespective to social context. To take nothing from the private, interior experience of religion, such is not the prevailing understanding of religion operating in this book. I understand religion (particularly when speaking in communal and institutional terms) and even notions of the sacred to be mutually reinforcing modalities that find expression as the cultural production of their adherents. Far from being passive observers of religion during the Great Migration, black Christians actively produced a religious cultural expression that reflected social, cultural, and political concerns. Responding to the crisis of migration and the demands of urban life, many members of Chicago's African American religious community shaped a religious culture that was thoroughly cognizant of the human condition. They were particularly aware of the plight of the city's black population and understood that the context of the faithful must influence the content of religion. The book also reveals a new theological orientation developed during the migration signified by themes of exile, sojourn, deliverance, and the moral obligation of black Christian churches to the black community. In this way, the book is a religious history that is also a cultural analysis and a social history of black religion. It works from the perspective of a number of disciplines that often by way of their divergent methods and discourses speak past each other.

The most crucial aspect of the book centers on the interplay between southern migrants and mainstream black Protestant churches. The pragmatic attempts by mainstream black Protestant churches to address the temporal needs of southern migrants and the migrants' insistence upon infusing these congregations with their own sense of religion characterized this exchange. The interplay was often fraught with tensions that were grounded in issues of class and region, but it effectively altered the church music and worship patterns in many mainstream black churches, allowing for greater degrees of emotionality and more focused programs of social service. Prior to the migration, the majority of Chicago's black Protestants openly discouraged emotional worship for the way it reflected "African" and "slave religion." Nor did they consider social outreach to be a priority. With the migration, black gospel music emerged as a prime example of the new climate of expressive religious worship. It also highlighted the rural/urban tension and dichotomy. As a musical genre, black gospel predated the migration and had its origins in the rural South. It was also primarily characteristic of Pentecostal "storefront" congregations in the urban North and Midwest. But black gospel music as performed by artists such as Thomas A. Dorsey and Mahalia Jackson only came into prominence when it was introduced into mainstream black Protestant churches as a response to the worship demands of southern migrants. From these churches, it spread by mass communication and marketing practices drawn from urban culture. The same is true for "folk" or vernacular preaching, which was the companion religious expression to black gospel music. Social service and community outreach targeted for southern migrants became integral parts of the Christian mission and gauges for institutional relevancy. Black Chicago churches were far less "otherworldly," escapist, quietist, and otherwise socially disengaged than the normal depictions of early-twentieth-century African American religion.[14] Indeed, many black churches across a wide denominational spectrum embraced a new pragmatism about "worldly" matters in deference to southern migrants. In a few cases, this new pragmatism was clearly influenced by the tenets of the Social Gospel.[15] Some African American ministers even suggested a new set of institutional priorities that placed the material needs of new migrants at the center of urban church work. This view signaled a profound reconception of African American Christianity.

The reconception of African American Christianity shaped the cultural production of the period in black Chicago, contributing Chicago's rich tradition as an entertainment capital. As Norman Spaulding has argued, a disproportionate number of theaters, taverns, clubs, and lounges dotted the Loop and South Side beginning in the 1890s, many featuring black musicians and entertainers.[16] In the first part of the twentieth century, black Protestant churches added to this rich and vibrant culture of entertainment and performance. Black churches, particularly among the poor and working-class, became proving grounds for local singers such as Sam Cooke and Lou Rawls, who went on to national fame. Gospel artists such as Sister Rosetta Tharpe passed seamlessly between the constructed categories of sacred and secular, indecipherably merging the genres of gospel and swing. Choirs staged fierce competitions, with the highest marks going to those with the best overall presentation, including who had the best choreography and who could best "shout the church."[17]

The advent of gospel music and radio broadcasts provided the opportunity for some Chicagoans to market black religion to a wide audience. Radio preacher Wilber Daniels put it succinctly: "I realized a long time ago that if I was to spread the Word, radio would reach more people and get the message across to more people. Religion can be sold as well as other products."[18] This new thinking regarding the church's place in the wider world of Chicago not only spread the Word, however; it also created a space for new theological and social stances regarding issues of gender and sexuality. Many black women rose to take positions of clerical leadership, usually outside the ecclesiastical mainstream. In doing so, they defied conventional gendered thinking about "women's place" and "man's work." Some of these ministers outside the mainstream were rumored to be homosexual, even if they did not claim a homosexual identity. At the very least they espoused nonnormative sexualities. From among these churches came the richest contributions to the city's cultural production.

Black Chicago's new sacred order fractured older notions of church life and instituted new ones. Since the late nineteenth century, black churches in Chicago had usually comprised members from the same or similar economic backgrounds and social status. Worship across class lines rarely took place, and it was not encouraged. With the influx of black southerners, however, this level of class division among and within churches was simply impossible to maintain. Class lines in black Chicago churches began to blur as people from various socioeconomic backgrounds clustered into the same congregations. A middle-class religious establishment that had developed among mainline black Protestants had to gradually yield preeminence to a dynamic and class-diverse religious culture, as these churches found in their midst growing numbers of southern migrants, who were overwhelmingly poor and working class.

Similarly, the migration of black southerners to Chicago began to mitigate the historic competition between African American religious institutions and civic organizations.[19] Throughout the late nineteenth century, the institutional life among the city's blacks had become bifurcated into neat categories of sacred and secular. The few commercial and media ventures that existed, along with a number of political and civic organizations, occupied the public (secular) realm, while churches occupied the private or semipublic realm. Attempts to bridge the two worlds generated great tensions and was met, at times, with open hostility. The demands the migration placed on the resources of most black Protestant churches, however, made this level of institutional and philosophical division untenable. Many churches began to develop intimate alliances with local civic groups, such as the Chicago Urban League and the Travelers Aid Society, fraternal orders, national social service organizations, and black businesses. In some instances, black Protestants even cooperated with white-owned businesses eager to tap into the resources of the city's growing black congregations. They initiated and maintained these alliances to better assist new migrants, and the alliances soon became a barometer of the commitment black churches held not only toward southern migrants but also toward racial betterment generally. It became apparent that the degree to which black Protestant churches responded to the needs of southern migrants, as well as to the altering religious scene, signaled their interest in social change and indicated their vitality as religious institutions.

By the time of the migration, few black Protestants in Chicago would have disagreed with W. E. B. Du Bois, who stated in 1903 that the "problem of the twentieth century is the problem of the color line." But these same black Protestants would also concur with a lesser-known, yet equally prescient statement Du Bois made a decade later. He said the "Negro problem" in America was also a theological problem, a "test for the church."[20] Although what Du Bois meant by the "Negro problem" transcended the Chicago context, the statement was relevant to the city's migration-era black churches. The migration of black southerners tested the resourcefulness, fortitude, and spiritual vigor of black Chicago churches in the way Jim Crow segregation had done for all black American churches in previous years. And as in the days of Jim Crow, migration-era black Protestants appropriated extant racial ideologies that tended to encourage not only outreach to southern migrants but also programmatic and policy changes in their congregations. The primary racial ideology many black Chicago Protestant churches followed was the doctrine of self-help, which had by the second decade of the twentieth century become the standard creed throughout most sectors of the black community. For many black Protestant churches, the migration of black southerners provided the basis for practicing the tenets of self-help in their congregations and in the network of organizational alliances they established. Black Protestant churches, for example, became crucial stopping points to the "Spend money with our own merchants" campaigns started by the *Chicago Defender* editor Robert S. Abbott in the mid-1920s.[21] As an ideological approach to racial progress, the doctrine of self-help greatly influenced Chicago's black churches during the migration era. And although it was often ineffective, it also provided a system of thought and action which proved useful to black Chicago churches during a chaotic time of population growth and broad cultural shift.

Use of the term "migration era" interchangeably with the "Great Migration" is an attempt to span the range of analysis over both phases of the mass movement. Past studies of the Great Migration have claimed to cover the entire exodus but have actually concentrated only on one of the two phases. In this study, "migration era" indicates that the periodization covers the first phase spanning from 1915 to 1930 and the much larger one that occurred during the Second World War lasting until the early 1970s. This study considers both as one singular phase. Although the number of black southerners migrating to the urban North decreased during the Depression, the migration by no means ceased. Rather, it "continued throughout the depression years," as St. Clair Drake noted, at a slower pace that came to full throttle with the availability of industrial and manufacturing jobs at the outbreak of the Second World War.[22] Indeed, the outmigration from some southern states, though less than it had been in the previous decade and would be in the next, was still substantial during the 1930s. Mississippi experienced a net loss of more than 68,000 blacks between 1930 and 1940. During the 1920s the loss was 83,000, and during the 1940s the number totaled nearly 315,000 persons.[23] Furthermore, migrants did not draw a distinction between the two phases of migration. This has long been an interpretive convention (invention) of scholars, not the perspective of the participants in migration. Migrants themselves registered no indication that they viewed the movement to have slowed or ceased during the 1930s. Neither did scholars who were observing the exodus at the time acknowledge a break in the mass movement during the 1930s. In 1940, for example, prior to the second wave of migration, Horace Cayton, Jr., presented a paper titled "Negro Migration" at a hearing of the U.S. Congressional Committee on Interstate Migration held in Chicago. He detailed several causes and conditions he considered key factors in the continuation of the exodus. The year before, Cayton had assisted the *Chicago Defender* in publishing a series of articles on the migration titled, "Is the South Doomed?"[24] St. Clair Drake further asserted that migrants continued their quest northward "due to the collapse of cotton tenancy in the South, inadequate relief for Negroes in those regions, and the availability of WPA employment."[25] The time is right to dispense with the ahistorical and unhelpful periodization of the Great Migration. Although this study does not extend as far as the early 1970s—it covers all of the interwar period and ends with the death of Elder Lucy Smith in 1952—treating the years between 1915 and 1952 as part of a single "Great Migration."

Not only is there confusion about the phases of the Great Migration, there is little agreement as to how best to measure it, and whether the period is the proper domain of sociologists, anthropologists, demographers, or urban historians. The answer, of course, is that it is the proper domain of each of these fields, and this book, although primarily a religious history, takes a multidisciplinary approach, relying heavily on these other perspectives. A multidisciplinary approach is not only warranted, it is necessary because students of the Great Migration have long recognized that the mass movement was not simply about the vast numbers and the demographic shift in population. What warrants the superlative in the characterization of the exodus of southern blacks to northern cities is the wide-ranging impact the mass movement had on individual African Americans, specific black communities, and on American society as a whole. The account that follows is not an attempt to paste the lives of churchgoing southern migrants onto the master narrative of the Great Migration, but a suggestion that looking at migrants' religious experiences and the concurrent transformations to African American religious culture calls scholars of all relevant fields to rethink our assumptions about the movement entirely.

Building on a small body of scholarship that deals specifically with the impact of the Great Migration on African American religion, this study pushes the analysis further and in different directions.[26] What follows is as much a work of religious history as it is a work of social and cultural history that analyzes the relationship between urbanization, migration, and African American religion. As a work of religious history, it chronicles the development of the organizational forms of black Protestant religion in Chicago. The social history aspect of the study quantifies that development in terms of rates of church growth vis-à-vis the migration. It teases out the intricate alliances and tensions maintained in and among these institutions and with the larger community. The study is also a critical discussion of the relationship between religion and culture. I use the term "critical" because past studies of African American religion have often elided an analysis of this relationship. As a cultural history of African American religion, it is concerned about religious practice, objects, and symbols and the various meanings attributed to them by black Chicago Christians. It is an exploration of the structures of significance that emerge from an analysis of the forms of black religious expression developed during the migration era. Also, given my conviction that history must tell a story, the study integrates analysis with a narrative that is ethnographic, chronological, and thematic. This is particularly significant for a religious history because religious history, as all sacred texts will testify, is told in story form. It avoids overreliance on the socioeconomic theories that have long shaped the field of African American religion in order to underscore religious meanings, human agency, and the resiliency of religious community. Religious communities are not necessarily like other communities, and often operate with different assumptions and different priorities. Put simply, in consideration of the development and transformation of Chicago's African American religious community during the migration era, the structural forces of racial oppression, economic deprivation, and spatial limitation were at work, but they did not prevent African American Protestant Christians from forming religious communities with all the accompanying dynamism, tensions, and contradictions.

In arguing for the cultural dominance of lower- and working-class southern migrants over the mainline religious establishment of black Chicago, the book suggests a new way to think about how class operated in these institutions. The evidence strongly suggests that the class composition in many black churches became more complicated and harder to decipher. Although the categories of "upper-class," "middle-class," and "lower-class" churches did not disappear entirely with the influx of black southern migrants, these designations became less meaningful and far less accurate. Also, the emergence of a black working class or industrial proletariat—unknown in Chicago before the migration—further complicated the composition of these congregations as well as the relationships between class categories. Moreover, an understanding of the influence of black southerners, who enjoyed a "more emotional ritual," over many mainline African American churches, challenges the previous propensity by some scholars for socioeconomic compartmentalization of religious practice. Not all black Chicago churches became "shouting" churches, but one of the most profound effects of the Great Migration on Chicago's Protestant religious culture was the way mainline churches altered various aspects of their religious rituals to "make some concessions" for the religious inclinations of black southerners. By the 1930s, with the dawn of "gospel blues," the influence of the "South in the city" within Chicago's black churches, encouraged by this ever-increasing religious diaspora, was deep and pervasive.[27] During the migration era, black Chicago Protestants—southern migrants and long-term residents alike—reconfigured the religious culture according to specific social conditions. They adapted and reinterpreted religious practices to fit the new urban setting. In the context of the urban North, ecstatic religious worship took on new depth and meaning, while social service attained a new urgency.

Chapter 1 expands the depiction of the migration of black southerners to Chicago beyond the master narrative of a demographic shift prompted by socioeconomic "push-pull" factors. Historically, these factors have been understood as the "push" of southern racism, mob rule, discrimination, and ecological disaster and the "pull" of northern economic opportunity and personal liberty. As the historian John McMillen succinctly asserted, black southerners were "drawn as well as driven" to the North.[28] Establishing first the centrality of Chicago to the Great Migration, the chapter shows that the mass movement had a profound impact on all aspects of black life, especially upon African American religious institutions.[29] But even beyond issues of rapid congregational growth and alterations in church policies, there developed significant changes in the very conception of black religion. Lastly, the chapter places the book historiographically, arguing that cultural and religious analyses of the Great Migration have been overlooked in the interest of sociological ones—to the detriment of a comprehensive view of the movement and of southern migrants.

The second chapter shows the specific ways black southerners influenced religious worship and church policies. It demonstrates how the presence of black southerners muted the voices and perspectives of an African American middle-class Protestant religious establishment that had existed since the nineteenth century. In its stead, a diverse religious culture emerged that was essentially "southern" and "folk" in ethos, and the very margins of the religious culture were moved to the center. The chapter demonstrates that a key factor to the pervasive spread of this southern folk ethos in black churches was the way migrants insisted on sustaining their southern identities in the urban North. Rooted in the experiences of southern migrants, the chapter chronicles the ways black southerners understood themselves to be dispersed from the religious communities of their former homes—becoming a significant aspect of a new sacred order. They were, in effect, a religious diaspora.

Chapter 3 shows how the core of the new sacred order was a pragmatic religiosity instigated by the presence of new migrants, opposing the static typologies of twentieth-century black urban religion as compensatory, escapist, and socially disengaged. This chapter reveals the various ways many black Protestant churches faced the challenge of an expanding and materially desperate black community. From this new pragmatism among black churches arose greater support for black businesses and what some came to call "a business approach to religion." Similarly, many of those same congregations established for the first time programs of social service, even hiring professional social workers. Social service attained a central place among the black churches of Chicago like never before, becoming an integral part of the new sacred order. Chapter 4 expands this discussion of the new sacred order, chronicling the ways worship in the new order acquired a decidedly southern folk sensibility. Patterns of worship, preaching, and music were augmented to fit the tastes of black southern migrants. The marketing of black gospel and the rise of black-oriented radio became key factors in the spread of a vernacular religious culture.

In chapter 5 the focus turns exclusively to the African Methodist Episcopal Church. The Chicago AME Church lagged behind black Baptists in terms of congregational growth and lost much of the prestige they had previously enjoyed. Whereas black Baptist churches launched aggressive recruitment initiatives, even to the point of establishing organizations designed specifically to reach southern migrants, AMEs remained ambivalent at best. The chapter shows how, by the 1920s, the ambivalence of the historic black denomination led to rebellion within the ranks as several AME ministers bolted from the denomination to form "Community Churches." The Community Church Movement, launched after World War I by white Protestants (mostly business leaders), was a liberal religious expression committed to social outreach as its central premise. The movement afforded former AMEs the theoretical basis, the spiritual impetus, and the institutional means to address the chaos of migration and the temporal needs of southern migrants. African American Community Churches in Chicago flourished as a critique of the AME church, asserting by their existence that the level of institutional intransigence demonstrated by that wing of black Methodism was out of step with the times.

The sixth and final chapter compares the lives and the work of two of migration-era Chicago's most prominent African American women pastors. It maps out the theological and cultural means, as well as the institutional complexities implied by the presence of women in positions of ministerial leadership. Profiting from the opportunities afforded by the new sacred order, Elder Lucy Smith and the Reverend Mary G. Evans rose to unprecedented levels of ecclesiastical authority and ministerial prominence during the migration era. They were unrestrained in their efforts to build and lead two of the city's largest congregations, All Nations Pentecostal Church and Cosmopolitan Community Church. These churches illustrate the way the new sacred order was a female sacred order. Composed almost entirely of women, who, like Smith, migrated to Chicago from the rural South, All Nations became one of the South Side's most vibrant congregations. Southern migrants' attraction to Smith's down-home manner and the popularity of her broadcast, "The Glorious Church of the Air," ensured its spread. The rise of "black gospel" and radio broadcasts like Smith's demonstrate the ways African American religion became a key component in black cultural production during the migration. Questioning the depictions of African American Pentecostalism as "otherworldly," the chapter shows how Smith's brand of Pentecostalism, rooted in the early Pentecostalism of Azusa Street, contained a pragmatic element.[30] Not only did Smith form relationships with local black businesses, she also became the first African American pastor in the city to use church facilities to provide food to area residents during the Depression.

Elder Lucy Smith and her All Nations Pentecostal Church embodied the dynamic and pluralistic religious culture of Chicago for close to four decades. Smith's death in 1952 and the subsequent (and literal) collapse of the All Nations church a few years later were an emphatic coda to an era of phenomenal religious institutional transformation. It was an era when the new urban religious practices and traditions developed among the black Chicago churches became encoded onto the very fabric of African American Christianity. It had become the way both to "do" and to "have" church in the city.

CHAPTER ONE

"Mecca of the Migrant Mob"

With a migrant people came a migrant church.
—Sydney Ahlstrom

When the Negro migrated north his church came with him.
—Robert Lee Sutherland

ONE OF THE MOST profound commentaries on twentieth-century African American religion appeared in a most unlikely place. In 1929, the Reverend Lacey Kirk Williams wrote an editorial for the *Chicago Tribune*, where he made a direct connection between urbanization, the northward migration of black southerners, modernity, and religious change. Titled "The Urbanization of Negroes; Effect on Their Religious Life," the editorial publicly acknowledged that the Great Migration had extended its sphere of influence to what was seemingly immutable in black life, African American religion. In language worthy of the well-educated minister and seasoned orator that he was, Williams addressed what he considered the "palpable inexcusable neglect" of black southern migrants by northern black churches "in matters of practical charitable work." According to Williams, the most recent arrivals to northern cities were being drawn away from established religious institutions by "semireligious" organizations and commercial recreation, unable to "adapt themselves to their new religious environment."[1]

Few African American ministers at the time could speak with more authority about the relationship between black southern migrants, urbanization, and African American church life than Williams. Having been born in 1871 in Barbour County, Alabama, Williams was reared in Texas. His father figured that the family had a better chance for economic advancement in the West, so he moved them there in 1877. The relocation set in motion a pattern of migration that would eventually take Williams to Chicago. After teaching in a number of rural schools and receiving his ordination as a Baptist minister in 1894, he settled first in Dallas to become pastor of Macedonian Baptist Church and then in Fort Worth to head Mount Gilead Baptist Church. The moves to Dallas and Fort Worth completed Williams's own rural-to-urban migratory experience, which his father had begun. (See figure 1.)

Williams became concerned about migration and its impact on the entirety of black life when he moved to Chicago in 1915 to lead the historic

Fig. 1. Lacey Kirk Williams. Williams assumed the pastorate of Olivet Baptist Church in 1915 and was elected president of the National Baptist Convention, Inc., in 1922. He held both posts until the time of his death in 1940. His pragmatic approach to the work of the church epitomized Chicago's African American Religious culture during the Great Migration. (Source: Chicago Historical Society)

Olivet Baptist Church. Under his direction, Olivet, the oldest black Baptist church in the city, became actively involved in the work of recruiting black southerners to Chicago and in providing for their needs once they arrived. Another article Williams wrote for the *Chicago Whip* nearly a decade before, titled "A Square Deal for the Negro," was the first in a series that discussed the migration and its causes.[2] In that article, Williams asserted that southern migrants had come during the First World War and were still coming to Chicago "for noble purposes." Their labor had been welcome during the war effort, as it helped to "keep the home fires burning" (a phrase from the immensely popular WWI tune by Lena Ford and Ivor Novello), and their continued exodus from the South chastised the region for its harsh social customs and discriminatory policies toward African Americans. The exodus had also stimulated black cultural and institutional life in the North. The responsibility to help and welcome these newcomers belonged to the whole community, but especially to African American churches. For Williams, the responsibility to "make efficient and assimilate a rural element into modern city life" belonged to black churches and represented their most important work. The rigors of the Chicago winter would not be the most difficult problem faced by southern migrants; it would be a new and strange industrial economy, new social and political systems, new personal freedoms, and a new religious climate. In effect, modern existence in a city setting posed the greatest challenge. Helping migrants make the adjustment was tantamount to a moral duty. It was the "golden opportunity" and the religious obligation of all "humanity-loving and God-fearing men." Black churches must be prepared to meet the full range of needs temporal and spiritual that recent migrants would doubtless encounter. Williams was resolute about this point. Along with concerns for prayer and preaching, he further asserted in the *Chicago Tribune* editorial, "city churches" must implement programs that take into account the "religious psychology" of black southern migrants, as well as the material needs of this "struggling humanity." African American urban churches must be, Williams declared, "passionately human, but no less divine."[3]

Not surprisingly, Williams's editorial is not well known among scholars and students of African American religious history.[4] We are not accustomed to looking to mainstream white newspapers for commentaries on African American religion. But the piece must take its place among an expanding body of documents that testify to the particular development of African American urban religion during the twentieth century. Penned by one of the most eloquent and politically active black ministers of his day, the editorial is a crucial document for several other important reasons. Williams's editorial was one of the first times a black minister, by way of the mainstream press, linked African American religious cultural and institutional change to black southern migrants and the process of urbanization. It underscored, in other words, the ways city life and the migration had begun to impinge on African American religion. The migration as a significant demographic shift aggravated by economic and social factors had been a topic of discussion by both the black and white press since 1915. The white press warned of its potential dangers and its threat to the status quo; the black press heralded it as a mass protest movement. But this editorial went further than that, eclipsing those concerns. It indicated clearly from the perspective of an African American minister that the movement was also having a profound effect on the church, black America's central cultural institution.

The circumstances as to why and how Williams's essay came to be published in the *Chicago Tribune* are unclear. Given his high profile in the city and his vast social connections, he could have been asked by the newspaper to write the piece. The former Alabamian had been tremendously influential to black Protestants in the preceding decade. He had turned Olivet Baptist, which had been established in 1844, into a thriving congregation and the mammoth National Baptist Convention USA, Inc. (NBC), into a formidable and well-run organization. His involvement with the Commission on Race Relations in 1919 and winning the prestigious Harmon Award in 1928 further bolstered his national reputation. Established in 1922 by the real estate mogul and philanthropist William E. Harmon, the Harmon Award acknowledged black achievement, usually in the categories of music, the arts, literature, education, race relations, and science. Williams won the award (and the $400 prize money) in recognition for his distiction in religious service. Williams was well-known, even revered, and his words captivated thousands. If the *Tribune* asked him to write the article it was most likely because they considered him to be someone who reflected the paper's conservative views. They were correct in part.[5] Although he was progressive on issues of race, Williams was a staunch social and political conservative. Much of his writing and many of his speeches up to that point included articulate stances on fair labor, unobstructed access to the ballot, and denunciations of segregation.[6] But the Baptist preacher frequently railed against "cheaters," policy players, gamblers, and "society matrons." His fight against the "curse of liquor" was particularly focused. Fighting to uphold the Eighteenth Amendment, Williams established no fewer than eighty-seven temperance and Prohibition organizations by 1922.[7] His political views would align him with the Republican Party, which he called "the party of the finest ideals," well into the 1930s when most blacks had bolted to become Democrats.[8] Indeed, he died in a plane crash in 1940 on his way to a political function in support of the Republican presidential nominee, Wendell Willkie. Most likely, Williams published this article in the *Tribune* (whether by invitation or his own initiative) not only to clarify the relationship between the migration and religion change, but also to make that relationship a matter of wider public discourse. The *Tribune's* large readership would bring attention to the national crisis of migration and its impact on black institutional life. Williams's editorial was a public introduction of a new black church and a new wave in African American religion.

As a "documentary witness" to the development of African American religion during the twentieth century, Williams's editorial is even more important for what it revealed about the changing character of black religion and its expansion beyond traditional conceptions.[9] The strongest implication in the piece was that African American religion and religious institutions were confronting far-reaching transformations, incited by the migration of southern blacks. Migrants were generating certain changes in many black Chicago Protestant churches as they sought to transport and reconstitute a religious culture, forged in southern and rural contexts, to the urban north. They were also those most likely to establish and affiliate with the vast number of independent Holiness-Pentecostal congregations, as well as other innovative, nonorthodox, and marginally religious groups burgeoning on the South Side. It was not immediately obvious to many Chicago black churches from among the historical and mainline Protestant denominations—Methodists, Baptists, Congregationalists, Episcopalians, and Presbyterians—that the influx of southern migrants into the city and their congregations necessitated a response at all. This was Williams's primary complaint about Chicago and black Protestant churches in other northern cities. With regard to black southern migrants, the established black churches were losing ground to nontraditional and non-Christian religious groups, including "followers of Mohammed" (by which he meant devotees of Noble Drew Ali and the Moorish Science Temple), Free Thinkers, Christian Science, and the Catholic Church. Many of these groups, he recognized, had not existed among blacks in urban centers before 1915, and their numbers were growing exponentially each year. Just as black America was fast becoming characteristically urban in the 1920s in the way it had been characteristically rural throughout the nineteenth century, so too, black religion as practiced in many of the city's black churches transformed in the wake of migration and the urbanization of Chicago's black citizens. Ironically, the influx of rural blacks into Chicago changed the city's African American religious culture into a characteristically, perhaps even uniquely, urban expression. That urban expression differed significantly from historical conceptions of black southern religion in its complexity and multidimensionality. What it meant to be a church, what it meant to do church work, what it meant to be religious, and who became the voices of spiritual authority all augmented and shifted throughout this era because of the presence of southern migrants.

In suggesting that a religious culture was "passionately human, but no less divine," Williams was not merely replicating a notion of the duality of black religion. Although it would seem that this is another binarism suggestive of the classic models of duality in the study of African American religion, the structure of the phrase is a question of both language and theology. Williams was not suggesting that black churches exist on two oppositional poles, one "human" the other "divine." His use of the word *but* (as a conjunction not as a preposition) is meant to suggest that these two aspects of the religious culture are actually the same in nature and in function—at the same time: passionately human *even as* it is simultaneously divine. And here is where the issue of theology surfaces. The notion of duality or binarism in black religion lends credence to the secularization theory, which views the work of the church as either sacred or secular. It also understands the work of churches to be on a trajectory toward secularization, mostly as a sign of progress. However, "passionately human" and "no less divine," as Williams was asserting, comprised the totality of the nature of church work, indeed the nature of the church. In theological terms, this construct is reminiscent of the doctrine of *homoousios* (Greek: of the same substance or same nature).[10] The church, therefore, is not secular, nor does it do secular work. The work of the church, even that work in the world, is made sacred by the acts of those who perform it. The work of the churches Williams envisioned, in the realm of the human and the realm of the divine, was of the same substance, forming the same function. This was the new urban religion.

As to what this new urban religious culture meant for established and mainline black Protestant churches, Williams was clear. They must posit themselves differently within the black community at large and substantially change the way they operated. More than merely a charge to northern black churches to become more sensitive to the demographic shifts influencing their congregations, the editorial encouraged profound changes in the ideas about what constituted Christian social responsibility. These changes had implications for every aspect of church life among black Protestants, from worship patterns and preaching styles to church polity and community outreach. Importantly, however, Williams suggested a reordering of priorities that put social concerns ahead of religious worship. Note the order of requisites he deemed that black Protestant churches needed in light of the migration of southern migrants: "a more comprehensive program, better qualified workers, plants adequately equipped for recreation, Christian education, and the social needs of the community, and for worship."[11] In short, northern black Protestant churches had to adopt a new programmatic and institutional dynamism that matched the dynamic shifts occurring in the religious culture broadly. During the era of migration, social concerns had to take preeminence over the "things of the sanctuary." A religious institutional approach that offered "a Godward and heavenward gospel, and too little of the manward and earthward," Williams claimed, would no longer suffice. Black Protestant churches must strive for comprehensiveness and be attentive to the "every day problems" of people as well, no longer fashioning themselves as suitable only for "paying, praying, and preaching."[12] Williams's was a new religious vision and institutional approach for African American urban Protestant churches that was systematically pragmatic, rooted in the exigencies of city life and the influx of black southern migrants. It was also a process already in force among many African American churches in Chicago by the late 1920s, including Williams's own church. Olivet Baptist and a number of other established and mainline black Protestant churches that chose to respond to the influx—recognizing its significance and potential—found themselves participating in one of the richest moments in history for the development of African American urban religion.

LIKE NO OTHER CITY in the urban North or Midwest, Chicago shouldered the full force of the Great Migration. Already a major industrial metropolis by the early twentieth century, comprised of ever-expanding and tightly knit populations of Germans, Scandinavians, Poles, Irish, and Italians, the city assumed near-mythic significance for the thousands of southern blacks making their way to what many had dubbed "the promised land." By 1920, the African American population of Chicago had climbed to 109,594, an increase of 148 percent over 1910. Fifty thousand southern blacks migrated to Chicago during 1917–1918 alone, and by midcentury, the city's black population had swelled to 492,000.[13] Comparatively, the total black population of New York just topped 340,000. In Philadelphia blacks comprised about 370,000 of the total population, and Detroit's black population was 335,000. Many black southerners came to Chicago with the idea that they would find not only higher-paying work but also new kinds of work. What they actually found was a different matter. Although the city's packinghouses, stockyards, and clothing factories employed thousands of blacks, the largest percentage of black workers were restricted to domestic service. This was particularly true for black women from the south, who constituted two-thirds of the domestic workforce between 1920 and 1930.[14] Although the percentage of men in domestic service had fallen from a high of 45 percent in 1910, primarily due to the availability of industrial jobs, it still hovered around 25 percent in 1920.[15] Non- and semiskilled jobs were plentiful but the rapid rate of population increase among African Americans nevertheless strained the job market. Competition for jobs became fierce, generating tensions within the black community as well as with native whites and ethnic minorities. The explosive race riot of 1919 most likely resulted as much from pulsating tensions among the city's labor force as it did from competition for limited housing and social space. Walter White, the longtime executive secretary of the NAACP, considered "economic competition" among his "eight reasons" for the outbreak.[16] Black political culture attained a whole new tenor during the migration era. Using a larger number of black votes as leverage, Republican and Democratic politicians such as Oscar DePriest, Arthur Mitchell, and William L. Dawson developed powerful political networks on the South and West sides of the city.[17] Similarly, black businesses flourished.

Numerous shops, grocery stores, and entertainment and financial establishments emerged, responding to the material needs of both southern migrants and "old settlers." Jesse Binga's bank boasted more than one million dollars in assets generated from among its exclusively African American clientele. Binga's real estate business also profited from the increase of Chicago's black population. The Supreme Liberty Life Insurance Company grew to become the most successful black business of any kind in black Chicago. Few could have imagined at the onset of the migration the indelible mark the influx of black southerners would leave on African American life in the city.[18]

The impact of the migration on Chicago's African American religious culture and black churches was even more significant. The number, size, and variety of black churches during the migration era were nothing short of staggering, contributing to Chicago's long-standing reputation as a city of churches. By the late 1940s, conservative estimates placed the number of African American churches in Chicago at about five hundred. This number included hundreds of smaller "storefronts."[19] Although the vast majority of these were Protestant religious institutions, Chicago also boasted at least two African American Catholic churches, chapters of Marcus Garvey's Universal Negro Improvement Association (UNIA), the Nation of Islam, Noble Drew Ali's Moorish Science Temple, and Father Divine's Peace Mission. The UNIA was never as strong in Chicago as it was in New York City, but there were two divisions operational in Chicago, one on the West Side and the other on the South Side. A struggle for control split the group after Garvey's arrest in 1925, but the movement did not entirely disappear from the Chicago scene, increasing to six, albeit smaller, divisions by the late 1930s. North Carolinian Timothy Drew (a.k.a. Noble Drew Ali) originally founded the Moorish Science Temple in Newark, New Jersey, in 1913 as the Holy Moabite Temple of the World. Its name change to Moorish Holy Temple of Science and finally to the Moorish Science Temple of America, however, happened in Chicago, where in 1923 the movement formally organized and became a national phenomenon. Although Arthur Huff Fauset gave no specific numbers in his ground breaking book, *Black Gods of the Metropolis*, he confirmed the overwhelming popularity of this movement among black Chicagoans by asserting that "many Negroes on the South Side of Chicago flocked to the new teacher."[20] Father Divine made rare appearances in Chicago and his missions remained small. His infrequent visits, however, did not prevent enthusiastic praise of "father" by his primarily female followers. In worship services that were rife with sexual tension, women devotees testified that they were able to feel their leader's presence in their bodies. By 1934, the Nation of Islam had relocated its headquarters from Detroit to Chicago, claiming many converts from among new migrants. The message of the black nationalist group struck a responsive chord with a cross-section of black Chicagoans. As St. Clair Drake and Horace Cayton noted in their classic 1940s study, *Black Metropolis*, "the spirit of Bronzeville [was] tinctured with religion."[21]

The city of Chicago was central to the process of migration and has been pivotal to the written history of that process. Most studies of the mass movement agree that Chicago was the symbolic if not actual destination of the majority of black southern migrants. As James Grossman asserted, "it was Chicago that captured the attention and imagination of restless black Americans."[22] Even for those migrants who were simply passing through Chicago en route to other northern cities, or for those not venturing through the city at all, Chicago came to represent, in African American author and educator Charles S. Johnson's words, the "Mecca of the migrant mob."[23] Stories that reached the Deep South by informal networks of communication, labor agents, and Robert S. Abbott's *Chicago Defender* told of an abundance of factory jobs, equal education, and clean housing. They also spoke of radically new social arrangements wherein blacks exercised unprecedented levels of individual and collective freedom. Although many migrants quickly discovered that the North fell far short of its stated promises, they believed Chicago to be a place supportive of their dignity and humanity. As one southern migrant writing home to Mississippi in 1917 reported, "there isn't any 'yes sir' and 'no sir' its all yes and no, Sam and Bill." This same migrant confessed with obvious pride, "I just begin to feel like a man." Recalling his own departure to Chicago as a young man, southern migrant and "son of the blues" Sterling Plumpp proclaimed, "I thought Chicago must be heaven."[24] Bessie Smith, "Empress of the Blues," and Robert Johnson, perhaps the greatest blues artists to ever record, immortalized Chicago as a destination for southern blacks. Smith, a Tennessee native, recorded "Chicago Bound Blues" in 1923, singing:

> Late last night I stole away and cried,
> had the blues for Chicago
> and I just can't be satisfied.[25]

The song, released the first year of Smith's professional recording career, expressed an insatiable longing for Chicago that could only be eased with a journey there. It also showed that already by the early 1920s Chicago had become lodged in the creative imagination and national psyche of black Americans. Johnson's "Sweet Home Chicago," recorded in 1936, stands as nearly an iconic anthem for the entire mass movement.

> Oh, baby don't you want to go?
> Oh, baby don't you want to go?
> Back to the land of California, to my sweet home Chicago.

Now one and one is two, two and two is four
I'm heavy loaded baby, I'm booked, I got to go
Cryin' baby, honey don't you want to go?
Back to the land of California, to my sweet home Chicago.[26]

A rather personal account between two lovers—a plea for one to join the other—also expressed a longing for Chicago as a place of escape and possible refuge. The confused geography in the song suggests that Johnson had never actually been to Chicago. If that is the case, Johnson is equating Chicago to California as a metaphor representing the "land of milk and honey," adventure, and opportunity. This was certainly the perception about "the Golden State" in the 1930s. Referring to a place he had never seen as his "sweet home" only reinforced the city's mythological stature among blacks. Other blues artists appropriated this theme, proclaiming in song the symbolic importance of Chicago during the migration. Some even drew a direct connection between the meaning of Chicago and their demoralizing experience in the Jim Crow South. Several years before Robert Johnson's recording, Alabama native Charles "Cow Cow" Davenport compared the "sweetness" of Chicago to the acerbic quality of southern black life in "Jim Crow Blues." In Davenport's song, the longing cut both ways. His determination to leave the South was just as compelling as his determination to get to Chicago.

I'm tired of this Jim Crow,
Gonna leave this Jim Crow town,
Doggone my black soul,
I'm sweet Chicago bound,
Yes, I'm leavin' here,
From this ole Jim Crow town.[27]

Numerous songs, migration narratives, and historical and sociological studies attest to the central place Chicago has held in the Great Migration, indicating the city as a site of incredible significance to black southern migrants.

The Great Migration emerges as a movement of affirmation as much as protest when one realizes that the letters written by black southern migrants to and from Chicago contain a great deal of religious content. Religion and faith were prominent themes in the lives of the hundreds of thousands of blacks who left the Southland for the midwestern metropolis. The majority of the migrant letters Howard University's Emmett J. Scott published in the *Journal of Negro History* in 1919 contained some reference to God, the church, personal faith, or morality. Scott claimed that he had gathered the letters from nearly every region of the South and that they were "based on almost every topic of concern to humanity." Indeed, many of these letters written to either the *Chicago Defender* or the

Chicago Urban League were from men seeking to establish their church affiliation or moral character as evidence of their fitness for work in the North. A man from Rome, Georgia, wanted to convince the editor of the *Chicago Defender* that he was "not a tramp by any means." "I am," he insisted, "a high class churchman and businessman." A potential migrant writing from Atlanta in 1917 echoed this sentiment, asserting that he was "a good strong moral religious man" with "no habits." An office worker from Memphis, Tennessee, wrote that he was a "Christian, Baptist by affiliation" and included specifically that he was a member of the Canaan Baptist Church.[28] To be sure, many migrants wanted to convince their northern benefactors that they were respectable, and therefore, worthy of the help they sought. As historian Victoria Wolcott has shown, some northern leaders required as much from black southerners. But to read these proclamations of faith and church affiliation as mere assertions of respectability deprives them of spiritual meaning and of a larger intent. Migrant letters with religious content established more than good moral character. For some letter writers, the prospect of leaving the South for Chicago was at the core a journey of faith. A potential migrant from Texas wrote, "I ask you to help me that much the lord will help you. I am a christians [sic]. I try to make a honest living. A man ought to help another when he try to help his self." He added, "I am motherless and fatherless I don't care when I go I am gone trust in the Lord."[29] Proclamations like this demonstrate that many southern migrants linked the process of migration to their experience as people of faith.

The letters of southern migrants also indicate that many who made it to Chicago kept close ties to their home church communities and in many cases attempted to remain active participants in those communities. Churchgoing southern migrants constituted a religious diaspora in the way they viewed themselves as sojourners from their southern religious communities and the migration as a shared experience around which to identify themselves. Their letters reflected their sense of dispersion and were replete with longings for reunion, appeals to migrate, and inquiries about the home church community. Though undoubtedly many of these letters were simple examples of nostalgia and loneliness, they nevertheless substantiate Milton Sernett's depiction of the Great Migration as an event of salvific proportions. Speaking of the movement as a whole, Sernett proclaimed that "the exodus from the South during the Great Migration years was tantamount to a religious Pilgrimage out of the Wilderness into the Promised Land."[30] For many black southerners escaping the harsh living conditions, severe discrimination, and mob rule, the migration was very much a religious sojourn. The biblical imagery of "the Exodus," "flight from Egypt," "crossing over Jordan," and "bound for the promised land" were routinely invoked by black southerners to characterize their own migration. Churchgoing southern migrants seemed to indicate that they viewed the migration as a religious sojourn and an act of faith. The Reverend Charles Cook, father of the soul singer Sam Cooke, indicated as much when he was interviewed about his own passage north from Clarksdale, Mississippi. The aged Church of God (Holiness) minister resolutely proclaimed, "the Lord told me to come to Chicago."[31]

Beyond the conventional push and pull factors that have historically been cited as stimuli for the migration, religion was a central motivation. Indeed, the sheer number of migrants and the apparent spontaneity of the movement gave it a divinely providential air. George Edmund Haynes, the first executive secretary of the National Urban League, intimated as much in his governmental report on migration in 1919. "This movement of the Colored people is striking in many ways. . . . The movement is without organization or opportunities. The Negroes just quietly move away without taking their recognized leaders into their confidence any more than they do the white people about them." He continued, "A Negro minister may have all his deacons with him at the mid week meeting but by Sunday every church officer is likely to be in the North."[32] Ironically, it was the "leaderless" aspect of the movement that contributed to its providential ethos. There was no Moses in this black migration. Even many African American intellectuals and ministers recognized that the exodus was occurring without the sanction or control of the church. W. E. B. Du Bois noted as early as 1917 that one of the most important things about the exodus was that it was "a mass movement and not a movement of the leaders." "The wave of economic distress and social unrest," he claimed, "pushed past the conservative advice of the Negro preacher . . . and the colored laborers and artisans have determined to find a way for themselves." Alaine Locke concurred with this assessment a few years later in *The New Negro*, adding that "in a real sense it is the rank and file who are leading, and the leaders who are following." A few black ministers, such as Adam Clayton Powell, Sr., of Harlem, celebrated the leaderless character of the Great Migration saying, "let it first be known that the Negro Church did not start this exodus, and neither can it stop it."[33] The letters of southern migrants reveal their religious perspectives and the role their dispersion played in the development of Chicago's African American religious culture. They are further confirmation of our understanding of migration as a complex phenomenon and that migrants chose to relocate for various reasons. We must specify religion as one of those motivations, for as Miles Mark Fisher observed as early as 1925, "they came for religious reasons."[34] A Chicago African American minister, Harold M. Kingsley, confirmed this observation less than a decade later in his "spiritual interpretation of an economic problem." As to motivations for the migration, "the economic was immediate," he asserted, "but the spiritual and social was primary and fundamental."[35]

THE LITTLE THAT HAS been written about migration-era black religion in Chicago is important and informative. This literature, however brief, gives us not only composites of black church life at the time but also some understanding of the methods used to study black urban religion. The earliest of these works coincided with broader analyses of race in America being produced by the federal government and attempted to reckon with Chicago's African American religious culture vis-à-vis the influx of southern migrants. The first of what Joe William Trotter has recognized as "three distinct, but interrelated, conceptual orientations in black urban history," the race-relations model of analysis was interested in the role migration played in the rise of interracial conflict. These studies concluded that black southern migrants contributed to racial conflict but that they were also of tremendous value to the effort of postwar economic development.[36] The drawbacks to these analyses were just as striking. Typically, they were heavily influenced by deterministic sociological theories that assumed class structure as the overarching influence on the formation of Chicago's black church culture. They often did this over issues of regional heritage, racial ideology, gender, or religious faith. However, the tendency to categorize African American Christians, religious practice, and institutions by socioeconomic class has retarded long-needed discussions about religious meaning. This structuralist approach has been one of the key factors that has disallowed black southern migrants to speak in the deepest way about the central event of their lives. These studies have also tended to polarize the African American religious community along a strict binarism during a moment of dynamic pluralism. Further, these analyses, in their concentration on race and class, have not sufficiently recognized that the nature of religion is change. Nor have they appreciated the agency of black Chicagoans in constructing religious practices that reflected a full range of issues, including, but not limited to their economic status or aspirations. Churchgoing southern migrants were, in the words of Nell Irvin Painter, "choosers, makers, and doers."[37]

The Negro in Chicago, compiled by the Commission on Race Relations was the first of these studies, and in many ways the written history of Chicago's African American religious culture began with this report. Typical of the race-relations model and highly sociological in nature, The Negro in Chicago documented the findings of the commission after the race riot of 1919. Although black religious life was a relatively brief discussion amid a larger examination of the "causes and conditions" underlying the riot, which had left thirty-eight people dead and more than five hundred wounded, the report marked the first serious attention given to the study of Chicago's black churches. The commission's report affirmed that the city's black churches were a "great value in promoting the adjustment of newcomers," a conclusion doubtlessly drawn primarily from an observation of Olivet Baptist. Lacey Kirk Williams, pastor of the church, served on the commission, the only African American minister to do so.[38] The exhaustive study required hundreds of researchers who documented every aspect of the lives of black Chicagoans. They visited 80 percent of the known black congregations on the South Side, representing the first time any organization or group had attempted to account for the number of black churches in Chicago. The commission's report concluded that there was a decided difference between northern and southern churches and that storefront churches were particular to migrants.[39] Equally important, *The Negro in Chicago* established the analytical method by which black religion would be studied for years to come. Investigations of black religious life would be conducted from a sociological and socioanthropological point of view, involving case studies, interviews, neighborhood surveys, and data from a variety of civic and federal sources. This method came to the commission by way of Charles S. Johnson, who took a leave from his duties with the Chicago Urban League to assist with the study. Although the social reformer Graham Taylor served as executive secretary of the Commission, Johnson, as associate secretary, was the real guiding force. A student of Robert E. Park at the University of Chicago, Johnson initiated the study of black religion in Chicago as the enterprise of sociologists.[40]

Studies that emerged in the 1930s and 1940s focusing specifically on black Chicago churches followed the sociological framework set by the commission. For instance, although Robert Lee Sutherland wrote his 1930 University of Chicago dissertation, "An Analysis of Negro Churches in Chicago," for the Department of Christian Theology and Ethics, in the strictest terms it was neither a theological nor an ethical analysis. It was, rather, a sociological, quantitative study with large amounts of information compiled from interviews, case studies, and Sutherland's "street by street survey."[41] The great value of Sutherland's work is that it gave the first glimpse of the increasing diversity of black churches during the migration era. By the time his study appeared, every major denomination was represented in the African American religious community. He did not, however, mince words and allowed his biases to surface, demonstrating a particular insensitivity to what he considered "lower class" and "uneducated" preachers. Of uneducated black preachers, Sutherland claimed, "the absence of education in such men is easily recognizable in listening to their sermons," which he described as "all-action-no-thought." Educated black ministers faired little better. "The ease with which many of these men can exchange pulpits with some of the most progressive white ministers," he asserted, "is possibly the best attestation of the character of their preaching."[42] Deterministic sociological theories influenced Sutherland's study, although it is not clear how, given that he did his work in the department of Christian Theology and Ethics. Sutherland understood the role the South played in the formation of black church life in the North, stating, "when the Negro migrated north his church came with him," but he compartmentalized black religious institutional life according to class.[43] For Sutherland, black Chicagoans worshiped according to their class interests, in churches that reflected their class positions. The language of pathology he used to describe storefront churches, for example, revealed his view that storefront religion was the religion of the poor and socially marginalized.

Both Charles Johnson and Robert Sutherland seemed particularly inspired by the early writings of Robert E. Park. Park was born in Pennsylvania in 1864 and began his career as a reporter after finishing college at the University of Michigan, studying under John Dewey. He gave up his career as a reporter after a few years (but not his interest in investigative reporting) to study under George Simmel in Heidelberg, Germany. After obtaining his doctorate in 1904, Park went to work with Booker T. Washington at Tuskegee Institute, becoming Washington's trusted aide and ghostwriter. While in the South, Park developed a keen interest in black people, saying of his time there that "I became, for all intents and purposes, for a time, Negro myself." When he arrived at the University of Chicago in 1914, he developed an interest in the city, which he called "a state of mind" and "a product of nature," and in the interaction between racial groups. It was from these interests that Park formed his thoughts about blacks and their capacity for city life. As the leading light among the Chicago school sociologists, Park inferred that because of slavery, historical discrimination, and inexperience with modern life, black Americans faired worse in cities than other immigrants. Although he remained hopeful that the city could provide the civilizing factor blacks needed, Park's inferences tended to construct strict classifications among blacks according to class and social experience. Indeed, Park rarely talked in terms of classes. But his methods and discursive modes prompted many of his students to characterize black life in terms of pathology and social fragmentation. Religion, which they held to be inherently regressive in some forms, was particularly susceptible to this framework.[44] Analyses of black religion in Chicago that followed Sutherland's demonstrated the influence of the Chicago school of sociology even more clearly.

By the late 1930s, it was confirmed that sociologists at the University of Chicago had developed a particular interest in black Chicago life. If Chicago was a great laboratory for urban study, the South Side was the center of that lab. Scholars such as Louis Wirth, Robert Park, and Ernest

Burgess supervised studies covering a wide range of topics in black Chicago life. Several of these dealt specifically with African American religion in the city and their notions about class formation and social division among blacks reflected the basic assumptions of the Chicago school of sociology.[45] The best example of this was a dissertation written by Vattel Elbert Daniel, titled "Ritual in Chicago's South Side Churches for Negroes." Daniel's exhaustive study drew from five thousand interviews he conducted over a period of three years. He, too, was concerned with "counting the churches," but his primary aim was to analyze the development of religious ritual in black Chicago congregations. The rituals that concerned him most were those involving sermons, prayers, music, the offering, testimony, and "demonstrative behavior." Daniel also had a lot to say about the expansion of the South Side black community, about what accounted for the increasing numbers of black Chicago churches, and about storefront churches. Black mobility and white discrimination were the combined forces that swelled the black community, pushing it ever southward. This increase in the black community resulted from the migration, which was having an impact on the size of black congregations. The large increase in congregational sizes, he asserted, was attributable to the "transplantation of tens of thousands of rural Negroes to Chicago."[46] Daniel, like Sutherland, viewed the storefront phenomenon as particular to poor southern migrants and, perhaps because of that, reserved his value judgments solely for storefront religion. Storefronts, he maintained, were "not aesthetically pleasing," and "it is difficult to conduct an artistic church service in an ugly box-like room surrounded by filth and noise."[47] The notion that "ritual differentation" was akin to "class stratification" comprised the core of Daniel's argument. He attempted to demonstrate that religious ritual varied among blacks according to their class status and that the meanings attributed to certain rituals in black churches depended on the class position of the congregants. Simply put, class determined ritual practice. "Upper class church behavior," for example, "means restrained behavior: behavior which manifests considerable self-control." The opposite, of course, was true for "lower class" churches, the "ecstatic cults" that practiced no form of self-control in worship.[48] Attentive to the deterministic sociological theories of the Chicago school, Daniel held that "class lines" superseded all other influences on the development of the city's African American religious culture.

Daniel's fellow classmate, Samuel M. Strong made similar claims about the relationship between black religion and class in "Social Types in the Negro Community of Chicago: An Example of the Social Type Method." Working under what he called the "surveillance" of Park, Burgess, and Wirth, Strong argued that Chicago African Americans ordered themselves in the black community along several "axes" of life, including "race pride," "color differentiation," "the sporting life," and "religion." Where one stood socioeconomically determined one's response to and participation in these axes. The "sporting life," for example, was the exclusive domain of the poor and working class. Entertainment venues were geared to their tastes and they were the most likely to become involved in the vice and illegal activities prevalent in the "Black Belt," the name that had been used since the beginning of the twentieth century to identify Chicago's South Side.[49] African American religious culture was similarly stratified. According to Strong, black Chicago churches could be divided neatly among the higher class, middle class, and the lower class. Class interests and social values assured that there would be little interaction between churches. Indeed, there were "sharp and well-defined" cleavages "between the segments of the community based on the principle of the type of church one attends."[50]

Typically, however, for all his concern for the various kinds of churches emerging in black Chicago during the time, Strong concentrated his analytical efforts on the "social types" found in lower-class churches. Those types included: "the healer," "sanctified or holy person," "spiritual reader," "voodoo or hoodoo man," and the "numerologist." In an extremely long section of his work, Strong gave detailed accounts of these types and their social function. He also interviewed numerous black Chicagoans who were obviously from the middle class to ascertain their opinions about the lower-class types. He offered no interviews from among those who represented the types. In this way, Strong expressed greater confidence in what a "social worker," "stenographer," and "graduate student" could say about healers and numerologists than in what those groups could say about themselves. Like his fellow University of Chicago classmates, Strong documented the increase in the number of black Chicago churches and the growth of particular congregations, similarly attributing the expansion to the influx of southern migrants. Unlike his previous classmates, however, Strong added a "color" component to the class differentiation among black Chicago churches, a format that would be duplicated in later studies. "It is pointed out that the lower class churches," he claimed, "are frequented by the darker Negroes who constitute the largest number of the lower class groups." Middle-class churches were the domain of "the brown variety of Negroes" and "Pale Negroes" attended upper-class churches.[51] Samuel Strong's "social type" method was perhaps the most formulaic and generalized of the studies of black religion to date. It was also perhaps the most strictly attentive to the Chicago School's theories of class differentiation, pathology, and social marginalization. But it contributed much to a small and growing body of work focusing on Chicago black religion and religious institutions during the interwar period.

Continuing the work done in the late 1930s, the most thorough examinations of black Chicago churches appeared in the 1940s. St. Clair Drake, an anthropologist trained at the University of Chicago, produced the first of these examinations, titled "Churches and Voluntary Associations in the Chicago Negro Community." It was an official project of the Works Progress Administration (WPA), the agency established by Franklin Delano Roosevelt during the Depression to provide work for millions of unemployed Americans.[52] With additional sponsorship from the University of Chicago and the Institute for Juvenile Research, it was the first time a study of black Chicago religion received federal funding. Drake's expertise in research led to a position in the sociology department at Roosevelt University in Chicago in the mid 1940s despite his lack of formal training in the field. He remained there until he left to establish the Afro-American studies department at Stanford University. Deeply influenced by the thoughts of Robert Park, Louis Wirth, and W. Lloyd Warner, who served as advisers to the project, Drake drew attention to the "cultural and psychological factors" that accounted for the development of racially separate institutions in black Chicago. He worked from the premise that America was a nation of "joiners" and that affiliation with a particular organization stemmed from an individual's racial and class identification with that group. Black Chicago churches proved a perfect arena to test this hypothesis. Utilizing numerous charts, graphs, maps, and drawings, Drake established the importance of the institution of church to Chicago African Americans, attributing the increase in the number of churches to the migration. Drake appeared to differ from his previous Chicago cohorts, engaging the work of Robert Sutherland in particular. Rather than emphasizing the class types of churches in the manner of Sutherland, Drake devoted much of "Churches and Voluntary Associations" to explaining the competition for space and status among black churches. He even seemed at points to suggest that the typologies were not as fixed as others had suggested, noting that the city had a "secularizing effect" on black Chicago churches that prompted social mobility up the class scale. Black churches were arenas that gave a "sense of place" and provided a way to "change place."[53] In the final analysis, however, Drake sided with Sutherland, stating that Sutherland's class typology had "some validity" since most migrants and their churches comprised the lower class. By the time of Drake's WPA study, class as a determinate factor in church worship and affiliation had become the definitive way to discuss and to describe black church life.

St. Clair Drake joined Horace Cayton, Jr., a fellow University of Chicago student and grandson of Hiram Revels, in the mid-1940s to write what remains the authoritative account of black life in Chicago up to that time. Not since the work of W. E. B. Du Bois in *The Philadelphia Negro*

(1898) and *The Negro Church* (1903) had there appeared so exhaustive a study of urban black American life. Utilizing scores of material collected under the auspices of the WPA, Drake and Cayton aimed to touch on every aspect of the lives of black Chicagoans. What resulted was a staggeringly comprehensive study, which in many ways eclipsed Gunnar Myrdal's encyclopedic *An American Dilemma*, published a year earlier. One reviewer claimed the book contained "all the stuff of which our culture is made." Although *Black Metropolis: A Study of Negro Life in a Northern City* was not exclusively about the city's African American religious culture, it contained ample discussion of black church life. In typical fashion, *Black Metropolis* divided the black church community into socioeconomic classes. A "higher proportion of the upper stratum" in black Chicago, the authors contended, belonged to Presbyterian, Congregationalist, and Episcopal churches. These churches were "devoid of the cruder emotional tricks" found among the "lower class" churches, which they took to be exclusively of the storefront variety. In the manner of Samuel Strong, on whose study they had served as consultants, Drake and Cayton also suggested a correlation between the religion of the upper class and skin color, noting that while not entirely "blue vein," many among those who attended elite churches were of light complexion. The opposite, of course, was true for those in lower-class churches. Moreover, the largest segment of the black population, the poor, belonged to Pentecostal, Holiness, or "Spiritualist" congregations, they argued, and unlike the upper stratum were given to venting their emotions without restraint. It was among Chicago's black middle-class that Drake and Cayton recognized variation. Some middle-class churches tended to cater to "high-toned people" (a possible double meaning regarding both skin color and worship sensibility) while others differed little from the churches of the lower class. Even with this nuanced regard for "middle-class religion," Drake and Cayton as exemplars of the Chicago school of sociology remained wedded to the notion that socioeconomic class determined religious affiliation and ritual practice.[54]

There was a larger implication or consequence to the socioeconomic taxonomy of black churches that arose from the works of the Chicago school scholars. In the end, they fostered a dichotomy between northern modernity and southern premodernity with regard to African American religion. This rigid binarism infused each project. They each worked from the premise that the religion of the city was progressive and modern, while southern, rural black religion was of a primitive nature. W. E. B. Du Bois, influenced by the teachings of Hegel, must shoulder some of the responsibility for this and other binarisms in black culture, but the juxtaposition of northern modernity and southern premodernity in black religion can be linked directly the Chicago school of sociology.[55] And the binarism found its fullest expression in the writings of Richard Wright, who on more than one occasion acknowledged that he was greatly influenced by the theoretical models of the Chicago school. In Wright's migration narratives—*Native Son, American Hunger,* and *12 Million Black Voices* —black southern migrants were depicted as racially subjugated by structural power and white domination.[56] Only those migrants who acquired what Wright called a "critical consciousness" through their northern experiences could, in his words, "march into modernity." Wright apparently believed that developing this "critical consciousness" was difficult, if not impossible, for black southern migrants. As Farah Jasmine Griffin has noted, a dominant theme in the migration narratives of Richard Wright has been the "inability of the majority of black people to understand and enter civilization."[57] The march into civilization and modernity required a break from the premodern folk traditions of the South, and according to Wright, nowhere was the inability or unwillingness to do this more clearly demonstrated than in the churches of migrants. Wright depicted the churches of migrants, which he viewed exclusively as storefronts, as provincial and nonprogressive. They were "safe spaces" where southern migrants kept alive a sense of themselves "in relation to the total world" in which they lived. They were also "the orbit of the surviving remnants of the culture of the south, our naïve, casual, verbal, fluid folk life."[58] Though somewhat ambivalent about their value on the whole, Wright understood these "safe spaces" of migrants to be without any potential to challenge the social order, as islands of southern religious folk practice that prevented their assemblage from facing the modern world. Further, Wright's view of migrant churches implied that black women, particularly, were primarily premodern since it was well established that these smaller churches were overwhelmingly attended and run by women. According to Wright, "the consciousness of vast sections of our black women lies beyond the boundaries of the modern world, though they live and work in that world daily."[59] Black migrant women, therefore, held the strongest link to the folk past and were the greatest hindrance to modernity among black southern migrants.

In his now classic introduction to *Black Metropolis,* Wright acknowledged his debt to the Chicago school of sociology for the structure of his thought regarding black urban life. He wrote, "it was from the scientific findings of men like the late Robert E. Park, Robert Redfield, and Louis Wirth that I drew the meanings for my documentary book *12 Million Black Voices,* and for my novel, *Native Son.*" The influence of the Chicago school was also evident in his tendency to privilege structure over agency and to depict black southern religion as provincial and premodern. His friend and contemporary, Horace Cayton, held the same views. Cayton spoke of the "acids of modernity," a phrase coined by Walter Lippmann in the late 1920s, which he hoped would "weaken the otherworldly faith brought from the South."[60] Although he was not a sociologist by training, Wright incorporated a tremendous amount of sociological theory into his fiction and social commentary on black life. As a chief proponent of the dichotomy between northern modernity and southern premodernity, he cast his lot with a specific group of social theorists during the first half of the twentieth century who had begun to examine and to explain the social function of black urban religion in Chicago.

ALTHOUGH BRIEF AND SPARSE when one considers the iconic importance of Chicago to the Great Migration, the analyses of black religion by Wright, Drake, Cayton, Strong, and others held great value. The first value is that they confirmed in various ways that Chicago sat at the center of the process of migration. Chicago indeed was the "Mecca of the migrant mob." Second, we have from them the initial composites of black faith in the urban midwestern metropolis. It is from this literature that the contours of black church life begin to take shape, including some understanding of the challenges posed to congregations by the influx of southern migrants. Third, we see clearly the methods used to study and to discuss black religion in Chicago. And it is here that we encounter a significant shortcoming in these analyses. The sociological methods used to study black Chicago religion, with their emphasis on class determinism and normative ideology, obscured a more dynamic picture of black religion that was emerging in their midst. Lacey Kirk Williams perhaps inadvertently spoke to this dynamism when he warned of the numerous other religious movements that possibly vied for the attention of new migrants. He almost certainly overstated the prospect of mass defections from conventional black churches for alternative groups, but like most Chicagoans, he was well aware of the existence and relative attractiveness of these new religious expressions. Also, social class was by no means the sole factor in determining one's church affiliation or religious sensibility. Neither were black Chicago churches comprised of a single social class, as had been the case in the previous century. Class was perhaps the least among a variety of factors that influenced church affiliation and ritual practice during the Great Migration. As we shall see with storefront churches, economics and class played a lesser role in the development of storefronts as compared with the desire to exert regional identification.

The sociological methods used to study black religion during the migration era also tended to disregard human agency in the construction of black religion. The religious passivity that emanated from these writings reflected a misunderstanding of something fundamental about religion, perhaps black religion in particular. Black urban religion in Chicago was constructed contextually through social networks. It was the end result of human arrangements. The thoughts of anthropologist Clifford Geertz are applicable on this score. Geertz has held that all aspects of religion must be understood as social in origin, providing meaning to a wide variety of human experiences, individual and communal.[61] The Great Migration provided the context wherein Chicago African Americans, southern migrants and long-term residents alike, constructed black church culture according to specific historical, economic, and social conditions. The pervasiveness of a southern religious ethos over the entire religious scene and the cultural dominance of black southerners were intrinsic to that dynamic. The new urban religion envisioned by Lacey Kirk Williams had taken hold in black Chicago during the migration era, even as important aspects of it eluded the view of some scholars. It was an urban religious expression, necessarily pragmatic as it attempted to meet the temporal and spiritual needs of the new migrants. It was also one where conceptions of religious progress were represented in the "old-time religion" that many poor and working class southern migrants espoused. The religion of migrants simultaneously revealed continuity with the past and a confrontation with the present and in the process radically transformed black religion in Chicago.

CHAPTER TWO

The South in the City

> *The city is a world of rapid change. Such a tempo of life affects even religious behavior profoundly.*
>
> —St. Clair Drake

> *Of all aspects of community life religious activities were most profoundly changed by the migration.*
>
> —Allan Spear

THE DEATH of Julius Nelthropp Avendorph in 1923 marked the end of an era in black Chicago. Having come from Mobile, Alabama, in 1884, Avendorph by the time of his passing was "one of the best known men" within the city's African American social circles. No social gathering of any note was complete without the presence of this meticulous man of style and manners. Debuts and "coming out" parties were deemed failures if Avendorph could not be secured as master of ceremonies. In his role as the "social arbiter of Chicago colored society," Avendorph edited the society page of the *Chicago Defender*, and helped establish the Columbia and the Half Century clubs. He also founded the prestigious Appomattox Club, which was run on "a pretentious scale," providing social life and recreation for an exclusive list of members. The guest lists for his private social occasions included African Americans of national prominence, such as Booker T. Washington. Befitting his status as one of Chicago's black "aristocrats," Avendorph's funeral took place at St. Thomas Protestant Episcopal, "the church of the Negro elite," where he and his wife had been members.[1]

In the later years of his life, Avendorph lamented what he considered the demise of his world, the world of strict moral standards, decorum, and social distinction. In two articles published in the *Chicago Defender*, Avendorph expressed dismay not only at the loosening of social standards among Chicago's blacks but also at the intrusion by "questionable characters and social impostors" into elite circles. "Twenty-two years ago," he wrote in 1917, "Chicago could rightfully claim a real social set that stood for high ideals and did not hesitate to draw a line of demarcation." Expressive of what Hazel Carby has called "moral panic," Avendoph found distasteful the new social arrangements that allowed for such things as kissing in public places. Even more troubling to him, however, was the

blurring of social and class lines. In the Chicago of the 1890s, he editorialized, "class distinction" was the "cardinal rule." In the homes of that
generation's "society people," who provided the city's black leadership,
"exclusiveness permeated the very atmosphere."[2] That exclusiveness which
Avendorph recalled was intrinsic to late nineteenth- and early twentieth-
century black Chicago, where there was a strict demarcation of social
classes. A class-based racial hierarchy characterized the black community,
separating the city's African American elite from the masses throughout
the community's organizational structure, the city's African American
women's and men's clubs, social clubs, and choral societies. The rosters of
the men's clubs contained the most prestigious names in black Chicago,
and their formal balls and receptions were some of the city's grandest
annual events. Membership was restricted to middle-class professionals,
businessmen, and those who held a "responsible position."[3] Correspond-
ingly, membership in most of black Chicago's musical organizations, choruses, and choirs was strict and exclusive. With reputations to maintain
for music of the highest quality, involvement in each group was carefully
monitored and limited to the "highly refined." The performances by
these groups often deliberately targeted audiences of the "more cultured
class" and were by no means democratic affairs. When the Umbria Glee
Club gave its initial concert of the season in 1910 at Quinn Chapel AME,
it was to "a large gathering of Chicago's best society people."[4] In part to
reflect Victorian values of decorum and to counter notions of black inferiority, the Chicago African Americans that populated these organizations
preoccupied themselves with correct manners, high morals, and refined
public display. This was done primarily to distinguish themselves from, in
the words of Fannie Barrier Williams, "the rabble, the ignorant and the
uncouth."[5]

The timing of these articles suggested that Avendorph attributed both
the breakdown in social decorum and the disruption of class distinction in
Chicago to the influx of southern migrants. By 1917, black Chicagoans
knew that a great mass movement was taking place among them and that
Chicago was the destination for many of those trekking northward. Most
were aware of the city's long history as a migrant point of entry. It had
been since the antebellum era.[6] But it was clear that this latest demographic shift was qualitatively and quantitatively different. Daily, with almost every train on the Illinois Central, as well as by car and by bus,
thousands of new blacks filtered into Chicago.[7] For longtime residents
like Julius Avendorph, it seemed as if the entire South was coming to their
city.[8] Those who thought this were correct in a couple of ways. The number of black Chicagoans born in other states would overtake those who
had been born in Illinois during the nineteenth century. By 1920 more
than ninety-one thousand blacks were from outside the state, as opposed

Black migrants living in chicago outnumbered black native chicagoans

to the sixteen thousand born in Illinois, which is to say that 83 percent of blacks in Chicago during 1920 came from elsewhere. The largest percentage of those were from the states of Tennessee, Kentucky, Mississippi, and Alabama. More than five times as many people claimed Mississippi as their birth origin in 1920 as did in 1910.[9] By the time of the Second World War, black Chicago would be composed overwhelmingly of those whose formative experiences had taken place in the southern United States.

As significant as that is, it is more significant that black southern migrants brought to Chicago a distinctly southern ethos. Though dispersed from the South, black southern migrants remained committed to their home region and to southern ways of life. This commitment to southern cultural ties was the focal point of the tensions between southern migrants and "old settlers," and the primary means of self-identification by new arrivals. Southern migrants frequently referenced the South as "home" or "down home," indicating that the region maintained a tremendous hold on them culturally and emotionally. Even Richard Wright, who was as ambivalent about the South as he was about black southerners, confessed to the strong grip his southern heritage had on him. In his autobiographical novel, *Black Boy*, he asserted, "I knew that I could never leave the South, for my feelings had already been formed by the South, for there had been slowly instilled into my consciousness . . . the culture of the South."[10] Ideas about the meaning of the South served as the basis of solidarity among churchgoing black southerners as well as the tension between migrants and longtime residents.

The tensions that flared between new arrivals and longtime residents had as much to do with the region from which the migrants came as it did with their large numbers. Indeed, the bias some showed toward black southerners indicated a stern bias against the South. Primarily because migrants were from the rural South, longtime residents felt at liberty to scrutinize every aspect of migrant speech, dress, and behavior. They insisted new migrants conform to their own values of bourgeois respectability. Robert Abbott, who had encouraged the migration from the start, used the *Chicago Defender* to establish guidelines for migrant behavior. From 1917 up to the early 1920s, the African American weekly published lists titled "Some Don'ts," "A Few Do's and Don'ts," and simply "How to Act in Public Places," instructing black southerners in the ways of city life. Chief among the concerns was the apparent crudeness of migrant speech, mannerisms, and dress. "Don't use vile language in public places / Stop hooping from one end of the street car to another. You are not on a plantation, nor in a minstrel show / Don't go to market in your apron and wearing house-slippers and a boudoir cap."[11] In some ways this scrutiny reflected the actual habits of southern migrants, but in other ways it did more to reveal existing prejudices against the South. An editorial comment in the *Chicago Whip* expressed this clearly. "It's no difficult task to get people out of the South, but you have a job on your hands when you attempt to get the South out of them."[12]

Much of the thinking with regard to the backwardness of black southerners and the civility of urban blacks reflected slightly divergent interpretations of notions then emanating from the Chicago school of sociology. Influential African American writers and social theorists such as Horace Cayton, St. Clair Drake, E. Franklin Frazier, Charles S. Johnson, and Richard Wright, adhered to Darwinian metaphors with regard to rural existence and city life, or gemeinschaft and gesellschaft. This group added nuance to the thinking of Robert Part, their chief influence, by asserting the superiority of city life to rural life. Throughout much of his career at the University of Chicago, Park had actually attempted to demonstrate that rural existence maintained social and familial qualities that were mitigated or lost in urban settings. However, in attributing the values of "community" to rural life over against the attributes of "society" found in cities, he inadvertently constructed a hierarchy between the two. African American scholars and writers picked up on this. They began asserting that a central tenet of the Chicago school held that the communal ties of the rural South (gemeinschaft) were not only culturally debilitating and backward, they were also lower on the evolutionary scale than the voluntary association of city life or urban existence (gesellschaft).[13] Progress and "civilization" among black Americans, therefore, would only take place when they were released from the stranglehold of the rural "folk" past and embraced the liberating force of the city, a necessary adaptation to modern life. Certainly, some southern migrants, as Allen Spear noted, "seriously erred in their conduct in public places," lending credence to extant notions held by whites of black immorality and inferiority. Indeed, this was the greatest concern. For many black Chicagoans among the "respectable classes of Colored citizens," the "antics" of southern migrants demonstrated low breeding and a lack of cultural sophistication. So when Avendorph, "the Ward McAllister of the South Side," complained of relaxed standards and of "social imposters," there was little question of to whom he was referring.[14]

One could easily dismiss Avendorph's lament as merely "moral panic" or a romantic look back by an African American elitist to a lost and bemoaned time. On the deepest level, however, it expressed an awareness of one of the most important cultural shifts in the history of black Chicago. The demographic changes occurring with the Great Migration presaged a reordering or recharacterization of black life in the simplest terms from rural to urban, south to north, a permeation of a rural, vernacular sensibility into much of the religious institutional life of black Chicago. The

South was coming to the city both in terms of real numbers and through the means of cultural influence. It is doubtful that it came as any surprise to Avendorph that the migration was beginning to have an impact on the churches of black Chicago as well as on the religious culture in general. As a member of St. Thomas Episcopal, he would have been particularly concerned about this. St. Thomas had been established in the early 1890s to accommodate the tastes of the "ultra-aristocratic, proud and supercilious" among Chicago's black churchgoers. Although its building was not as imposing as even some of the Baptist and Methodist churches in town, it offered a highly liturgical worship service and a congregation consisting of many of the city's African American social and political leaders. The propensity for high liturgical worship developed from the influence of some of the church's earliest leaders, whose sentiments were more Catholic than Anglican. They were given to the sensuousness of Episcopal ritual—its sights, sounds, and smells—and were particularly fond of elaborate vestments. Church music was Eurocentric, sung by a "paid choir" of professional singers.[15] Quite simply, it was the church to attend for anyone concerned about social status and style, and it had been that way since it was founded. As a report on the church proclaimed in 1893, "the colored votaries of fashion single out St. Thomas from among the other churches as their particular place of worship."[16] The church's class consciousness extended to concerns about the neighborhood in which the building was located. In 1907, the congregation elected to vacate its edifice on Dearborn Street because poor and working-class African Americans had engulfed the area. They moved instead to Wabash Avenue, "one of the choicest streets of the city." This location suited the congregation better, for as Avendorph's fellow St. Thomas parishioner, Fannie Barrier Williams, remarked, it was "not an easy thing to be a real aristocrat on a street in the 'black belt.'"[17] Unfortunately for St. Thomas, as the number of migrants moving into the city pushed the residential area of African Americans ever southward, the church found itself again in the middle of the Black Belt, and eventually found within their congregation some of the southern migrants they had attempted to avoid.

The sweeping changes taking place in Chicago's African American religious culture and institutions touched Avendorph's family as well. When Georgia Avendorph died two years after her son did, her obituary hailed her as "one of the first to locate in Chicago," one of the city's "old settlers." A widow of advanced age, she was praised for her charity work in the latter years of her life. Tellingly, the obituary also noted Georgia Avendorph was a member of the Metropolitan Community Church and not of St. Thomas, which she had once attended along with her son. A group of former African Methodists who were dissatisfied with their denominations' ministerial policies as well as their diffident response to the migration founded Metropolitan in 1920. Of those who initially joined the congregation, thousands were recently from the South. As a community church, Metropolitan welcomed all classes of people, observed a non-liturgical pattern of worship, and had no official church creed. It was the very antithesis of St. Thomas Episcopal and a witness to the fracturing of strict class compositions in migration-era black Chicago churches.[18] In black Chicago's new religious order, Julius Avendorph's mother, a widowed "old settler" of obvious means, could leave the Episcopal church for Metropolitan, where she worshipped alongside new migrants and poorer black Chicagoans from the surrounding community.

The experience of Julius Avendorph and his family testified to the effectual disruption of one African American religious culture and the construction of another, one that was different in organizational form and in the way class operated within its institutions. Scholars have long noted that the Great Migration led to economic stratification or class differentiation among African Americans in the urban north. Social theorists began in the first years of migration to group urban blacks into categories of lower, working, middle, and elite classes. Blacks, too, began to recognize themselves clearly in distinction from one another along class lines. This stratification is perhaps one of the enduring legacies of the migration. But as a further consequence of its disruption of the middle-class religious establishment, the migration also complicated notions of social status. It blurred the criteria for social distinction.[19] Julius Avendorph worked his entire life as a messenger for the Pullman Company. Because of this relatively prestigious service position, in addition to his personal style and his religious affiliation, he was considered an aristocrat.[20] In a reciprocal process that had been in force since the early 1880s, Avendorph's membership at St. Thomas Episcopal signaled that it was a church for the black elite. Episcopal churches had been widely viewed since the antebellum era as the preferred church home of "aristocrats of color."[21] The church, in turn, confirmed his status as an aristocrat. After 1915, elite Protestant churches such as St. Thomas lost their ability to confer social status, as the criteria for social distinction changed from social decorum and length of time in the city to social capital, wealth, and profession. For Avendorph and others who shared his view, this development was tantamount to the end of society.

To complicate things further, new and newer kinds of churches outside the ecclesiastical mainstream emerged that challenged the primacy of established churches. On the extreme end were those churches that only marginally reflected orthodox Protestant Christian traditions. They were, however, large, wealthy, and well attended by a vast cross section of black Chicago citizens. The First Church of Deliverance, a Spiritualist congregation established by the Reverend Clarence Cobbs (see figure 2), began as a storefront on State Street, an area containing one of the densest populations

Fig. 2. Clarence Cobbs. Cobbs never hid his flamboyant style. Throughout his long career he was known to smoke the finest cigars, drive a "flashy car," and wear clothes of the "latest cut." (Source: Vivian G. Harsh Collection, Carter G. Woodson Regional Branch, Chicago Public Library)

of Chicago's African American poor at the time. Observing a new, radically demonstrative brand of Pentecostalism, Spiritualist churches practiced divine healing, psychic phenomena, and séances.[22] In other ways indistinguishable from a Pentecostal church, First Church of Deliverance heavily emphasized religious iconography (candles, incense, robes, sacred objects) and put communication with the spirit world at the core of its ministry. The church had many "mediums" among the congregation and Cobbs sold "blessed flowers" which promised to bring the wearer "good luck or some blessing." One WPA writer remarked that Cobbs's followers

THE WORLD OF THE LOWER CLASS

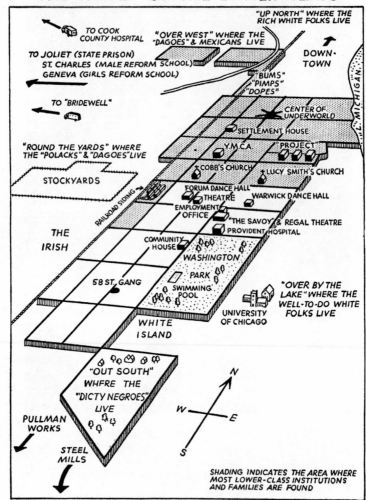

Fig. 3. The World of the Lower Class. Drake and Cayton used this map to demonstrate that Chicago's South Side was divided along racial, ethnic, and class lines. African Americans were further divided by class, which was reflected in their institutions. They depicted Clarence Cobb's First Church of Deliverance and Elder Lucy Smith's All Nations Pentecostal as representative of "lower-class institutions" even though by the 1940s those congregations were not made up entirely of "the lower class." (Source: St. Clair Drake and Horace Cayton, *Black Metropolis: A Study of Negro Life in a Northern City* [Chicago: University of Chicago Press, 1993])

obtained these pendants like "hungry children at a picnic." By the 1940s, the church—by then housed in an art moderne–style building—boasted more than two thousand members and one hundred officers. (Cobbs claimed the church had a "membership over 10,000"). The "soft-spoken" and "very polished" Reverend Mattie Thornton, or "Mother Mattie" as she was called, served as the church's assistant pastor. First Church of Deliverance claimed enough resources to send Cobbs on "an expensive vacation trip" each year. He often took these vacations with his male secretary, R. Edward Bolden, fueling the speculation that he was homosexual. The church became enormously popular during the migration and acquired a congregation comprising citizens across a wide spectrum, even though Drake and Cayton considered it representative of "the world of the lower class." (See figure 3.) Annual banquets sponsored by the church (usually held at Bacon's Casino, the former garage turned jazz club), as well as other special events, were elaborate affairs that attracted numerous civic officials and local dignitaries such as Mrs. Robert S. Abbott.[23] Cobbs sat on the executive committee of the Chicago branch of the NAACP and wielded significant political influence as well. Courted by politicians who recognized the potential of such a large and obedient following at his church, Cobbs received many rewards for "delivering the votes." Chicago activist Timuel Black recalled that "speaking out against Cobbs" at the height of his popularity was to "lose something" personally or professionally.[24] As politicians came to realize, the reverse was also true.

Not coincidentally, the First Church of Deliverance and Metropolitan Community Church share a history. Two of Metropolitan's earliest members, William Frank Taylor and Leviticus Lee Boswell, left that church in 1925 to organize the "mother church" of Spiritualist churches in Kansas City, Missouri—the Metropolitan Spiritualist Churches of Christ. This became the parent church of First Church of Deliverance.[25] In the same way that St. Thomas Episcopal had been the church of the fashionable in a previous generation, able to endow its members with a certain social standing, attendance at First Church of Deliverance came to wield similar power. Though the church appealed primarily to the city's poor, First Church of Deliverance generated a large following among the middle class, the young, and those "slightly above Bronzeville's average in education."[26] Members of the church became a new generation of "fashionable worshippers" with high social standing, which represented an important aspect of the dynamic shifts taking place among the black churches of Chicago.

THE CONSTRUCTION of a new African American religious culture in black Chicago based on differing notions of class and status was one of the most significant transformations to the religious scene. The most obvious development, however, involved the unprecedented increase in the number of churches and the rate of growth within existing congregations. Between 1916 and 1920 alone, the congregations of Salem Baptist Church increased by 51 percent, St. Mark's Methodist Episcopal by 100 percent, and Walter's African Methodist Episcopal church by 338 percent. By 1930, five black churches in Chicago—Olivet Baptist, Pilgrim Baptist, Ebenezer Baptist, Greater Bethesda Baptist, and Metropolitan Community Church—claimed memberships exceeding two thousand.[27] (See table 1.) Growth in memberships and in the number of churches was greatest among black Baptists. By the 1920s, Chicago contained more black Baptist churches than any other denomination.[28] The rapid rate of growth of the number of churches became the first concern of longtime residents, ahead of the pervasive spread of the vernacular religious practices that would soon follow. The number of black churches in Chicago grew steadily after the 1890s, but with the rapid influx of southern blacks beginning in 1915, the number of churches skyrocketed. Indeed, black churches became so numerous and varied that an accurate accounting became almost impossible. As the religious landscape continuously shifted, there was no conceivable way demographers could account for all black churches in the city. Many of them would not have been exactly sure what to look for at a time when the very definition of sacred space was in flux. By the end of the nineteenth century, there were about twelve black churches in Chicago, ranging from those such as Quinn Chapel AME and Olivet Baptist, which had been established since the 1840s and 1850s, to those such as Grace Presbyterian and St. Thomas Episcopal, which were established in the late 1880s and early 1890s. Between 1900 and 1915 the number of black churches in Chicago reportedly jumped to about twenty five, including ten "modern churches" costing between seven thousand and fifty thousand dollars each.[29] Miles Mark Fisher, son of Olivet's sixth pastor, Elijah John Fisher, estimated that twenty-two new African American churches were established in Chicago between 1915 and 1918. Allan Spear claimed that there were thirty-six Baptist churches and twenty-two Methodist churches in the city by 1916. Both of these estimates were most likely conservative ones, only taking into account traditional denominations and churches occupying standard worship spaces. Founders of many new black churches could not always be attentive to concerns for regular worship spaces and chose to establish churches wherever they could afford and in spaces convenient to their members. It was not uncommon for dance halls, outdoor tents, and school auditoriums to become worship spaces—often for extended periods of time. Storefront and "house churches," which began to appear in the Black Belt mostly along State Street as early as 1904, mushroomed after 1915. Easy to establish and transitory by nature, storefronts and house churches were perhaps the

TABLE 1
Black Chicago Churches with Congregations Exceeding 2,000 (1930)

1. Olivet Baptist

2. Pilgrim Baptist

3. Liberty Baptist

4. Ebenezer Baptist

5. Greater Bethesda Baptist

6. Metropolitan Community Church

Sources: "Pilgrim Baptist Church," WPA, FWP Files, box 182, Illinois Historical Library; "Ebenezer Missionary Baptist Church," WPA, FWP Files, container A125, folder: "Illinois Religion," Library of Congress; Amos Martin Meredith, Oneida Cockrell, and Dr. Daniel W. Hopkins, *History of the Olivet Baptist Church* (Chicago: Olivet Baptist Church, 1992); "The History of Liberty Baptist Church," WPA, IWP Files, box 18, Vivian Harsh Collection, Carter Woodson Regional Branch, Chicago Public Library; "Bethesda Baptist Church," WPA, IWP Files, box 18, Vivian Harsh Collection, Carter Woodson Regional Branch, Chicago Public Library; "Metropolitan Community Church, WPA, IWP Files, box 18, Vivian Harsh Collection, Carter Woodson Regional Branch, Chicago Public Library.

most difficult to tally and the easiest to escape view. Charles S. Johnson's assertion that by 1923 there were 200 black churches in Chicago, and Robert Lee Sutherland's more empirically based study, which found 278 black Chicago churches in 1928, were almost certainly still well short of the actual numbers.[30]

The migration affected every black church that had been operating in Chicago for any length of time. Bethesda Baptist is a case in point. Established by former members of Olivet Baptist in 1882, Bethesda purchased property on Wabash Avenue from a white Evangelical Lutheran church in 1907 to accommodate its modest congregation of about two hundred. By 1922, the congregation numbered in the thousands, including "several of the richest Chicago Negroes" such as Anthony Overton of Overton Hygienic Manufacturing Company and Mrs. Jesse Binga, wife of Chicago's most prominent black banker. Bethesda quickly outgrew its Wabash Avenue location and determined to build a new edifice or to buy larger quarters. In 1925, the congregation purchased the Isaiah Temple Israel, a former Jewish synagogue known to be "one of the most beautiful structures of its kind in the city." The purchase represented one of several cases where a former Jewish worship space became an African American worship space, melding in a unique way Jewish and Christian iconography and architecture. The building was located at 5300 South Michigan Avenue, a formerly white area that had because of racial transition become

almost entirely African American. In this instance, the transition was exclusively on racial terms. A coterie of middle-class blacks replaced the
middle-class white and Jewish population that had occupied the neighborhood, locating Bethesda's congregation "in the very heart of the better
strata of the Negro residential district." Despite its location and the presence of prominent blacks among the membership, Bethesda Baptist comprised many black southern migrants as well. It is likely that the church's
attraction to migrants figured secondarily as a motive when Bethesda was
bombed shortly after the congregation took occupancy of the building.
The primary reason these "die-hard segregationists," as the *Chicago Defender* dubbed them, "almost completely wrecked" the church was because
Bethesda Baptist occupied a former Jewish synagogue and was located in a
previously white and Jewish neighborhood.[31] After a vast cross-section of
Chicago citizens launched an intense and successful campaign to raise
funds to repair the church, Bethesda continued to acquire an enormous
congregation.

Ebenezer Baptist experienced similar growth. The Reverend John
Francis Thomas established the church in 1901 when he broke from
Olivet Baptist after a disagreement about the purchase of church property.
By 1921, Ebenezer was one of the four largest churches that were, as
WPA writers reported, "serving the Negro people of Chicago." Like
Bethesda, Ebenezer discovered that its present building had become inad-
equate and that it needed a new structure. With sufficient resources to
do so, the congregation also purchased a former synagogue, the Temple
Isaiah at Forty-fifth street and Vincennes Avenue, the last major work of
the famed Chicago architect Dankmar Adler. Adler, who has been over-
shadowed by his fellow architect and business partner, Louis Sullivan, designed more than a hundred buildings in his lifetime, including the Chicago
Auditorium and the Chicago Stock Exchange. While a claim of a WPA
worker in 1941 that Ebenezer maintained a membership of "more than
20,000 worshipers" was surely an exaggeration, Ebenezer's congregation
unquestionably ran well into the thousands and, like many churches of its
kind, included a significant number of recent migrants from the South.[32]

By far, Olivet Baptist Church received the largest number of southern
migrants into its ranks, becoming not only the largest church of any kind
in the city, but by some accounts "the largest Protestant church of any
race in the world."[33] Established in 1850, Olivet was the first African
American Baptist church in Chicago and in a real sense was the "mother
church" of many black Baptist congregations. In 1915 the church, located
at Twenty-seventh and Dearborn, claimed an enrollment of four thousand
members. That number was already incredible by early twentieth-century
standards for black congregations, but in 1917 the membership leaped to
seven thousand, forcing the need for a new building. Under the direction

of its new pastor, Lacey Kirk Williams, the congregation relocated to the First Baptist Church, the former home of the oldest white Baptist congregation in Chicago, on the corner of Thirty-first and South Park Way.[34] The First Baptist Church readily agreed to sell its building to Olivet because the surrounding neighborhood was quickly transitioning and its congregation dwindling. As a report made by First Baptist regarding its sale to Olivet stated, "The Negroes coming from the South by tens of thousands, lured by the promise of high wages in the packing houses, mills, and railroad yards of Chicago swarmed to the blocks surrounding the church building." As a result, the membership of the church declined to just over four hundred. The church faced "catastrophe," the report concluded, because "no eloquent preaching, no social service, could save a [white] church in a community that was 100 percent Negro." On the day the members of Olivet moved into their new church home, they celebrated the acquisition of the building by staging a parade of thousands that stretched from Dearborn Street to South Park Way. Williams and his ministerial staff led the parade. A year after taking possession of the building, Olivet Baptist added 2,670 members and, by the mid-1920s, estimates of Olivet's membership ranged from eleven thousand to fourteen thousand.[35] Williams, employing his phenomenal leadership skill and an abundance of financial and personnel resources, helped Olivet negotiate its meteoric rise in membership with an ease that eluded other mainline black Chicago churches.[36]

In addition to swelling the ranks of long-established mainline black churches in Chicago, the Great Migration generated myriad new mainline churches, organized specifically for new migrants. Many of these were the outgrowth of regionally specific "migrant clubs" and prayer groups that met in houses. Black Baptists, in particular, found these methods effective in developing a diasporic and regathered religious community in Chicago. The history of Pilgrim Baptist Church typified that of many mainline churches organized during the initial wave of migration, starting as the Union Grow Prayer Club in the home of Mr. and Mrs. J. A. Fink in 1915.[37] The church became a roving congregation for many years before establishing a permanent church building. Monumental Baptist Church also developed from a "prayer band." E. J. Jackson started the congregation in the home of Mrs. Ida Windsor in 1918 and it quickly grew into a small church pastored by Reverend J. H. Smith. Attempts to merge with the Come and See Baptist Church failed in 1920, and Smith left. In 1921 the church called a Reverend Madison, formerly of Montgomery, Alabama, whose presence drew "many Alabamians" to Monumental. One of those Alabamians later testified as to how the worship at the church reflected the practices familiar to those from that region. In an interview with a WPA worker in 1939, a migrant from Tuskegee reported that she had "received the Holy Spirit" one Sunday while sitting in Monumental Baptist when she began to "speak with tongues."[38] A group of lay members also founded Liberty Baptist Church in 1918. The group was explicit about why it formed the church, judging that "more churches were needed to accommodate the hordes of immigrants from the rural south." The church grew "with rapid strides" and was soon forced to seek a larger building. The congregation agreed to purchase the old Olivet Building at Twenty-seventh and Dearborn in 1924, a Renaissance-style structure designed by one of the country's first African American architects, J. M. Higginbotham. By embedding a Star of David in a circular window on the larger of two unequal towers, Higginbotham made the building unique among original African American church structures. He also presaged the melding of Jewish and African American religious iconography that would typify many aspects of Chicago's black religious culture during the migration.[39] The congregation called Dr. D. Z. Jackson, a former Mississippi pastor who had come to Chicago in 1923. Jackson, who had already merged the Centennial Church and the Christian Home Baptist Church at Twenty-fifth and State, proved himself a capable pastor and recruiter of southern migrants. Over the next decade, Liberty's membership grew from one hundred and twenty to over three thousand.[40]

Chicago became so ripe a field for creating new churches that some were established before there were any members. Many church officials demonstrated great faith that the influx of black southerners would quickly fill empty pews. They had every reason to believe that their prospects for finding congregants were good, since the vast majority of migrants would likely be churchgoers. It was deemed safe to work from the principle that no African American church in the Black Belt would ever sit empty for very long. The Reverend Pettis T. Gorham had no members when he opened the Indiana Methodist Church in 1928. Bishop Clement of the African Methodist Episcopal Zion (AMEZ) church had attempted to purchase the property from the City Missionary Society, of which Gorham was the district superintendent, but the society wanted it as "a place of worship" for Methodists, particularly those "just moving into the neighborhood."[41] In 1928, Charles Palmerton Anderson, bishop of the white Protestant Episcopal Churches of Illinois ordained Samuel J. Martin as deacon and charged him with a new ministry on Indiana Avenue, a mission church named St. Edmund's. The bishop's charge to Martin was forthright: "I can only offer to you a building, there is no congregation. It will be up to you to secure your congregation. I am tremendously interested in this new mission among colored people; I count upon you." As white Episcopalians moved out of the area, vacating the church, the bishop saw the potential to build a black Episcopal congregation on the South Side. The building otherwise would have sat empty, and this provided the Episcopal Church with an opportunity to gather a congregation from "the greatly increased Negro population in the vicinity."[42] It was a daring move on the bishop's part, considering that, St. Thomas notwithstanding, few working-class black southern migrants were likely to affiliate with the Episcopal Church on their own initiative. During the antebellum period, the Episcopal Communion in the United States had claimed a sizable black membership, especially in the South and particularly in the rural areas of Virginia, the Carolinas, and Georgia. Nearly half of all Episcopalians in South Carolina in 1860, for example, were black. After emancipation, however, there was a "wholesale exodus" out of the denomination—and its white control—into predominately black denominations. The relationship between African Americans and the Episcopal Church became so tattered that it prompted W. E. B. Du Bois (who was confirmed in the Episcopal Church) to proclaim in 1903 that it had "probably done less for black people than any other aggregation of Christians."[43] Martin, a former Alabamian and Baptist took readily to his new charge. When St. Edmund's opened its doors for worship in 1929 he canvassed the neighborhood recruiting new members. His efforts were met with success. In the late 1930s, the church's communicant list was close to a thousand, and more than three hundred considered themselves regular members. By 1946 the congregation purchased the former home of St. Constantine Greek Orthodox Church on South Michigan Avenue.

St. Edmund's is also significant for the way it demonstrates the tenacity of a perception of class homogeneity within congregations, despite the class fragmentation occurring in most congregations. These tensions bubbled under the surface at all times, particularly in the historical denominations. Farm Security Administration (FSA) photographers Jack Delano, Russell Lee, and Edwin Rosskam fixated on St. Edmund's during 1941 and 1942, taking dozens of photographs. Their pictures seem to represent a "fashionable Negro church" composed exclusively of the black elite. Indeed, the church's roster did contain the names of many black professionals, actors such as Richard B. Harrison of *The Green Pastures* fame, and politicians such as Earl B. Dickerson. Such events as the annual flower and fashion shows and the regular teas, complete with ice sculptures, tended to bolster the church's elitist air. But as his daughter recalled, not only did Father Martin deliberately seek out the poor and working class to join the congregation, the neighborhood around the parish could not have sustained a congregation composed exclusively of the black elite. The congregation was "mixed," she asserted, despite its elite characterization and denominational affiliation. And it was the poor and working-class members of St. Edmund's that primarily benefited from the church's many programs, including its parochial school, employment agency, and "social service guild."[44] (See figure 4.)

Fig. 4. St. Edmund's Episcopal Church. The first African American Episcopal church in Chicago, St. Edmunds started with no members in 1928. By the 1940s, the church was thriving and multifaceted with a class-diverse congregation. (Source: Library of Congress)

The story of Chicago's migration-era African American religious culture is about more than the phenomenal increase in the number of churches and their congregational sizes. The larger significance lies in the changes that took place within congregations. The jump in the number of churches and the swelling of black congregations is not to be underappreciated, for nothing like it had occurred in the history of the city. But in many ways, it was a natural consequence of the population increase by a largely churchgoing group from the South. The phenomenon of church and congregational growth was taking place in other northern cities—such as Washington, D.C., New York, Philadelphia, Detroit, and Cleveland—during the same period. Cleveland's Antioch Baptist Church, for example, grew from a congregation of five hundred to fourteen hundred by the mid-1920s. Shiloh Baptist Church, also located in Cleveland, added three thousand members, taking its congregation to five thousand people.[45] What was more remarkable was the specific ways the interplay between the migration and city life began to cast black Christianity in a more dynamic light. St. Clair Drake hinted at this in the 1940s when he surmised that "the city is a world of rapid change. Such a tempo of life affects even religious behavior profoundly."[46]

The clearest evidence of that interplay was the rise of the storefront church and the pervasive spread of storefront religion—the religion of black southern migrants—into mainstream churches.

THE STOREFRONT CHURCH represented the most common type of church established during the migration. An original institutional creation among urban blacks in the twentieth century, storefronts signified unequivocally that the new religious culture emerging among the city's blacks was rooted in the African American religious culture of the rural South. The worship practices of the vast majority of storefront devotees made this clear. At the same time, storefront churches were decidedly expressive of the urban experience. Everything about them, from their location, to their physicality to their social policies, connoted city life. More than any other religious institutional development, storefronts indicated that urban space—the streets themselves—would be contested space. Each time a storefront church was established, usually along the State and Federal streets corridor, the congregation demarcated a bit of sacred space alongside commercial ventures, entertainment venues, and vice. In this way, Chicago's storefront churches were just as much products of urbanization as they were exemplars of the newly emerging religious culture.

The exact origin of the term "storefront" is not known, but it came into common parlance in the early twentieth century to describe vacant stores converted to resemble and function as traditional church edifices. Because they were easy to establish, storefronts became popular among southern migrants, who could organize quickly, and thereby in some instances, simply "reestablish their [former] churches in the Northern metropolis."[47] In most cases, a fresh coat of paint, some chairs, and a bulletin board proclaiming the new church were all that was required. James Baldwin provided an apt description of how a storefront church was formed in his migration narrative, *Go Tell It on the Mountain*.[48] His vivid prose designated the territorial constestation and the evangelical fire that was fueled by the scrabble for sacred space in the urban north, in this case New York City's Harlem.

> It was a store-front church and had stood, for John's lifetime, on the corner of this sinful avenue, facing the hospital to which criminal wounded and dying were carried almost every night. The saints, arriving, had rented this abandoned store and taken out the fixtures; had painted the walls and built the pulpit, moved in a piano and camp chairs, and bought the biggest Bible they could find. They put white curtains in the show window, and painted across the window TEMPLE OF THE FIRE BAPTIZED. Then they were ready to do the Lord's work.[49]

Usually these churches took shape when several members of the same southern congregation were joined in Chicago by their former pastor. Southern migrant Junius Gaten recalled that just as African American *following livelihood*

musicians were following their audiences north during the Great Migration, "so too were preachers who'd see their whole flock take off for Chicago." Other ministers migrated along with their congregations. The Reverend R. H. Harmon arrived from Mississippi with his wife and twenty-eight members of his congregation, declaring that they were in Chicago "for keeps."[50] Vacant stores emerged during this era as often the first—and sometimes the permanent—houses of worship for black southerners. Contrary to those scholars who claim that storefronts do not exist as a "substantive category" of black church, storefronts represented one of the most viable expressions migration-era Chicago religious institutions. They expressed a unique ontology of black churches.[51] And for many black southerners, storefronts best represented their identity as religious people. The long length of time some congregations chose to occupy storefront edifices seems to corroborate this. Although some congregations worshiped in storefronts for only brief periods of time, until they moved to a regular edifice, others remained seemingly committed to the physicality and social placement of their churches long after they were able to relocate. Various congregations on the South Side chose to expand existing storefront edifices rather than abandon them, even when it was financially possible.

The prevalence of storefront churches did not escape the attention of social scientists, demographers, and ordinary Chicago citizens. As one middle-class African American interviewee complained to Drake and Cayton, "there's a store-front everywhere you turn."[52] This was not true, but storefront churches far outnumbered those in regular edifices, and they dotted every commercial street on the South Side. They were often located two and three in a row. (See figure 5.) "One street alone," Drake and Cayton further reported, "had 90 to a three mile stretch, or 1.9 per block."[53] Affordability only partly explains the prevalence of storefront churches. Other reasons reached deeper into the structure of these new institutions. Storefronts were absolutely autonomous in many cases, which allowed for a great deal of innovation and theological eclecticism. They ordinarily did what they wanted when they wanted in terms that were set by the founder of the church or someone among the leadership. The autonomy of many storefronts usually meant that the founder of the church or the founder's family owned everything in the church, including chairs, hymn books, and sacred objects. This unilateralism rendered splits among storefront churches particularly vicious. Their theological eclecticism often matched their institutional inventiveness. It was not uncommon for congregations to pick and choose among the major tenets of the Christian faith. Church iconography and vestments sometimes reflected a random mix of Catholic, Protestant, and Eastern Orthodox traditions. Nomenclature and the structure of church hierarchies were equally imaginative, including categories of "seekers,"

Fig. 5. Storefront Religion. In 1941, WPA worker Arthur Weinberg compiled a booklet titled *Storefront Religion: An Impressionistic Account of the Negro Cult in Chicago.* Weinberg cast storefront churches as small businesses dedicated to "selling religion." The success of storefronts at doing so, he explained, accounted for their ubiquity. The drawing by Charles Fencel suggests the large number of black Chicago storefronts, which were often in close proximity to one another, and equates them with other commercial ventures. (Source: Center for Family and Community History, Newberry Library Archives)

"saints," "bishops," "prophets," and even "apostles." By the late 1930s, none of the churches among the traditional denominations were housed in storefront edifices. A high percentage of Baptist churches were. Many of these churches, particularly among the Baptists, had simply transplanted from the South and were affiliated with an overseeing denominational body. This, however, was not true in most cases. Many of these smaller Baptist churches and the host of various Pentecostal and Holiness churches maintained no connection to a governing denominational head. In many cases, they represented the start of an entirely new, fledgling denomination altogether. Often the model of leadership and organizational structure only loosely resembled that of mainline or evangelical churches. The highest percentage of Baptist storefronts in 1938 (27.8) were of "no special designation," meaning they were not connected to any governing denominational body.[54] (See table 2.) The traditional autonomous nature of black Baptist, Pentecostal, and independent churches and the openness of urban culture allowed for the great inventiveness in Chicago's African American religious culture, as well as the prevalent spread of storefronts.

As storefront churches began to outnumber those in regular buildings, complaints surfaced suggesting that there were simply too many black churches in the city. While that may have been the case from the standpoint of the ratio of the number of churches to the actual population, the content of these complaints revealed that the concern was not so much about the number of mainstream churches but the kinds of churches and

TABLE 2
Negro Religious Bodies in Chicago, Storefronts (1938)

Group	Denomination	Number	Percentage
1.	Baptist (no special designation)	62	27.8
	Missionary Baptist	40	17.9
	Primitive Baptist	3	1.3
2.	African Methodist Episcopal	4	1.8
	African Methodist Episcopal Zion	4	1.8
	Colored Methodist Episcopal	–	–
3.	Methodist Episcopal	–	–
	Episcopal	–	–
	Presbyterian	–	–
	Congregational	–	–
	Seventh Day Adventists	–	–
	Catholic (Roman)	–	–
	Lutheran	–	–
	Church of Christ Scientist	–	–
4.	Community Churches	2	.9
5.	Church of God in Christ	20	9.0
	Church of Christ (Holiness U.S.A.)	1	.4
	Church of Christ (no designation)	–	–
	Church of God (no designation)	4	1.8
	Church of the Living God	2	.9
	Church of God (Holiness)	2	.9
	Church of God and Saints of Christ	4	1.8
	Apostolic and Pentecostal	17	7.6
	Pentecostal Assemblies of the World	2	.9
	Old Time Methodist	–	–
	Holiness (miscellaneous groups)	18	8.1
6.	Spiritual and Spiritualist	27	12.1
	I.A.M.E. Spiritual	9	4.0
7.	Cumberland Presbyterian	1	.5
	African Orthodox	–	–
	Christial Catholic	–	–
	Liberal Catholic	1	.5
	Others	–	–
	Grand total	223	100.00

Source: St. Clair Drake Papers, box 57, Schomburg Center for Reasearch in Black Culture, New York.

the people who occupied them. These complaints extended beyond anxieties about the number of storefronts to the issue of their constituency, physicality, and most important, their worship practices. For many longtime black Chicago residents, the problem with storefronts was threefold: there were too many of them, their buildings didn't resemble regular church edifices, and the people who attended were most likely poor and from the South. These concerns revealed a bias that conflated issues of class and region.

On the surface, the evidence would seem to suggest that the conflict over storefront churches was solely about socioeconomics. A closer examination shows that it involved other factors as well. Because storefronts tended to concentrate in, as Drake and Cayton noted, "run-down, low-rent, business streets," they became associated with "the religion of the lower class." Indeed, the membership of storefront churches was disproportionately poor and female, and many storefronts occupied buildings that were in a state of great disrepair along commercial stretches of the Black Belt that also were physically dilapidated. The physical condition of these buildings accounted, in part, for their affordability.[55] But the designation of storefronts as the religion of the lower class was as much a pejorative statement about southern migrants and their worship proclivities as it was a commentary on their economic status. We know this because most but not all storefront churches were located in low-income commercial areas. A study done in 1938 found that 66 percent of Chicago's reportedly one hundred and seven Holiness churches were of the storefront variety. Although 24 percent of all Holiness churches were located in the "worst" areas, usually along State Street, 22 percent were located in "mixed" areas and 17 percent were located in the "best" areas.[56] (See figure 6.) Though primarily clustered in the most economically depressed areas of the Black Belt, storefront churches were not exclusively located in these areas, and they drew their memberships from among those in the "mixed" and "best" neighborhoods. Clearly, the easy generalization of storefront churches as belonging to the religion of the lower class had to do with their patterns of worship, no matter where these churches were located. It was storefronts and storefront religion that were at the heart of the apprehension some Chicago African Americans felt about the growing number of churches during the migration. The discomfort some black Chicagoans registered about storefronts had as much to do with the black southerners who occupied them and the loud, demonstrative worship they practiced as with the church's physical structure.

Although steeped in regional and class biases, the concern about the constituency of storefront churches and their worship practices was not entirely unfounded. The worship practices of most storefront churches differed substantially from patterns that had been in place in the city since

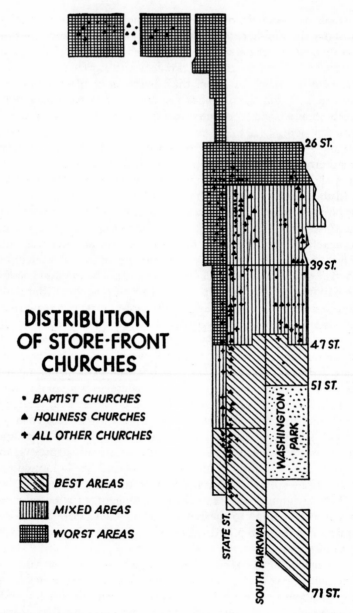

DISTRIBUTION
OF STORE·FRONT
CHURCHES

· *BAPTIST CHURCHES*
▲ *HOLINESS CHURCHES*
✦ *ALL OTHER CHURCHES*

BEST AREAS

MIXED AREAS

WORST AREAS

26 ST.

39 ST.

47 ST.

51 ST.

71 ST.

WASHINGTON PARK

STATE ST.

SOUTH PARKWAY

Fig. 6. Distribution of Storefront Churches. Although the majority of storefront churches could be found concentrated along commercial streets in the "worst areas" of the South Side, they were also reasonably well dispersed in some of the more affluent areas. (Source: St. Clair Drake and Horace Cayton, *Black Metropolis: A Study of Negro Life in a Northern City* [Chicago: University of Chicago Press, 1993])

the late nineteenth century. Black southern migrants reintroduced to Chicago such worship practices as "shouting," hand clapping, foot stomping, and enthusiastic congregational singing. "Shouting," the most common form of African American ritual practice, refers to what Marsha Natalie Taylor called "the dance of the black church," which has been integral to black worship since the slave era. The services would most often be accompanied by "the noise of guitars, tambourines, and drums," in the words of Drake and Cayton. Healing services, speaking in tongues, and vivacious testimonies of deliverance from sin unto salvation were also commonplace. As Brother Martin Jones proclaimed in his late 1930s testimony, "when the Holy Ghost strikes you, you will either jump and shout, or you'll fall out and roll over and over on the floor."[57] Although such forms of religious worship had been common in nineteenth-century evangelical revivalism, they had fallen into disfavor in the late nineteenth century among many black Chicagoans. They regarded these worship practices as vestiges of the African and slave past. Both Quinn Chapel and Olivet Baptist had practiced emotional worship styles with a conscientious connection to Africa up until the late 1870s. One chronicler of the early worship patterns of Quinn Chapel asserted that the "emotional and revivifying" worship services at the church were held, in part, to "promote African prayer life."[58] By the 1880s, black Chicagoans in mainline Protestant churches expended great effort to exemplify a refined spirituality and bourgeois decorum in order to demonstrate the religious and cultural progress of the race. They also wanted to distance themselves from notions of African religiosity. The Reverend James Alfred Dunn Podd, who obtained the pastorate of Olivet Baptist in 1882, broke from the church within a year to establish Bethesda Baptist, citing his preference for "formal theology rather than emotionalism." A former Episcopalian, Podd was partial to high liturgical worship and had "no sympathy for the African survivals in American Negro churches."[59] Grace Presbyterian Church, the first of this denomination among African Americans in Chicago, was organized in 1888 by a "Presbyterian club" that grew "dissatisfied with the African tendencies of the Negro Methodist and Baptist churches" in the city.[60]

In the South, however, enthusiastic worship inextricably tied to notions of "the folk" remained the norm among black Christians, many of whom had direct experience with slavery, slave religion, and the emancipation. As William E. Montgomery argued, "emotional exuberance" was fundamental to the sacred worldview of slaves. African slaves appropriated demonstrative religious practices as a means to counter the "drabness of their daily lives." It was also a way slave Christians took ownership of their faith—through the use of their bodies in worship—and distinguished their worship patterns from that of their oppressors.[61] What W. E. B. Du Bois called the "frenzy" of African American southern worship and Nell Irvin Painter considered "a rural, non-literate folk culture" persisted into emancipation, resisting efforts of would-be reformers.[62] Many former slaves rejected a more restrained worship as "white" and inauthentic. Cordelia Anderson Jackson told her interviewers, "I stays independent of what white folks tells me when I shouts. De Spirit moves me every day, dat's how I stays in. White folks don't feel sech as I does; so day stays out."[63]

For the most part, postemancipation black southern Christians were children of revival, influenced by the emotive expressions of "slave religion" and the emotional exorbitance of the Holiness movement. The Holiness movement coincided with and was a crucial aspect of the religious revivals that cascaded across various portions of the United States and especially the rural South during the late eighteenth and early nineteenth centuries. It was rooted in the teachings of the Anglican minister John Wesley.[64] Wesley's teachings were targeted at the Anglican Church, which he thought was ripe for reform, and though he never left the Church of England his reforms, or his "method," led to the formation of the Methodist church in 1784.[65] By the early nineteenth century, there were those who felt that the newly formed Methodist denomination was also ripe for reform. Wesley's teachings were, therefore, reapplied to a perceived lapsed church, resulting in a movement to restore it to "holiness." Wesley's most important teaching had to do with the doctrine of "sanctification." He asserted that in addition to a dramatic conversion experience, there needed to follow an equally dramatic experience of sanctification, whereupon the believer was "entirely" delivered from sin by way of a "second blessing."[66] The movement and its teaching touched virtually every denomination and generated many revivals or "camp meetings" that attracted large numbers of blacks and whites. The worship patterns and the interracial character of these meetings were their distinctive features. Typically, Holiness "camp meetings" were a festival of emotional display. In part because Wesley's doctrine required that both the salvation and sanctification experience be dramatic, holiness worship involved moaning, shrieking, fainting, groaning, cries for mercy, running, holy dancing ("shouting"), jumping, and even laughing. Although whites also practiced these "enthusiastic" worship forms, by the late nineteenth and early twentieth centuries they were more closely identified with black Christians, as they were believed to reflect African religious traditions.[67]

This highly emotional worship emanating from the Holiness movement touched every denomination among blacks, particularly in the rural South. It was more common among black Holiness churches and in Pentecostal churches, which, in addition to the "second blessing," practiced a "third blessing" that included the experience of "speaking in tongues."[68] But even black Baptist and Methodist churches in the South were known for their emotional display. Among African Methodists, emotional worship sparked much debate and initiated campaigns of worship reform.[69] Though these campaigns were successful in some ways, in large part they did nothing to stop the spread of emotional worship, which became the signature feature of black southern religion. Indeed, the failed campaigns launched by the "advocates of respectable religion" attested to the resilience of ecstatic worship among freed people and their descendents. The African American minister H. T. Kealing noted in 1904 the appearance of a younger crop of southern preachers who rendered intellectual and sedate sermons, yet these preachers complained of the "wide-working leaven of old-time shouters." While reformers had made some headway by the era of the Great Migration, the vast majority of those black Christians entering northern cities were steeped in a very different religious culture than their northern coreligionists. As a congregant of a southern black Baptist church that had come under the influence of reformers in the late nineteenth century put it, after hearing a "powerful good" sermon, "it most [almost] killed me to hold in them shouts."[70] By the late 1910s, it was clear to longtime African American residents of Chicago that migrants were importing distinct forms of worship from their southern homes and practicing them in the churches they established. By the 1940s, it was clear that this emotional worship had even permeated the larger, mainstream black churches. One "high school trained" woman reported that she belonged to one of the city's black Baptist churches and was generally satisfied. "The only thing I dislike about the church," she further elaborated, "is the shouting of the members. . . . The men as well as the women have outbursts. They run up and down the aisles shaking and yelling, overcome as it were with emotion."[71] The woman discovered that her church had begun to embrace a form of worship that could rightly be attributed to the presence and the influence of black southerners.

African American scholars and longtime black Chicagoans reacted viscerally to storefront religion, in part, on the assumption that it was antimodern and "otherworldly." Novels like those of Richard Wright and scholarly journals, which pitted folk culture against urban culture, shaped and dispensed the notion that storefronts were antimodern. Coeval to this notion was the assertion that black southern religion was inattentive to temporal concerns and dealt in rhetorical abstractions. Many of those observers determined what a number of sociological studies later attempted to confirm—that the beliefs and practices of southern migrants in storefront churches were merely sentimental and ethereal in nature. As one African American Presbyterian minister intoned, they were "just another place to go to express pent-up emotions." A collection of reactions gathered in the 1930s characterized storefront practitioners as "fanatical" and blinded to "practical and real life."

To be sure, the theology of many of these churches often dictated that they be "in the world, but not of it." Some storefronts maintained strict prohibitions against a number of "sins," including drinking, dancing, gambling, adultery, premarital sexual activity, and all kinds of "worldly amusements." These prohibitions even extended to concerns about the proper attire for women and men and about what social engagements were proper to attend. Typically, storefront devotees were biblical literalists. Ministers were socially and politically conservative and at times unabashedly antiscientific and antimodern. In a study he did for Howard University in the late 1940s, Hiley H. Hill found a storefront preacher who taught his followers that the earth was flat. "Therefore it is foolish to think that the world is round and turns on an axis," the preacher explained, "for everybody knows that if the worlds were framed, then this world of ours must be square because a frame is square, not round."[72]

At the same time, however, the religion of southern migrants moved in concert with modern, urban life. It had a pragmatic element to it, particularly with regard to social concerns. Devotees of storefront religion were often attentive to concerns of a this-worldly nature due to the exigencies of urban life and the trauma of migration. The emotionally demonstrative worship did not preclude a concern for the temporal world. It necessitated that type of concern. Worship services in some storefront churches, for example, included searches for those who had become lost in the chaos of the mass movement. The testimonial services of Robert's Temple Pentecostal Church of God in Christ included not only "vigorous clapping and dancing," but also a regular "missing persons" ceremony. Those who had lost contact with a relative or friend gave descriptions of the person to church workers who attempted to locate them. By 1938 the church claimed to have found five hundred people. The material lives of blacks were a deep concern for most storefront churches. They placed issues of clean housing, employment, and education at the very center of social programs in a way that mirrored the values of those who targeted black southerners for reform. The needs generated by the Depression seemed to give these churches a unique opportunity to fuse religion with social outreach. The programs they developed targeted individuals and families who had fallen victim to the economic downturn but were unaffected by the various government initiatives. Some storefront churches raised money to assist needy families, viewing such efforts as expressions of their faith. As the wife of a Church of God pastor told a WPA worker in 1940, "These people are not lazy, they've tried to get work but couldn't. They haven't been able to get on relief and it's our duty to help them all we can. Let's practice our religion right here."[73]

It was not uncommon for storefront devotees to make known as widely as possible their concerns for the material lives of Chicago blacks. Beginning in the 1930s, Elder Lucy Smith incorporated a system of charitable distribution into the weekly program of her church, All Nations Pentecostal. (Although she and her congregation never occupied a storefront, Smith epitomized storefront religion for many black Chicagoans.) Staged each Thursday, the charitable outreach effort distributed food and clothing from the church basement. Many of the material goods were provided in response to Smith's appeals on her weekly radio program, *The Glorious Church of the Air*. In response to the broadcast, contributions regularly poured into All Nations and many people made their way to the church to reap the benefits. Smith often spoke of the long lines outside the church consisting of the hungry and the destitute from the surrounding community and beyond. By the later 1930s, the lines increasingly included members of her congregation, who were struck just as hard by the economic downturn. Perhaps the first African American minister in Chicago (male or female) to recognize radio's potential for charitable solicitation, Smith used *The Glorious Church of the Air* broadcast to gather goods, which she then gave to needy Chicagoans. She seemed especially aware that her church had become a center of charitable distribution during the Depression and rarely failed to mention it to interviewers from the Federal Writers' Project.

In an unprecedented move, Smith wrote the *Chicago Defender* in November of 1935 to rebuke Chicago blacks who had written the paper the previous week expressing opposition to the Public Works Administration's plan to clear much of the area around Langley, Vincennes, and Rhodes avenues to make way for a public housing project, the Ida B. Wells Homes. Those in opposition to "this great project," she declared, "don't seem interested in their race." Smith's support for the Ida B. Wells Homes stemmed from her observation of the living conditions in the area.

> Why the homes some of our people are living in are a disgrace to our color and are not fit for any human being to live in. On Langley there are houses and buildings without windows, without water, lights or gas. They have to go to the nearest park for the use of toilets. For water they go to the fireplug with old buckets and bottles to drink. Now is this sanitary for our people?

Smith ended her editorial with an appeal for black Chicagoans to "wake up" to the conditions of "our poorer classes." Only then could necessary improvements be made in the lives of poor blacks, which should begin with "healthy living quarters," and vast sections of the Black Belt could be free of the stigmatic designation of "slums."[74]

Such pragmatic concerns were integral to the experience of storefront religion and to the creation of a commonality among churchgoing southern migrants. Storefront churches were not only a way black southern migrants reorganized their former churches and practiced emotionally demonstrative worship. Their churches tended to reinforce a collective identity and a notion of themselves as a religious diaspora. The term "diaspora" is used here in the sense that black southerners were dispersed from communities to which they conscientiously maintained tight communal and associational bonds. Richard Wright was correct on the point that storefront churches resuscitated "the close and intimate folk culture of the South."[75] Black southern migrants demonstrated a keen sense of religious alliance that esteemed their common regional origin as a central unifying element among them. A migrant woman from South Carolina, for example, left Salem Baptist Church after joining in 1924 because of a rift in the church over pastoral leadership. Attending no church for several years, she joined a storefront on Thirty-fifth Street after visiting a revival near her home. "I started going to that revival," she reported to a writer for the *Chicago Defender*, "and soon became interested in their services and what convinced me was when I heard a preacher from South Carolina."[76]

Most churchgoing migrants viewed the Great Migration as a shared experience, which allowed them to closely identify with others who had come to Chicago from the South. Those who made the journey relayed assurances to their loved ones back home that Chicago was a safe haven from racial violence and a place where they could find the type of spiritual sustenance to which they were accustomed. A letter from a migrant written to the sisters in her former church poignantly evoked this sense.

> My Dear Sisters: I was agreeably surprised to hear from you and to hear from home. I am well and thankful to be in a city with no lynching and no beating. The weather was a great surprise to me. I got here just in time for one of the greatest revivals in the history of my life—over 500 joined the church. We had a holy ghost shower. You know I like to run wild at the services—it snows here and even the churches are crowded. . . . Hurry up and come to Chicago it is wonderful.[77]

Certainly, many southern migrants who made it to Chicago kept close ties to their home church communities. A woman from a Baptist church in Georgia was apparently in the habit of keeping her friend, who had relocated to Chicago, abreast of the happenings in the home church. A letter she wrote in 1917 captured the sense of union she still felt toward her friend. "We had a souls stirring revival this year. I miss you so much. . . . May if I don't come to Chgo I will go to Detroit. I don't think we will be so far apart an we will get chance to see each other agin." Another woman writing to her "sister in Christ" from Chicago reported that she had arrived in the city just in time to attend a great revival. The work she had found making sausages left her little time to play, but the $1.50 per day was good. What she missed, however, was her home church community. She reported to her friend, "I will be delighted to look into your face once more in my life." A southern migrant writing his pastor in Union Springs, Alabama, demonstrated the sense of religious diaspora even more clearly.

"Dear Pastor I shall send my church some money in a few days. I am try-ing to influence our members here to do the same. . . . Let me know how is our church I am anxious to no. My wife always talking about her seat in the church want to know who accupying it." Though residing in Chicago and apparently active in one of the city's African American churches, this man's connections to his church in Alabama remained strong.[78] This letter to Union Springs also inadvertently illustrated the transformation in the physicality of sacred space in northern cities. His wife's inquiry about her pew suggests that their home church comprised pews belonging to entire families. Many churches like this also had family grave plots in the churchyard where generations were laid to rest. Hence, sometimes migra-tion from rural church communities involved leaving a sacred space im-bued with the familial and constant reminders of one's heritage. By contrast, the physicality of sacred space in the North often differed only slightly from commercial venues where the most rudimentary of daily transactions took place.

The diasporic motif is the most fitting and appropriate characterization of churchgoing black southern migrants because of the way it reveals the dialectical nature of the mass movement. It is also appropriate for the way it situates migrants in relation to the South. The motif allows us to see that the process of migration was about both change and continuity, and that southern migrants understood this. Black southerners under-stood that the process of migration changed them and that they changed the established churches they joined as well as those they newly orga-nized. The process of transformation was never a matter of transferring their religious practices to the urban North unreconstructed (although in many cases this was the deepest commitment). In the process of transfor-mation, it was just as important to look back as a reference point as it was to look forward. They looked back to the South as a common cultural point of identification—a South that was in some cases real and in some cases imagined. This look to the South as cultural identifier gave them a sense of distinction from the North and northerners. This indeed was one of the largest benefits. Black southerners understood themselves as a dis-tinct group from the people they found in Chicago's urban metropolis. The cultural connections they maintained with the South, southern ways of life, and worship became a viable aspect of the strategies developed for coping with the perils of the urban North and with black northerners. In diasporic terms, storefront churches were indeed "islands of south-ern culture" as black sociologists dubbed them. They were meant to reflect southern, rural religious culture in every way. At the same time, however, they were re-creations, the primary institutional expression designed to help mediate a religious diaspora's entrance into the urban environment.

The diasporic motif was not limited to storefront churches. Nor was it limited to the majority of migrants who espoused storefront religion. Those migrants who joined mainstream black churches also endeavored to maintain strong associational ties to their home churches in the South. An interview conducted with Mrs. G. W. Neighbors, described as a "club-woman and wife of a photographer," showed that southern migrants in the larger churches were just as prone to consider their former churches as their primary religious institutional affiliation. Mrs. Neighbors, who had been a member of Olivet Baptist since she came to Chicago from Kentucky, informed her interviewer that she thought "store front churches are next to nothing." She particularly targeted Father Divine and Elder Lucy Smith for rebuke—the preachers she most closely associated with storefront churches. When asked about her impressions of Olivet, how-ever, Mrs. Neighbors made a point to bring the conversation to the sub-ject of her home church in Lexington, a church she had left twenty-seven years before. During a recent visit to the church, she discovered that a club started under her direction was still in existence and that the congre-gation remembered her. "I used to teach Sunday school in this church too," she remarked, "and when they introduced me to speak they men-tioned this. It all made me feel good." Though a member of what was at the time the largest Protestant church in Chicago, Mrs. Neighbors' most immediate emotional bond was to a church in Kentucky she left almost three decades previously. The basis of her identity as a church worker was built on that experience and early association.[79]

Southern identity was also invoked as an explanation for the occurrence of frenzied worship in mainstream churches. Blacks in mainstream churches made direct associations between these emotional outbursts and southern religion. After an outbreak of "considerable shouting," a Methodist minis-ter was quick to remind his audience, "We don't have conferences like this up here in the North. These are the kind we have down home!"[80]

Viewing churchgoing black southern migrants as a religious diaspora reveals new levels of meaning to the lament of those migrants who found the worship services of the larger black churches distasteful. Some may have found these services cold and impersonal, but contrary to the asser-tions of the black sociologists of the 1930s and 1940s, this had less to do with class and strict typologies of religious practice than with regional association and identity. Black southerners and longtime residents often used the language of class to discuss differences in worship that were more appropriately attributed to perceived regional differences. Complaints like that of one migrant who reported, "I have not enjoyed a good service since I left the southland. . . . The meetings down home were soul-stirring," were not only rooted in differences in worship tastes, they also had psy-chological, spatial, and regional implications as well. The trauma of being uprooted by the migration left many black southern migrants longing for churches that were "more like the churches in the South." It left them longing for the basis of their formative identity and psychological association. This can be seen in the many uses of the rhetoric of "home"—and perhaps even in the use of family residences as churches. Many of the references in music, testimony, and sermon to "going home" referred primarily to heaven and the afterlife, but complaints by southern migrants that they did not feel "at home" in larger mainline churches held a more earthly or earthbound meaning. At the same time, this sentiment expressed the extent to which many migrants failed to find in, or impute to established black churches the intimate, familial qualities to which they were accustomed in their southern churches. In the summer of 1938, an African American pastor from the South visited "a little prayer service" in Chicago organized by former members of his church. The service was conducted in the house of one of the members who was moved to declare, "I have not felt this way since I left my home church. Let's have another meeting with our pastor before he returns." Moreover, as much as some longtime residents belittled migrants for their religious tastes, most southern migrants considered their "old-time religion" superior to that which they found in northern mainstream black churches. In the late 1930s, a woman stopped attending one church because it had fallen short of its responsibility to shepherd its flock. "At home," she declared, "whenever I didn't come to Sunday School they would always come and see what was the matter." Another southern migrant, identified by Drake and Cayton as one of those in "revolt against heaven," expressed a similar comparison and an even more biting complaint. "I don't like these preachers standing up saying things and you don't know what they're talking about, all hifalutin. I like the preaching like we had down in Alabama."[81] A woman attending one of the city's Church of God in Christ (COGIC) congregations not only thought that "the old meetings that she attended in Lexington, Miss. were better," but also attributed the differences between southern and Chicago churches to institutional values. The fiscal concerns of northern churches had a direct impact on worship, she suggested. Churches in the South, she told her WPA interviewers, were "free of debt," whereas the "large salaries" of black Chicago ministers and their desire for bigger church buildings kept congregations under financial strain. "Good meetings," she therefore concluded, were "pushed in the background."[82]

As a religious diaspora, southern migrants established their churches as islands of southern religious practice and community. More than an economically and socially derived phenomenon rooted in the exigencies of urban life, storefront churches were evocative of an uprooted and regathered religious community. Ultimately, as Evans Edgar Crawford claimed, storefront churches and the worship practiced in them indicated "the most characteristic" element of the impact of migration and urbanization on black southern religion and the impact of southern religion on migration and urbanization.[83]

Black southern migrants may have found in storefront churches a way to reflect their home churches and to distinguish themselves from northerners, but the existence of storefronts generated serious complaints from African American scholars and the general population. A Chicago African American resident took particular issue with "house" churches in 1921, maintaining that "in view of the large number of churches there is positively no excuse for church members converting their private homes into places of public worship." Worship services and prayer meetings, the resident contended, were "very proper when held in churches," but "loud and noisy declamations and moans and groans from sisters and brothers until a late hour in the night are not only annoying but an unmistakable nuisance." In a study done in the early 1930s, the African American sociologists Benjamin E. Mays and Joseph Nicholson were less concerned with loud demonstrative worship than they were that black Chicagoans were "overchurched." There were too many churches, they concluded, more than were reasonably necessary for the black population. Given that about 75 percent of Chicago's black churches were of the storefront variety (usually averaging fewer than twenty-five in membership), they created unnecessary competition among themselves and assured their own financial ruin. Lay observers were often less generous, alleging that the "self-appointed" ministers of these small churches preyed upon their congregations "in the guise of religious piety instead of earning their living by honest labor." Ira de A. Reid, a sociologist and the first African American to teach at Haverford College, famously posited this notion in his 1926 essay "Let Us Prey." An African American businessman still voiced this view in the forties, asserting flatly that "there are too many Negro churches in Chicago and too many false preachers."[84]

Complaints about the staggering number of churches among African Americans and the rise of storefronts alluded to an awareness of broader changes in the religious climate in the city. Prior to 1915, the religious culture of black Chicago had been fairly homogeneous, led by a few mainline Protestant churches and a coterie of dominant male clerics. The growing number of Holiness, Pentecostal, and "Spiritualist" churches after 1915, as well as the growing number of autonomous black ministers and independent black churches, began to fragment that homogeneity and frustrate long-held notions of black ecclesiastical leadership. On the one hand stood a number of street corner preachers who worked not only outside accepted ecclesiastical boundaries, but also outside the confines of a physical space altogether. A woman who regularly preached at the corner of Thirty-first and State in 1917 incurred the wrath of a *Chicago Defender* commentator who called her an "old woman mock preacher," and her preaching "a regular vaudeville show."[85] By the late 1930s, street preaching was commonplace, usually performed by those who went on to establish storefront churches. A healer, spiritual adviser, and Tennessee native known as Reverend Aplin, for example, was a fixture on the corners from Thirty-ninth to Thirty-first before he established the "Sunlight Church of the Sabbath" in front of his barbershop.[86] On the other hand stood men and women preachers, "spiritualists," and "divine healers," such as Father Clarence Cobb, Elder Lucy Smith, Madam Cassyain Fletcher, Mother Naomi Bagby, Reverend Sadie B. Owens, and Reverend F. A. Alexander, who carved out substantial spaces for themselves on Chicago's African American religious scene. The ability of this eclectic group to rise to ecclesiastical power, albeit outside the mainstream, grew from the open-ended, laissez-faire nature of black urban culture during the initial years of the migration. A Memphis native, Father Clarence Cobb was widely rumored to be gay, yet served without restraint as head of the thriving First Church of Deliverance for five decades. Cobbs never publicly professed his homosexuality because it was customary that homosexuals within black churches remain silent about their sexual orientations. But as Timuel Black remembers, "he [Cobbs] didn't deny it and made no apologies for it."[87] The only African American minister in Chicago who was simply called "Preacher," Cobbs made sure that both he and the church were alive with fantastic display. The building was a showpiece of the art moderne style and Cobbs wore several robes of different colors often in the same service.[88] The number of women in ministry witnessed to a steady, though unstable disruption of conventional ideas about women in religious leadership.[89] They exerted great influence especially among the city's poor, challenging the male-dominated moral authority and cultural dominance of mainline Protestant black churches.

Such figures typically played on their southern roots as a basis for their appeal. When asked to account for her large following among southern migrant women, Elder Lucy Smith responded in one breath, "I'm from the South, I'm a Christian."[90] F. A. Alexander advertised that he was "formerly of Selma, Ala.," and Reverend M. E. Wofford, working out of his Michigan Avenue apartment, proclaimed that he had healed many "through[out] the country," but mentioned specifically the states of Kentucky, Arkansas, Tennessee, and Mississippi, states from which a large proportion of Chicago migrants had come. Chicago received a greater portion of southern migrants from the Tennessee valley and the Mississippi delta than any other northern city. By 1920, twenty-three thousand had come from Tennessee and nineteen thousand from Mississippi alone.[91] In the same way that regionally specific "migrant clubs" used common origin as means to foster migration to Chicago, some ministers and laity used it as a means to regather in the city.[92]

Black Chicago ministers of mainstream churches worried about the impact the influx would have on the city's religious culture when they recognized that the majority of new churches among African Americans were established by and for recent migrants. They disagreed about their responsibility toward "newcomers," and some disparaged southern migrants and their religious practices altogether. One black minister in Samuel Strong's study of black "social types," gibed, "if I had my way, I would ship every one of these ignorant Negroes back down South from where they came." The Reverend H. P. Jackson was more sympathetic to the economic component that gave rise to these smaller bodies, seeing as they were composed primarily of "the lower class of people." Still, Jackson considered storefronts "demoralizing to the race" and those that attended them "in the first stages of insanity." Another black minister went still further, asserting that storefronts and house churches undermined the "intellectual and religious standards" among the city's blacks. He argued that laws should be enacted to prevent "these types of Negroes" from opening "these little store front churches." For this minister, storefronts and house churches were merely "a scheme to beat these poor ignorant Negroes, who are constantly coming here from the South, out of their hard earned money."[93] The reverend was not entirely wrong. A number of "jackleg preachers" did set up storefronts merely to siphon the earnings of their congregants, particularly during the 1930s, as Drake and Cayton noted, to avoid going on relief.[94] The tone of the comments made by black ministers from mainline churches and ordinary citizens alike, however, betrayed a deep anxiety about the migration, as well as ambivalence about the South and southern migrants. Though the term "jackleg" was meant to connote something about the character of these ministers, as they were renown for shady financial practices within their churches, many African Americans drew inexorable links between jacklegs, storefronts, the city's religious poor or lower class, and the South. The definition of a Jackleg given by a black Chicagoan in 1940 encapsulated all of these elements. "As I understand it a 'jack-leg preacher' is a man who lacks training and has very little education. He is an individual who may have gotten the 'call' to preach and because of a combination of religious and financial reasons found it a more pleasant way of living than steady work. This type is often found in the South." He went on to say that jackleg preachers preyed on congregations that lacked regular ministers. They usually were occupied with some other work during the week, generally as unskilled laborers, and preached in storefronts on Sundays. The jackleg preacher is "decidedly lower class," he concluded, "and looked down upon by all orthodox preachers."[95] In addition to revealing biases against the South and black southern migrants, comments like these demonstrated the degree to which the religious sensibilities of poor and working-class southern migrants had already become culturally pervasive.

THE DIVERSIFICATION OF CLASSES, or class stratification, among African Americans emerges as perhaps one of the more enduring legacies of the Great Migration. Since the first years of the mass movement, scholars have noted class distinctions and antagonisms among urban African Americans, grouping them into categories of lower, working, middle, and elite classes. Indeed, during this time blacks began to recognize themselves in distinction from one another in terms of social capital, education, and income. But the categories were not fixed, nor were they always an accurate indication of behavior, aspirations, values, and institutional affiliation. The elite class was no more prone to exclusively attend Presbyterian and Episcopal churches than the poor to exclusively attend storefronts. What accounts for the fact that storefront churches were largely the domain of poor blacks from the rural South? To say that it was class, or even primarily class, as many scholars have done is to miss a larger point. Although black southerners migrated for different reasons, the Great Migration was the central event in their lives and the South, not the urban North, was the focal point of their identity. The defining element most southern migrants used to distinguish themselves from what they found in Chicago and to construct collective identity was their common origin, their southern heritage. Groups form identity in unpredictable ways, and that effort certainly does not yield passively to sociological theories. We must also consider that the metaphors for an African American religious diaspora in Chicago are not Darwinian, they are dialectical and synthetic. Richard Wright and scholars of the Chicago school correctly assessed storefront churches as expressions of the intimate folk culture of the rural South. They were not correct in suggesting that these expressions contrasted the progress, civilization, and modernity of urban life. The very existence of storefront churches and storefront religion bore witness to the dialectical and synthetic process of migration, the interplay between the past and the present, North and South, rural and urban, or gemeinschaft and gesellschaft. The very openness of urban culture allowed for the proliferation of storefronts, but those within these congregations drew spiritual, psychological, and emotional sustenance from their southern, rural roots.

Behind complaints rendered by some ministers of Chicago's mainline African American churches about "too many churches," "ignorant" southern blacks, and "loud" demonstrative worship stood anxiety about a mass movement that undermined their authority while it fragmented the broader African American religious culture. They had come to realize, like most of black Chicago, that the religion of the South had taken a hold on the entire black religious culture in their city. The balance of cultural influence was tipping towards black southern migrants who were coming in greater numbers daily, making their presence known in all aspects of black life and their religious inclinations felt in churches of nearly every type and denomination. The religious world black southern migrants instigated in Chicago during these years was one Julius Avendorph would have reviled, but it was one he would have been compelled to face.

CHAPTER THREE

Southern Migrants and the New Sacred Order

We propose a fearless, sane, intelligent gospel, designed to quicken men to better living, a democratic evangelization of a new and complex community; a full, working, six-day Christian ministry touching every phase of man's life.

—Harold Kingsley

More business in religion and more religion in business.

—M. L. Breeding

THE GREAT MIGRATION constituted the most significant event in black American life since the emancipation and Reconstruction. As early as 1917, the journalist and author Ray Stannard Baker deemed it the "most noteworthy" occurrence in black life. The historian August Meier, writing years later, considered the migration "after emancipation . . . the great watershed in American Negro history."[1] In many ways, the geographic and social mobility afforded by the migration resulted from these previous events. But in terms of its immediate impact on the entirety of black life, the Great Migration was equally important, and more so in many ways. The emancipation of 1863 did not at once release all blacks from chattel slavery, and although liberty for all black Americans came rather quickly after the proclamation, debates about the meaning of freedom ensued for many years after. Indeed, there were "competing visions" regarding what constituted true liberty for African Americans, and if there was any agreement at all it was on, as Eric Foner has written, "the ambiguous nature of freedom itself."[2] The occurrence of just as many reversals as improvements in the social and political lives of African Americans complicated the legacy of Reconstruction. Although there were significant congressional and judicial achievements during this era, namely the Fourteenth and Fifteenth Amendments, the time is best characterized as a social process that never quite rose to its promise. To make matters worse, the Reconstruction era, not coincidentally, concurred with the rise of scientific notions of race and racial difference, which thwarted advances toward black citizenship and provided the justification for social separation in all areas of life. Diversions from that social system were very often met by the real threat of mob violence.[3] The Great Migration, however, was nothing short of a complete revolution in black life. Beyond the all-important demographic shift were significant social, economic, political, and cultural changes. The mass movement transformed millions of individual black lives, as well as the very core identity of black America.

The development of a dynamic and pluralistic African American religious scene epitomized the Great Migration's impact in Chicago. Everything about this scene was undergoing steady and often unstable augmentation, from the site of sacred space to the means and the music of worship to the very nature of church work. Attempts to reach southern migrants and to attend to their religious tastes generated phenomenal shifts in the notion of church work. These attempts also put primacy on social service, often performed for the first time by professional social workers. They also reoriented the church's place in the wider world, particularly with regard to the world of business. There emerged a religious pragmatism among some black Protestant churches that mirrored many of the socially responsive values of the Social Gospel. Although few African Americans by the start of the migration era would have considered themselves Social Gospelers in the strictest sense, many within black Protestant churches initiated programs that were social in focus. They put primacy on the material conditions of their congregants, bringing institutional resources to bear on the lived experiences of those in the surrounding community. Churches that had the means and chose to respond in any way to the influx practically converted their churches into centers of community outreach. Alliances between the black business community and the religious community had existed since the nineteenth century. Indeed, there was significant overlap between the two as traditionally black ministers were also the ones most likely to engage in entrepreneurial and commercial enterprises. Concern for links with the black business community and the drive to integrate business principles into black religion intensified during the migration era as churches sought financial help to support their programs and to encourage notions of self-help at the emergence of an independent parallel economy on the South Side. The twin and mutually reinforcing impulses toward pragmatic social service and black business among the city's African American Protestant churches constituted important features to a new sacred order in black Chicago.

In light of the significant changes already evident by the first years of the migration era, some established mainstream black churches dramatically altered their posture towards migrants and the migration. While it is less clear that actual attitudes about the South and southern migrants changed much, a more supportive approach by the old-line churches conceded to a mass movement that they neither started nor were able to stop. Certainly, motivations varied in terms of exactly why mainstream churches began embracing southern migrants. Some hoped to opportunistically tap into the flow of people in order to increase the size of their congregations. Others wanted to claim a sense of control over a rapidly fragmenting religious climate. Still, there were some mainstream churches that viewed the whole phenomenon as a chance to promote African American religious unity and racial betterment. Whatever their motive, many of these churches began "making some concessions" toward the concerns of southern migrants and altering their stances toward the migration.[4] These cautious initial undertakings reflected a wellspring of religious change in mainstream black churches.

The first step made by those churches choosing to embrace the migration was to depict the distinction between longtime residents and new arrivals as an artificial barrier, an imagined division. In 1917, Grace Presbyterian invited the African American attorney Eugene J. Marshall to speak to the Young People's Lyceum. Marshall titled his talk "Great Opportunities" and argued that "newcomers" were "kith and kin" to Chicago's longtime African American residents. "It behooves the race," he further claimed, "to look after them: that the golden rule should be observed in reference to them." Marshall went on to applaud the *Chicago Defender* for "urging the race to come north and better its condition." Lastly, he challenged the members of Grace to use the migration as an opportunity to "make good."[5] For Marshall, the Great Migration represented a unique opportunity for the racial advancement of all Chicago blacks in economic and social terms. It also represented an opportunity to practice a Christian ethic that put primacy on unity among all African American Christians in the city, regardless of denomination or theological persuasion. To be sure, this unity was often predicated on paternalism directed toward southern migrants. The way some longtime residents juxtaposed the behavioral display of southern blacks over against what northern black churches could do to correct that behavior made this clear. In a *Chicago Defender* editorial titled "Go Clean Up North," one minister wrote: "In the south a premium was put on filth and uncleanliness." But black Chicago churches, he insisted, were teaching southern migrants "the things that will make for their best interest." Despite paternalistic and pejorative sentiments such as this, however, a fragile sense of community among "old settlers" and "newcomers" began to emerge. Some longtime residents even suggested that in light of the way southern migrants had begun to suffuse all aspects of black life in Chicago, including the religious culture, the labels be disbanded altogether. There was, they maintained, "no such thing as a 'new comer' and an 'old timer.'"[6]

Many of the smaller mainline churches began to employ this new position regarding southern migrants with the express purpose of quickly enlarging their congregations. They were very often richly rewarded for doing so. Michigan Avenue Congregational church underwent "remarkable growth" in one eighteen-month period after it decided to become more involved in meeting "the demands of the New Negro."[7] The most immediate benefit to enlarging one's congregation was a larger take in the weekly collection plate. A substantial congregation translated into more money for the pastor, his staff, and the church's general expenses. That was the perception, at least, if not always the reality. The "remarkable growth" of Michigan Avenue Congregational, for example, most certainly referred to an expansion in the church's programs and a newly energized congregation as a result of claiming more southern migrants as members. It did not necessarily refer to an increase in the church's financial resources, although this did sometimes happen. A larger congregation also meant greater visibility on the South Side's black ecclesiastical map. It was a chance to reflect some prestige and distinction in a section of the city that was nearly overrun with churches, with new ones being established almost daily. For many smaller mainline black churches, the growth was swift enough to tax their resources beyond any hope for a timely and reasonable recovery.

It was Chicago's largest black churches that led the way in the direct recruitment of southern migrants. They were the ones most likely to initiate efforts or expand existing programs designed to address migrants' concerns. Churches like Institutional African Methodist Episcopal (AME) and Olivet Baptist, with their sizable congregations and substantial resources, were the best prepared for this level of involvement with new migrants. Institutional had been operating a number of social services since 1900 under the direction of Reverdy C. Ransom, but the migration presented an opportunity to expand the work of the church's employment and housing bureaus, day nursery, kindergarten, sewing clubs, and gymnasium. Ransom, an early exponent of the Social Gospel, had demonstrated a keen interest in black southern migrants to Chicago some years before the start of the mass movement in 1915. He established Institutional AME as a "social settlement," modeled after Jane Addams's Hull House and Graham Taylor's Chicago Commons, and specifically targeted his outreach to newcomers to the city. His contemporary and onetime parishioner Ida B. Wells extolled Ransom for bringing a "new gospel to the city" and for "seeking strangers, visiting the sick and feeding, clothing and making havens for the poor and needy."[8] After his departure in 1904, the leadership of Institutional went against the tide in the AME church to continue Ransom's initiatives, which served greatly to increase the church's membership rolls. The active way they recruited new migrants and made pragmatic attempts to confront the material concerns they faced in the urban environment more accurately explains the seemingly natural growth of Institutional, Olivet, and others like them.

If Olivet Baptist could claim to be the "largest Protestant church of any race in the world" by 1920, that distinction came not without considerable effort on the part of the church's leadership and laity. Located in one of the most densely populated areas of the Black Belt, Olivet outdistanced other mainline black Protestant churches in assisting southern migrants' transition to the city and in enrolling them as members of the church. Olivet was one of the first churches in Chicago to take a systematic approach to reaching new arrivals and to use the phenomenon as a means to transform its approach to Christian ministry. The effort to reach southern migrants stemmed from a relatively recent commitment on the church's part to maintain a more active presence in the community. Like other middle-class mainstream black churches, Olivet had become removed from its socially responsive commitments developed during the antebellum period. By the 1890s, the church's institutional priorities reflected the values of other class-based racially hierarchical congregations, preoccupied with middle-class decorum and "respectability." It was not until 1908, under the ministry of Reverend Elijah John Fisher, that Olivet initiated a formal program of charitable work. Administered primarily by the women of the congregation, Olivet's charitable outreach provided food, lodging, and employment assistance.[9] By the time of the migration, Fisher's daughter and another member of Olivet were largely responsible for developing Olivet from a church into what they interchangeably called a "Christian," "community," and "religious" center. The adoption of this language indicated that S. Mattie Fisher and Jessie Mapp perceived a difference between the ordinary work of the church and that work which was done by a religious center. Or, it conveyed that a religious center expanded the work of the church into new areas of social service. Beginning in 1918, the two women conducted eight months of research and more than five thousand interviews with southern migrants, the results of which reshaped the very focus of Olivet Baptist. Their method of approach seemed typical of any social-scientific survey and tended to cover all the bases. They first inquired about the number of adults in the household and their church connection "if any." They then wanted to know how long the family had been in Chicago, their experience as Christian workers in their "home churches," employment situation, and number of children. Fisher and Mapp later reported to the Women's American Baptist Home Mission Society that the survey results became "the basis of all the other activities of the center," including the kindergarten, the "Mother's Circle," and the "Girls Community Guild." Fisher, one of the country's first African American women social workers, confessed how "timidly" she and Mapp approached the homes of new migrants, but she was unequivocal in her explanation as to what prompted her actions. "The city was not prepared at first to care for so many new people," she asserted, "many of whom having made no arrangement for themselves before coming and had no idea who would receive them or where they were to stay."[10]

As one might expect from two African American, middle-class women of the church, Fisher and Mapp worked from impulses that were both reformist and evangelical. Mapp, in particular, seemed concerned about what she called the "dreadful" condition of migrants' homes. The overcrowded apartments she visited were for the most part "poorly kept and very unsanitary" and the children had "scarcely any clothing." Because Fisher and Mapp primarily encountered women migrants and because it was their purpose to see that these women provide "the best Christian homes," there was a seamless conflation of the domestic arts and Christian values in the programs they started at Olivet. One of the most successful endeavors was the Girls Community Guild. This group of young women met once weekly for sewing class (and other "industrial work") and spiritual devotions consisting of Bible lessons. Special events included "practical discussions on home economics, child training, education in the home, laws of health," and "care of children." The Mother's Circle proved as popular with recent migrants as the Girls Guild. Geared toward women with one or more children of kindergarten age, the Mother's Circle assisted with day care, allowing women time to work. It also fostered networks of friendship among women in similar familial situations. One woman praised the group for being one where "mothers with five or six children can attend." Another simply claimed, "I feel encouraged now that I can attend these meetings, I do not feel so forsaken." Fisher's take on the work done for Olivet on behalf of southern migrants was decidedly evangelical. For her part, she was glad to be able to say "God used me to help that one find Himself."[11]

Fisher and Mapp's fieldwork yielded enormous rewards for Olivet Baptist in terms of conversions and increased membership. The two women understood that "many conversions and connections" with the church had been made because of their work and that they had been instrumental in reconceptualizing its Christian mission. Programs initiated in response to their survey obviated the need for Olivet to conduct membership drives or "go to church" campaigns among southern migrants. "Go to church" campaigns were commonly used by black Chicago churches in the 1920s and 1930s, as a means to promote moral responsibility and respectability and to boost membership rolls. "Those who found the church helpful in weekday affairs," Lacey Kirk Williams asserted, "gladly made it their place of worship on Sundays."[12] The annual reports stretching for more than a decade and written primarily by Fisher gave a strikingly clear view of the conditions under which many of those they targeted for service lived. Written in an almost Pauline epistolary tone, the reports to the Women's American Baptist Home Mission Society told of the quotidian struggles to minister to ever-growing numbers of people despite harsh winters, race rioting, staggering unemployment, domestic abuse, and general malaise.

The race riot of 1919, for example, proved disruptive to the work of the center, scattering Olivet members and halting regular services for weeks.[13] Olivet Church was turned into a "rescue center for the homeless and hungry," which generated so much work for Mapp that she suffered a breakdown in the process. Because of the poor and unsanitary condition of the homes on the South Side, sickness, disease, and death were constant factors. This prompted Fisher to proclaim that she had to serve "in nearly every way we count service—from nurse maid to funeral director." The work of these women greatly expanded what the church was able to do. Fisher said it best herself when she proclaimed in 1926, "there is no limit to the field of service as covered by the Olivet Baptist church."[14]

In addition to the efforts of Fisher and Mapp, Olivet Baptist went so far as to establish a para-church organization designed especially to assist new migrants in their transition from the rural South. Headquartered at Olivet, the Bethlehem Baptist Association offered its services "to the race coming from the south," and its sole purpose was to help new migrants adjust in every way to their new home. The association acted on the premise that few would arrive already possessing such skills. "Coming as you are," the ads in the *Chicago Defender* read, "to a section of the country, where the economical, social, and religious conditions are somewhat different to those from which you are coming, the association is desirous of helping you to adjust yourselves to the new problems that will confront you."[15] Because the *Chicago Defender* had a higher circulation in the South than any other northern black newspaper, these ads received an enormous response.[16] Many southern blacks wrote the association to "kindly send me a ticket at once" or to request "a suitcase to put things in." Most of the responses simply stated, "Meet me at the station." A staff of ministers, social workers, and other professionals bolstered the work of the association. They carried out a variety of social service programs that at times seemed overwhelming. A member of the organization recalled in the late 1930s that the Bethlehem Baptist Association quickly learned that the task of assisting migrants in their transition was formidable. "We put an ad in the paper to help the needy. Oh! was I sorry. I went down to the Union Station to meet them and there was a twenty-car train full of young men, old men, women and children." Attempting to cover the full range of migrant needs, leaders of the association considered adequate lodging to be a primary concern of new arrivals and made the provision of housing a top priority. In a move designed to foster economic independence and responsibility, as well as to secure housing in an overcrowded market, Lacey Kirk Williams opened a "savings department" in Anthony Overton's bank exclusively for southern migrants. This was done to, in his words, "establish the new Chicago[ans] financially that they might pay for the homes found for them."[17]

Not every black Protestant congregation had the vision or resources to radically reconfigure their social outreach programs during the migration in the manner of Olivet Baptist. Not every church developed a social service program. Indeed, WPA workers found great disparities among black churches with regard to social outreach, often within the same denomination. Aileen H. Dillon and O. Winkfield reported that Blackwell Memorial AMEZ Church was "opened daily and engaged in social and community service." But of Greater Walters AMEZ Church they surmised that "there seems to be a vast need of more community social work in this church, at least in the church's surrounding neighborhood."[18] And when these social service concessions were made in deference to southern migrants, they often had the ironic effect of exaggerating differences between longtime residents and new arrivals within many congregations. Despite this, a fragile support for migrants and the migration reaped for many mainline churches thousands of new members and generated new alliances with the wider African American community.

Because secular organizations like the Travelers Aid Society and the Chicago Urban League often succeeded in their attempts to orient new migrants to the urban North by the 1920s, scholars have argued that they supplanted the work of black churches during this time.[19] The argument suggested that black religious institutions had neither the will nor the resources to compete with secular organizations for the attention of new arrivals; such was beyond the scope of church work. But while many black Chicago churches lacking the resources of Olivet Baptist did falter in the wake of competition from secular organizations in attempts to assist southern migrants, others looked to organizations like the Travelers Aid Society and the Chicago Urban League as an opportunity to build alliances with them. Arvarh E. Strickland's definitive history of the Chicago Urban League confirmed these alliances with African American churches. He stated not only that many black churches became actively involved with secular organizations during the migration era but that women of black Chicago churches in particular "helped in this work" of assisting recent southern migrants in acclimating themselves to city life. Clearly, some churches viewed the alliances built with secular organizations as the only way to survive competition with them and as the best way to be engaged in the larger cause of race advancement. Anything less demonstrated a church's limited vision. This view was best articulated by Harold Kingsley, a former Alabamian and AME minister, who claimed never to have heard a "call to ministry," but sensed a deep need among black churches for "the best possible leadership." (See figure 7.) As pastor of the Church of the Good Shepherd Congregational, Kingsley concluded in 1933 that although black churches in Chicago remained the "largest organized unit in race relations," it was necessary that they link efforts with

Fig. 7. Harold M. Kingsley. Pastor of Good Shepherd Congregational Church and cofounder of the Parkway Community House, Kingsley appeared to WPA workers "more like a shrewd businessman than a clergyman." (Source: Chicago Historical Society)

"the wider undertakings in race relations." For Kingsley, those "wider undertakings" included the Chicago Urban league, an organization he believed "worthy of our co-operation."[20]

Kingsley may have found inspiration to extend the social services of Good Shepherd even further because of his alliances with secular organizations. Working closely with Horace Cayton, Jr., Kingsley transformed the outreach ministry of the church into the Good Shepherd Community Center. Organized in 1936 with the help of the WPA and the Chicago Board of Education, the Good Shepherd Community Center provided an array of civic and artistic programs. By 1942, the center was renamed the Parkway Community House (PCH) and contained a mother's clinic, an office of relief, literacy classes, sewing classes, music and writing work-shops, and the Henry George School of Social Service. Nearly 100,000 people came through the doors of PCH annually by the time of the Second World War. The place was a veritable wellspring of political, civic, and artistic expression. The Chicago Branch of the NAACP often held its annual membership campaigns at PCH, and a lecture series called "The People's Forum" highlighted the center's community involvement. The stated aim of "The People's Forum" was to "probe relentlessly for the truth" and to "suffuse action with understanding." PCH leaders considered the series "an adventure in collective self-analysis" and promised that each meeting would include "provocative questions" by the lecturers and a "free-for-all" discussion. Series organizers employed this framework in the fall of 1946 with a group of lectures that discussed the recently published *Black Metropolis*. Topics included, "The Negro Comes to Town" and "Bronzeville—The Fact and the Dream."[21] Other meetings and lectures at PCH were cosponsored by the AFL-CIO.

Artists such as W. C. Handy and Langston Hughes were regular visitors at PCH. Hughes, who gained some experience producing plays in Chicago when he was transferred from the Federal Writers' Project to the Federal Theater Project in 1936, founded PCH's theatrical group, the Skyloft Players. They were the first to perform his play *The Sun Do Move*."[22] Premiering in April 1942, it was the group's first production and Hughes's first religious play. Undoubtedly drawing its title from the famous sermon by the nineteenth-century African-American preacher John Jasper, the play simultaneously highlighted Hughes's interest in merging black music (in this case, the spirituals) with theatrical production and his support for the war effort. Although set in the Deep South during the time of the Civil War, the play sent a powerful message about the current conflict with clear nationalist overtones. When Rock, the protagonist of the play, announces to his wife that he has joined the Massachusetts 54, she proclaims: "I see my people everywhere, all over America, all over the world taking part in the making of a new life. Folks, the sun do move! I see you—black and white together, standing with me, working with me, singing with me. Come on! Everybody! Shout! March! Sing!" The play ends with the cast leading the audience in "The Star-Spangled Banner."[23] The "little theater group" at PCH reflected Kingsley's, Cayton's, and Hughes's conviction that the arts could be effectively used to dispense social, political, and religious messages. They were certainly aware that plays in particular have always had power to facilitate social commentary.[24] By the mid-1940s, Cayton was explicit in his aims for the Skyloft Players. "The group is interested not merely in providing entertainment but in fostering plays of social significance."[25] Throughout the group's long life at PCH, they merged notions of the sacred and the secular, and demonstrated the way African American religious culture participated in the overall cultural production of black Chicago.

The leaders of PCH concerned themselves particularly with the plight of new arrivals, providing a full range of services covering the most basic needs to the highly specific. Kingsley and Cayton started a birth-certificate service to help those seeking employment that required this documentation. By the early 1940s, they were handling a thousand cases a month. They built a "girls dormitory" to house single women traveling to the city alone, and a "literary course" for black men offered classes to migrant men classified by the armed services as "4F" because of illiteracy. The designation "4F" was army lingo for "unfit to serve" and could be used to classify individuals with a range of disabilities that would prevent them from serving effectively. Richard Wright did much of his research for *12 Million Black Voices* at the center and in 1941 wrote "The Negro and Parkway Community House," which became known as the "Parkway Statement." In that statement, Wright drew a direct connection between the migration and the work of PCH, identifying some of the themes he would also develop in *12 Million Black Voices*. Essentially, he argued that black southern migrants were caught up in a "great drama" with the urban North serving as the "industrial stage." As protagonists in this drama, migrants faced the enormous challenge of an urban existence against which they were not well equipped.

> These Negroes are truly a form of the modern refugee who has become so numerous a spectacle in our world today; they are refugees from a southern folk culture, from a static, warm, organic, simple way of life, where every man knew his fellow man; they are refugees fleeing the terrors of the plantation and seeking desperately to gain a footing in our highly complex and impersonal cities.[26]

Unlike *12 Million Black Voices*, however, the Parkway statement demonstrated Wrights' considerable concern for the stereotypical depiction of black southerners. On the "industrial stage" they are seen not as human beings but as "mammies and clowns," eliciting the nonproductive response by the wider community of either "laughter or tears." The "failure" of black southerners in the city, he further asserted, should be attributed to their southern mentalities as much as to the impersonal nature of urban life and racist stereotyping. Indeed, for Wright, black southerners' "folk mental equipment proved more of a detriment than a blessing." In praising PCH for its efforts to ameliorate the conditions faced by black southern migrants, Wright expressed the debt he owed to the Chicago school of sociology for shaping his thoughts. "The Parkway Community House is the first institution equipped with scientific knowledge of the urban situation among Negroes to attempt to control, probe, and disseminate facts as to the progress, meanings, causes and effects of urbanization."[27] For all its implicit pathologizing of southern migrants, Wright's thinking as expressed in the "Parkway Statement" set the tone for the work done at PCH.

While far from commonplace, alliances between social organizations and Chicago's black churches had emerged by the 1920s. The often un-even and erratic nature of that cooperation, however, indicated a basic mistrust of secular powers. It also indicated a determination by black churches to ultimately keep full organizational control over their own initiatives. A student of the University of Chicago sociologist Ernest Burgess surveyed an undisclosed number of black churches in 1929, all but two of which had regular programs of social outreach, many cooperat-ing with the United Charities, the Chicago Urban League, the juvenile courts, and "other such organizations." It seemed prudent to most of these churches to limit their association with social organizations or at least to limit the area of service. With the possible exception of Olivet Baptist, of which S. Mattie Fisher reported in 1926 that as a matter of course "as usual we are co-operating with the United Charities," most churches chose to restrict "charitable outreach" to their own resources in a way that reflected the basic assumptions of "self-help" ideology.[28] Lib-erty Baptist referred only a few cases to secular organizations, preferring to direct its charitable work to its own members. The Michigan Avenue Colored Methodist Episcopal (CME) Church worked exclusively with the Chicago Urban League. Good Shepherd Congregational offered "hand-outs, car fare, lunch etc. to those who apply," but all charity was at the dis-cretion of the pastor. When the needs exceeded Good Shepherd's resources, Harold Kingsley advised new arrivals "concerning the social in-stitution which can best assist them in ways in which they needed assis-tance." Black churches outside the mainstream observed no such limits in their cooperation with secular powers or the area of service and perhaps relied more heavily on civic aid. Elder Lucy Smith of All Nations Pente-costal, a church that built an impressive record of distributing goods to Chicago's poor, cooperated not only with local civic groups but also with federal relief authorities.[29]

Cooperation with secular organizations did not preclude many black churches from producing professional social service workers from among their ranks. Indeed, it may have encouraged it, particularly since coopera-tion did not always indicate mutual trust. The rise of trained social work-ers employed exclusively for one or more African American churches on the South Side connoted an entirely new development in black urban Christianity. It represented an expansion of the notion of church work as well as an added professional dimension. This was most relevant for black women, who exclusively comprised the group of African American social-service church workers during the first years of the migration. Social work became an acceptable route among a limited range of choices into public and professional life and church work. Usually the women were young, well educated, middle class, unmarried (by choice or circumstance), and from a prominent family. Olivet Baptist's S. Mattie Fisher typified a growing number of American women who entered social work professionally during the 1920s. By 1929, in addition to Olivet Baptist, Progressive Community Church, St. Mark's AME, Provident Baptist, and Metropolitan Community Church all employed full-time social workers. Operating under church auspices, these social workers were charged with the responsibility of establishing webs of cooperation with secular organizations, particularly with the onset of economic depression in the early 1930s. The social worker at St. Mark's, for example, cooperated with a number of organizations, including the Court of Domestic Relations, an organization concerned with juvenile delinquency. These women professionals also enlisted the help of the woman laity of their home congregations. At St. Mark's, a highly organized group of women calling themselves "the Master's Queenly Reserves" assisted the church's full-time social worker in bringing aid to needy members of the church, as well as to those on the far reaches of the South Side. The women adopted about one hundred and fifty "old, blind, lame or otherwise defective" persons living in the area of Chicago south of Roosevelt Road to 129th Street, east from Western Avenue to Lake Michigan. The area was divided into sub-districts, with each woman responsible for those located within one sub-district. The residents within each district received baskets of food, a trip to the church, and dinner four times a year. Any one of them with a need for food, clothing, or medical assistance during the interim needed only to contact one of the women of the group. It was a brilliant stroke of organizational savvy aligned with charitable outreach. These black women professional social workers and their lay assistants performed a vital function during the migration, identifying and meeting the needs of the growing number of poor and working-class blacks on the South Side.[30]

While not every black church with a social service program matched the work and vision of St. Mark's and the Master's Queenly Reserves, the rise in the number of social workers in black Chicago churches showed that many had come to realize the need for a professional social service staff. Or, as in the case of Harold Kingsley and PCH, they realized the need for their own independent social service organization. It also indicated the importance of alliances with secular organizations serving new migrants and the city's poor and the crucial role black women played in those efforts. Social work among African Americans easily became the domain of women because it fit conventional notions of womanhood and women's nature. Although it began as an effort coordinated by men and women, social work from the start reflected strongly held ideas about women as nurturers. As Clark Chambers asserted, women seemed "uniquely suited" for the "kindly visiting" social work required, assuming benevolence as a natural womanly instinct. This "gendered character of social work" generated an interesting paradox. As a "female profession," social work was a contradiction in terms. The most basic tenets of professionalization—rationality and objectivity—were perceived to be the ideological domain of men. The conflict of being both female and professional defined the early years of social work, and by 1930 about 80 percent of all those in the field were women. African Americans were not troubled by social work as an avenue into public life for black women, understanding black women to have few options and there being an "urgent need" for trained social workers. What annoyed some black Chicagoans was the apparent secularization of church work—the way Christian responsibility was seemingly usurped by secular powers.[31] Secularization did not pose a problem for the majority of black Chicagoans during the Great Migration, as it became clear that these discrete polarities were difficult to maintain under the circumstances of black life. Those working within church contexts concerned about the discourse of professionalization and secularization prompted by social workers, however, devised discursive strategies. One strategy was to depict the work of these women in terms of the church's traditional obligations for mission work. To give social work an evangelical cast, Pilgrim Baptist Church, for example, did not call its workers social service professionals, choosing rather to call them missionaries. Although in many cases these women were highly trained professionals, their assigned duties often reflected conventional notions of women's work. It was the job of the women missionaries at Pilgrim Baptist, J. C. Austin's son recalled, "to go out . . . into these tenements and hovels those folks were living in and teach them hygiene and how to care for their babies and make sure they had food."[32] Indeed, sometimes the women simply complied. Jessie Mapp had considered herself a missionary worker for the Women's Home Mission Society since the early 1920s and S. Mattie Fisher indicated "missionary" as her profession in the 1930 census.[33]

Black churches that employed social workers and cooperated with social and civic organizations were also those most likely to build alliances with the city's African American business community. It was not uncommon for black churches to support black-owned businesses by carrying advertisements in their church bulletins and newspapers, or by encouraging members to patronize certain retail stores, grocers, doctors, barbers, and undertakers. Black-owned businesses, in turn, often held citywide church contests, offering prizes ranging from small appliances to new cars. Black-owned businesses had been an important part of the institutional structure of black Chicago since the nineteenth century. Promotion of these enterprises had been a concern of the community since the turn of the century, when Booker T. Washington founded the Negro Business League.[34] By the early decades of the twentieth century, the South Side claimed enough political clout, numbers, and economic strength to build bridges of support for black businesses across institutional lines. Robert Abbott formed the Associated Business Club of Chicago (ABC) to be a support agency for black-owned businesses in 1925. The group encouraged black Chicagoans to "spend money with our own merchants," and used times of crisis like the bombing of Bethesda Baptist to promote a "closer relationship between churches, fraternal organizations and business men." There was a tremendous amount of interdenominational support for this organization, as its themes of "race pride," "self sufficiency," "cooperation," "business," and "religious responsibility" seemed to strike a chord with many of Chicago's black Christian ministers and laity. It was established with fourteen members but within a year possessed a thousand members. In 1926, the ABC launched a drive to grant a trip abroad to the pastor of the congregation that gave the most patronage to ABC businesses. The Reverend H. E. Stewart of Institutional AME and Reverend William Bradden of Berean Baptist took the opportunity at the opening of the drive to appeal for a "closer relation[ship] between the business and professional men and the churches."[35] In many ways, this accord between churches and businesses was an acknowledgment on the part of black Chicago churches of the rise of a separate black economy on the South Side. It also acknowledged the interdependency of black churches and black-owned businesses in the area. As early as 1923, the year in which Robert R. Moton, successor to Booker T. Washington, declared that "Negroes have more confidence in the business capacity of members of their own race," there were about eighteen hundred black business establishments in Chicago. Varying in size and character from "nondescript fly-traps called restaurants to the dignified Overton building," black businesses readily won the support and patronage of most black churches.[36]

By far, black Chicago churches maintained the closest relationship in the black business community with funeral homes and funeral directors. Although beauty parlors, grocery stores, and barbershops far outnumbered funeral homes, Drake and Cayton listed these establishments among "the ten most numerous types of Negro Businesses" in black Chicago by the late 1930s. They replaced the "burial societies" that many southern blacks had trusted with their final hours, and the large number of funeral establishments can be attributed to the needs of an ever-increasing black population for whom death was a constant visitor. Further, blacks ordinarily placed great importance on a good (and at times ostentatious) funeral and burial. This served to further bolster the status of funeral directors and the intimate connection between churches and funeral homes. The intimate association worked on two levels. First, the church and the funeral home tended to serve the needs of blacks from the cradle to the grave, often playing a big role in some of the most significant moments in the life of an individual or family. The support and solace one needed in the event of conversion, baptism, marriage, sickness, and death could be found in these institutions. Indeed, as Karla F. C. Holloway claims, "this collusion and community between the church and the burial business increased the intimacy of these professionals with private family matters."[37] Second, some funeral homes were owned and operated by men who were also preachers. (There are no records of any women-owned funeral businesses in Chicago during the migration era.) In these cases, the minister kept any funeral business within his own congregation. In other cases, funeral directors were careful to cultivate relationships with area ministers in the hope that they would recommend particular funeral establishments to the members of the congregation. These relationships were often richly rewarded, at times resulting in high-profile funerals at such prominent establishments as A. A. Rayner's and W. T. Brown's Funeral Homes. At Brown's own funeral in 1941, a coterie of area African American ministers attended, including Richard Keller of Beth Edan Baptist and Clarence Cobbs of First Church of Deliverance, testifying to their close association with the deceased business leader.[38]

The alliances built between the black business and religious communities more than represented an effort to strengthen the institutional base of black Chicago. They also indicated a fundamental shift in the racial philosophical approach of many leaders and laity within black churches. By the 1920s, many people within black Chicago churches had come to agree with the larger community that the expansion of a black business economy was crucial to the economic and racial advancement of Chicago blacks. For many within the black Protestant community, that advancement could only happen by adhering to Washingtonian notions of self-help that emphasized a racially separate and self-sustaining institutional life. This notion fueled an "Exposition of Negro Business" staged by South Side black businesses in cooperation with Pilgrim Baptist Church in 1938. Held on a Monday night at the Eighth Regiment Armory, the exposition showcased the wares of most of the major area African American retailers, including Knight's Shoe Store and Mae's Dress Shop. When called on for remarks, J. C. Austin, pastor of the church, warmed the crowd by making several explicit references to the southern origins of some of the proprietors, noting for instance that one of them was Edward Jones, aka "Vicksburg, Mississippi" Jones. He then implored the audience to give these local establishments their business, "for that is the only way we as a race will get anywhere."

Tomorrow I want all of you people to go to these stores, have your shoes repaired at a Negro shoe shop, buy your groceries from a Negro grocer, patronize these Jones brothers *and for God's sake buy your meats, pork chops and yes, even your chitterlings from your Negro butcher.*[39]

The following Sunday, Austin further explained his call for the support of black businesses during the exposition. Such support would not only create jobs for "young folks," it would also be evidence of "race respect" and self-help.[40]

Austin's plea for black Chicagoans to patronize area black businesses indicated that not everyone was inclined towards the self-sustaining, separate black economy that he envisioned. Despite efforts like the business exposition, by the 1930s, support by black Chicagoans for black businesses in Bronzeville was often weak. Indeed, it was because many Chicago blacks failed to patronize black establishments to a great extent that such expositions were necessary. (The same can be said for the earlier "spend your money with our own merchants" campaign.) The primary factor in this weak support was almost certainly economic. The economic downturn of the 1930s had a direct and deleterious effect on efforts for racial self-help and on an espousal of the creed. Blacks were not patronizing black-owned business with gusto; rather, a significant amount of black dollars were being spent in white establishments, as white-owned businesses within the area boasted a larger consumer base than black-owned ones. The numbers were chilling. A business census done in 1935 reported that of the eleven million dollars spent by blacks on groceries that year, only 5 percent was spent in black stores. And grocery stores were second only to beauty parlors in terms of the type of businesses owned by blacks. Another study done in 1938 found that although blacks owned nearly the same number of businesses in the Black Belt as whites (2,600 versus 2,800), black businesses received less than a tenth of the money spent on goods and services.[41]

Seemingly everyone was aware of this discrepancy in the economy of the South Side, but answers as to how it came about, why it persisted, and how to solve it depended on one's relationship vis-à-vis the business community. African American proprietors were convinced that black Chicagoans did not patronize their stores because, as recent migrants from the South, many blacks only knew of one merchant-client relationship—white owners and black buyers. As one grocer contended, "these people are used to living on the farm and trading with the white man. They don't know any better." Testimonials from black Chicagoans seem to lend this notion some credence, but others seem to suggest that patronizing white stores was also an act of defiance, or a show of power and role reversal. To buy in

a white store in Chicago was to enter into a new public space with economic power, placing whites in the serving position with the sole purpose
of meeting the most basic needs of blacks. As one woman told Drake and
Cayton, "it is like getting revenge for not having had the opportunity of
going into some white places in the South."[42] And while shopping at a
white-owned business indicated their social status, class position, or economic power for some black Chicagoans, it was a simple matter of price
and product quality for others. When asked why they shopped at white-
owned stores instead of black-owned businesses, many interviewees
evoked the harsh economic times as a primary reason. Indeed, some even
suggested that the Depression was a significant deterrent to their espousal
of "race pride." "I buy at the A & P where I can get food cheapest," one
interviewee stated. "I try to patronize my race, but I can't on my husband's
salary—$55 per month, WPA. My real friend is the dollar." "I try to pa-
tronize my people," another black Chicagoan similarly stated, "but when
it comes to saving a penny, especially at this time, I do so, even if I have to
buy from whites."[43] Customers who felt this way were more than likely to
be among those who also claimed that "the quality and variety of stock in
Negro stores are poor." White merchants made no apology for their success among blacks in the Black Belt. Many believed that their success was
directly related to the lack of business acumen on the part of black business owners. Their views even spoke to what many perceived to be the nature and psychology of black people. As one real estate agent concluded,
"the happy, carefree nature of the Negroes in seeking lines of least resistance in the conduct of their business is largely responsible for the high
credit risk tabulated against them." Another white merchant bluntly
stated, "as long as Negroes have enough money to spend on booze and
policy, they are happy."[44] These were the powerful odds against which
Austin and other Chicago ministers made their plea for blacks to support
black businesses as a show of race pride and self-help.

The state of black businesses like those in Chicago during the 1930s
was what inspired E. Franklin Frazier to pen some twenty years later his
polemical satire, *The Black Bourgeoisie*. In the section on black business,
Frazier ridiculed blacks for their faith in "salvation by business." For Frazier, a sociologist whose most respected work had been on the black family, this faith in the salvific power of black business was little more than a
"social myth."[45] Not only were black businesses powerless to "wipe out
racial prejudice," they were a mockery when faced with the "hard realities
of the Negro's insignificant achievements in business." The "hard reality,"
he insisted, was that black businesses across the board failed to match
white enterprises in terms of market share. Frazier argued that the social
myth of the efficacy of black business was inextricably linked to an even
greater faith in the possibility of a separate and parallel "Negro economy."

Since it was a "fundamental sociological fact" that Negroes ("gentlemen" and "peasants") lacked business acumen, they were doomed to fail in any business ventured, or to flounder in comparison with whites. Although it was never quite clear who or what Frazier implicated in the impossibility of black business, in sum he deemed racial self-help a dubious effort at best.[46]

The racial self-help of which Austin spoke at venues like the Exposition of Negro Business in 1938 was itself a difficult sell, particularly in light of the economic times. Mainstream black churches like Pilgrim Baptist, however, were on the forefront of those calling for continued patronage of black-owned businesses when support for these enterprises fluctuated among the black community generally. Indeed, black Protestant churches were the chief promoters of the philosophy of racial self-help, indicating a significant shift from the public posture of the African American religious culture during the previous century. Unlike the religious community of the last decades of the nineteenth century, few in migration-era black mainstream churches put faith solely in the demonstration of respectability and middle-class decorum as a viable format for racial and social change. Integrationist impulses made way for a new confidence in the development of an institutionally parallel, self-sustaining black community. Bolstered by a growing population of blacks and many more black businesses and organizations, many Chicago African American ministers and laity focused their attention on the potential for economic advancement. Harold Kingsley offered in 1933 what he termed "a new interpretation of the race problem" that no longer focused on "the shortcomings of the white man" and his "admitted injustices." His new interpretation instead turned from "the grievances against other people to the actual 'bread and meat' problems" that confronted the city's blacks. Kingsley, who appeared to WPA workers "more like a shrewd businessman than a clergyman," further stated that Chicago's blacks had three choices in conducting their economic lives: seek their place in the business culture of the city, set up more and stronger commercial enterprises in the Black Belt, or become "industrial serfs." For Kingsley, the key to better racial and economic conditions was for the city's black churches to encourage African American self-sufficiency by supporting black businesses and building institutional webs of connection with them. "The aesthetic, the political, the social, the economic," he asserted, "have a very vital and inseparable connection with the religious. The religious expression of a group's life is not going to be much higher than these other expressions."[47]

The emphasis on racial self-help seemed to sharpen the business focus of many black churches. They began to overtly embrace business principles in order to attract new migrants, build larger structures, and reduce debt. A few churches even took advantage of the new business climate for the purposes of entertainment and the financial support of specific church functions. In 1939, at the Fourth Annual Convention of the Young People's National Congress, members of Robert's Temple COGIC converted the church's basement into "commercial units." Desiring to benefit financially by providing food and services to delegates that had traveled from as far away as New York and California, they erected shoeshine and soft-drink stands, a post office, and an "information bureau." Outside, the church members operated a "thriving business" selling "frozen rockets," a type of ice cream.[48] More typically, however, the overall aims were higher. At Carter Temple CME Church, the Reverend Prentis A. Bryson oversaw a 100 percent increase in membership in the mid-1920s, as well as a sea change in the church's economic future. Recognizing the rapid increase of Chicago's black population as an opportunity to resuscitate Carter Temple, Bryson enlisted the aid of the businessmen of the community in a program combining "business efficiency with Christian leadership." Carter Temple had lost members and fallen into serious financial arrears, and the first priority in the program at Carter Temple seemed to have been the liquidation of debt as this would free necessary resources that could be used to bolster social outreach. Debt reduction became a concern not only for the committee of business and religious leaders created at Carter Temple but also for the vast majority of northern black churches during the late 1920s and early 1930s. Drawing from the study done earlier by Mays and Nicholson, St. Clair Drake and Horace Cayton contended that Chicago churches carried the second highest per capita debt of all northern churches in America.[49] In an effort to rise above this climate of indebtedness, acquiring sufficient funds to "tide over the most pressing obligations of the church," and building a "strong church treasury" became Bryson's chief concerns. Newly formed church clubs with names like "The Willing Workers," "The Busy Bee," and "The Trustee Aid Club" reflected that priority. In conjunction with this new push for financial stability, Bryson began to reconfigure the operation of Carter Temple to cooperate with numerous community outreach programs of a "broad based 'social service' nature." Fellow Chicago minister L. B. Johnson claimed the emphasis Bryson placed on "business efficiency" helped the church become one of the fastest growing among the CMEs in Chicago during the twenties and made it a "mecca for strangers and passersby." As word of Carter Temple's "relief work for needy families" spread, calls for assistance multiplied, and within a twelve-month period "the church around the corner" underwent a dramatic financial turnabout and greatly increased its membership. It later laid plans for a newer, larger church building.[50]

For Reverend John R. Harvey, the pastor of St. Mary's AME Church, the idea of combining business with Christian principles reflected not only a modern practicality, but also a brute necessity. Without immediate financial help, the church faced certain bankruptcy and closure. In 1921, St. Mary's, the third oldest AME church in Chicago, "with strong business as well as religious features," was carrying an enormous $30,000 debt that Harvey determined to liquidate. The financial obligations of the church were proving to be a heavy burden on a congregation that did not increase in membership despite the influx of new migrants into the surrounding neighborhood. To accomplish his goal, Harvey contracted with Alfred Clover, the general manager of the Public Life Insurance Company, who promised to contribute $5,000 if the members could raise the other $25,000. In addition to this arrangement, Harvey struck a deal with a local manufacturer, who pledged to give the church $20,000 if members sold 100,000 units of its carpet and wood renovator. Harvey explained his actions in an interview with a *Chicago Defender* reporter. "We are endeavoring to maintain a practical Christian work among our people in our section of Chicago." More defensively, he added, "there is no reason that I can see which prevents a church from closing a sensible business deal if it will enable it to do the work for Christ in a way to promote the cause of Christianity among our people." Harvey's campaign ultimately failed, and he left St. Mary's as a part of the larger exodus out of the AME church and to protest the conference's lack of support for his initiatives. Having formed the Cosmopolitan Community Church in 1923, he was free to carry out his belief that "the motives of Jesus" were "practicable in modern business." By the mid-1920s, as pastor of Cosmopolitan, Harvey was thoroughly ensconced in the South Side business community. The ABC invited him to address its members at its regular noonday Thursday meeting in June 1925. Harvey told the group that there was a "close relationship between the Bible and our salesman of the day." In a statement that clearly alluded to ministers, he further suggested that all men in business had something for sale, even if it was only "an idea for sale." He ended his talk by inviting Jesse Binga to be the principal speaker the following Sunday at Cosmopolitan.[51]

The attempt by some mainline African American churches to attach the "principles of business" to the work of their churches was consistent with the mood of the 1920s. The time was a period in which a business ethos permeated many American churches. President Calvin Coolidge articulated the spirit of the era when he uttered his famously misquoted pro-capitalist phrase in 1925: "The chief business of the American people is business."[52] Some historians have even suggested that during the 1920s "business values replaced religious values in the conduct of church affairs."[53] A pervasive business ethos found in many Christian organizations and some religious literature seemed to support this notion. The Interchurch World Movement, an ecumenical men's organization of the 1920s, stated that it was doing "the biggest business of the biggest man in the world." Advertisements for the organization further admonished that "He

(Christ) was always about His Father's business. Christ needs big men for big business."[54] A religious novel published in 1925 by an advertising executive and future congressman, Bruce Barton, did more than any other work of literature at the time to characterize the era. *The Man Nobody Knows* provocatively depicted Jesus as "the founder of modern business."[55] Barton, who wrote the book in response to images of Jesus he found "sissified," was greatly influenced by nineteenth-century liberal theology and particularly the Social Gospel. Wholly rejecting orthodox theology, he recast the Jesus of Scripture as not so much on a "divine mission," as on, in the words of James Neuchterlein, "a business errand." Barton's unqualified faith in the redemptive social value of Christianity and in the capitalist system prompted him to make an inextricable link between religion and business. Indeed, he viewed religion as the greatest business in the world and used business discourse to frame all things theological. The Christian Church, for example, triumphed by way of a "worldwide advertising campaign."[56] Although depicted and discounted by scholars as an insipid, inspirational, pro-capitalist text, the book worked on a number of complex and interrelated levels. As a product of Barton's liberal Protestant leaning, *The Man Nobody Knows* made a crucial contribution to extant endeavors to reject a "feminized" conception of the Christian religion. The Christ of Barton's creed was a "manly savior," who was more influenced by the rugged "man's man" carpenter Joseph than by his mother Mary. This Jesus possessed a firm physique and a masculine demeanor. The theology that emanated from this "muscular Jesus" was one that was entirely ethical and social in focus. As Leo Ribuffo asserted, ultimately the book was an attempt to "Christianize the social order."[57] With that attempt, however, the book curiously affirmed the basic assumptions of capitalism and the Protestant work ethic. It connected hard work and "positive thinking" to material prosperity long before that became a trend among Evangelical Protestants. The book became a huge popular success, selling 250,000 copies in the first eighteen months of printing. It remained on the bestseller list for two years and topped all nonfiction titles in 1926. Barton became a household name and his book a part of the corporate cannon.[58] Ultimately, despite its other complex levels, *The Man Nobody Knows* was an attempt to show the inexorable connection between religion and business, which was the spirit of the 1920s in both real and imagined ways.

The developments in the black churches of Chicago during the 1920s were consistent with these currents in American Protestantism. And in many cases, the effort to combine the impulses of Christian charity with "business efficiency" increased the church's stature in the community and its membership. Like Carter Temple, African American mainline Protestant churches in Chicago that exemplified this approach during the migration often buttressed their programs and attracted new migrants.

In 1925, Mt. Carmel CME Church adopted as its slogan "More business in religion and more religion in business." The Reverend M. L. Breeding, the pastor of Mt. Carmel, insisted that the slogan described "the outstanding need" of the city's black churches. In just one year of "remarkable progress," Breeding's efforts toward "systematizing the work of the church and of bringing it in line with the newest church methods" added hundreds to the congregation of Mt. Carmel.[59]

Whether to increase the size of their congregations, to reclaim a sense of control over the religious environment, or to genuinely attempt to promote religious solidarity, many mainline black Protestant churches reordered their institutional priorities to reflect the influx of black southern migrants. For many of them, this meant combining the principles of business with expanded commitments to social service. By the late 1920s, Breeding's comment to put "more business in religion and more religion in business" had proved prophetic. It had come to describe the ethos of many black Chicago churches in and outside the mainstream. The corresponding professionalization of social work within these churches became equally characteristic, as charity and social outreach became a civic as well as Christian responsibility. At the height of the migration, few in the black religious community would have drawn a distinction between their responsibility as citizens and their Christian faith. Harold Kingsley's proposals for a "fearless, sane, intelligent gospel, designed to quicken men to better living" and a "Christian community touching every phase of man's life" became typical.[60]

The reordering of the institutional priorities of these churches constituted a new sacred order in black Chicago. The process was uneven and fraught with tensions, as some churches were more successful than others in their attempts to transform church work. And the spoils of human capital usually went to those churches with the most aggressive, far-reaching programs and the most resources. These churches were also most likely to have the most intimate connections with the black community at large. Black southern migrants were key to all that occurred programmatically in black Protestant churches during these years. Churches rose and fell according to their stance on the migration and on black southerners. The enormous size of churches like Olivet Baptist, Ebenezer Baptist, Mt. Carmel, and Carter Temple (CME) testified to the position these congregations took on the migration as well as to their efforts to attract new migrants and address their concerns. Accompanying the programmatic changes instituted by mainstream black Protestant churches were transformations that cut even deeper to the core of black faith. The transformation of worship patterns, church music, and black preaching was integral to a new, dynamic expression of African American religion in the urban metropolis of black Chicago.

CHAPTER FOUR

The Frenzy, the Preacher, and the Music

> *"The Frenzy of 'Shouting' . . . was the last essential of Negro Religion and the one more devoutly believed in than all the rest."*
>
> *"The Preacher is the most unique personality developed by the Negro on American soil."*
>
> *"The Music of Negro Religion . . . still remains the most original and beautiful expression of human life and longing yet born on American soil."*
>
> —W. E. B. Du Bois

As THE NUMBER of southern migrants who attended mainline black Chicago churches surged, the worship patterns of those churches altered significantly. Indeed, with changes to the worship in mainstream black churches, the impact of black southerners on these congregations was complete. Southern migrants were fattening church rolls and exhausting as well as expanding financial and programmatic resources. They were also prompting a reconceptualization of the notion of church work through social service and alliances with the wider world. The capstone to all this transformation was how southern migrants helped shape the ways and means by which the faithful praised God. The anxieties of the dwindling number of "old settlers" who worried about the overwhelming influence migrants could have on black church culture proved well-founded. There were striking differences between the way churches operated in black Chicago in the 1890s and the way they did by the 1920s. And it was not so much about which people went to church; nearly all of black Chicago went to church, especially on Sundays. Drake and Cayton spoke to this when they asserted, "Sunday morning in Bronzeville is a colorful occasion." They went on to say that "Eleven o'clock service is the main event of the day, and some of the larger churches are filled by 10:45 A.M., when the older members start the pre-service prayer meeting." The congregants arrived at church by various means, including "jitneys" (illegal cabs), streetcars, buses, and "freshly polished" automobiles. "Church mothers" adorned with "little gray caps perched on their heads and secured by chin straps" conversed with the youth of the church "clad in their stylish Sunday best."[1] Scenes like this were repeated weekly in churches all across the South Side.

The issue with black Chicago churches during the migration era, however, was who went to what church amid the vast array of choices—or better, the diverse range of people one was likely to find in those congregations along regional, generational, educational, as well as class lines. The complexity of black Protestant churches during this era served as one of the new religious culture's signature features. It was this complexity, the fragmented or mixed nature of mainstream black Protestant churches that prompted the profound changes in preaching, worship patterns, and church music. For many of these churches, the adaptations were not only necessary; they also had an air of inevitability about them.

One of the primary aspects of the religious services in mainstream black churches to undergo adaptation was the way ministers conducted their sermons. In many ways, the changes started with the sermon for it was the historical centerpiece and lifeblood of black worship. Preaching held the key to all that happened or failed to happen in the worship service. Its form and content were firmly rooted in history and the black oral tradition.[2] In the South, the basic form of black preaching had remained fairly consistent since the mid-nineteenth century. Black southern migrants who came to Chicago would have been familiar with a preaching style that was unschooled, emotional, and theatrical. John Jasper typified the black southern "folk" preacher of the late nineteenth century. Born a slave in Fluvanna County, Virginia, in 1812, Jasper rose to become one of the most celebrated preachers of his day. Like many of his contemporaries Jasper had very little schooling, which may have, ironically, added to the power of his message and his delivery. Known most famously for his sermon, "Da Sun Do Move," in which he claimed that the sun revolved around the earth and that the earth was flat, Jasper delivered all his sermons in dialect or vernacular speech. Likewise, the theatrical use of his body in the pulpit held his audiences spellbound. Jasper's biographer, William E. Hatcher, described him as "a theater within himself." Upon first hearing Jasper, Hatcher wrote: "Shades of Anglo-Saxon fathers! Did mortal lips ever gush with such torrents of horrible English! Hardly a word came out clothed in its right mind. And gestures! He circled around the pulpit with his ankle in his hand; and laughed and sang and shouted and acted out a dozen characters within the space of three minutes."[3] In the twentieth century, southern black preachers continued in the tradition of Jasper, preaching theatrical sermons done in vernacular speech that were also highly emotional, theologically inventive, and socially conservative. Great showmen and stirring entertainers, many of these preachers recorded their sermons throughout the decade of the 1920s. The Reverend Calvin P. Dixon was the first to do so for Columbia Records in 1925. The most acclaimed sermon on record was done by Reverend J. C. Burnett of Kansas City, Missouri. His "The Downfall of Nebuchadnezzar" proved so enormously popular that it outsold Bessie Smith in 1926.[4] Perhaps the most acclaimed and certainly the most prolific preacher to record his sermons was J. M. Gates from Atlanta, Georgia. His many recordings, including such titles as "Death Might Be Your Santa Claus," "Women Spend Too Much Money," "Kinky Hair Is No Disgrace," and "Death's Black Train Is Coming," demonstrate the black southern sermonic tradition in all its elements, including the fabled "preacher's breath"—vocal interjections at the end of sentences. They also included "call and response" and chanting, or the "singing sermon."[5] Certainly, Du Bois had rural African American preachers working from this tradition in mind when he wrote "the preacher is the most unique personality developed by the Negro on American soil."[6] By the early 1920s, many mainline black Chicago preachers came to embrace aspects of this sermonic tradition in deference to congregations that held growing numbers of blacks from the rural South.

Prior to 1915, established black Chicago churches placed great emphasis on preaching that was "orderly" and worship that was "decorous." Although the lack of an "educated ministry" was a perennial critique both in the North and in the South after the Civil War, most ministers of Chicago's larger churches possessed ministerial degrees and had been trained in homiletics. Moses H. Jackson, Richard R. Wright, Jr., Archibald J. Carey, Sr., Elijah John Fisher, and James Alfred Dunn Podd, for example, were all prominent African American ministers who held advanced theological degrees during the late nineteenth and early twentieth centuries. Fisher, who had studied at the University of Chicago, was a scholar proficient in both Hebrew and Greek. Podd, a West Indian, came to pastor both Olivet and Bethesda Baptist in the 1890s after having finished a "classical collegiate course" in England in preparation for the Episcopal ministry. Miles Mark Fisher described him as an eloquent preacher with "pulpit ministrations" that were "brilliant" and "scholarly."[8] It was, however, the combined pressures of competition from other churches and from secular organizations for the attention of migrants who enjoyed "a more emotional ritual" that persuaded many ministers of mainline African American Chicago churches to adopt what Drake and Cayton called a "mixed type" preaching style.[9] Unlike the southern sermonic tradition, which was often done entirely in dialect, a sermon of the mixed type basically attempted to appeal to "two classes" of listeners in a congregation: the intellectually inclined and those who felt compelled to express their emotions freely and demonstratively.[10] On a deeper level, this new and innovative addition to the black sermonic tradition attempted to appeal to both reason (rationality) and to the emotions on the same occasion—if not at the same time. Olivet's Lacey Kirk Williams, for example, was said to be a "thoughtful, forceful, orthodox, interesting and emotional preacher" whose sermons simultaneously "satisfied the intellectual elite, convinced the skeptic and . . . electrified the washer woman." When a 1929 *Chicago Daily News* article lauded Olivet Baptist's extensive social outreach programs for southern migrants, Williams clarified that the church had not, in the process, neglected worship. "We have plenty of 'rousement,'" he maintained, "and I think at one of our services even one who believes as little as our good friend Clarence Darrow would be 'roused.'"[11] (A humanist and "freethinking" agnostic, Darrow made no secret of his disdain for organized religion and religious fervor. He would later write that he thought blacks to be too religious and their worship services to be "religious orgies.")[12] In tone, delivery, and intent, mixed-type sermons differed widely from those that had been preached among Chicago's African Americans prior to the migration.

Mixed-type sermons typically began at a slow, studied pace with the preacher reading from a prepared text. It was not uncommon for preachers during this portion of the sermon to illuminate their exposition with passages from the Bible, allusions to current events, or quotes from classical literature. The opening of "Reverend F's" sermon "was as erudite a discussion as one would expect to hear in a Hyde Park church," Robert Sutherland reported in 1930. The preacher, "one of the best educated ministers serving one of the largest churches," read from a prepared text on the subject "Christianity as a Mystery." Impressed with the minister's "style and thought," Sutherland excerpted heavily from the sermon: "The beauty without is a reflection of the beauty within. . . . A rose is beautiful because of our power of aesthetic appreciation."[13] As a mixed-type sermon progressed, the minister moved from text to extemporaneous speaking, the volume of his voice rising steadily. Decorum would soon be cast aside as he worked himself, and at least a portion of the congregation, to an emotional frenzy. Sutherland was not so impressed with the extemporaneous portion of Reverend F's sermon.

> After ten minutes of thoughtful preaching, Reverend F. began to wander occasionally from his manuscript, inserting now and then vivid descriptions with strong emotional appeal. This was merely a suggestion of what was to follow. Soon he rose to the height of enthusiasm. Manuscript and sermon subject was abandoned. With a skill I have never seen equaled, he played upon the emotions of his people. "God is everywhere. He is here. He is there. He is in the air. If a spiritual hand were out there I would grasp it."

Reverend F then began "gesturing" and "strutting" in the performance of his sermon. He blended singing and speaking as if carrying on a "face to face dialogue with the Lord." When he came to the "climax" of his sermon, Reverend F gave a "cry of abandonment" that referred back to the opening portion. "I am born of God," he exclaimed. "I can't be intelligent all the time. I've got to be myself. I've got religion. I've got religion." The congregation responded with holy dancing (one woman doing what Sutherland claimed was "not dissimilar to the Charleston"), and shouts of "Amen" and "Glory to God."[14]

Ministers such as Williams and Reverend F who became adroit at mixed-type preaching understood that the division between the "two classes" of listeners was not only along class or economic lines, but along cultural, regional, generational, and educational lines as well. As early as 1915, Theobald Smythe came under pressure from "two distinct classes of worshipers" in Bethel AME Church. Older members of the congregation wanted sermons that would "move them to shouting" while the younger congregants demanded sermons that were "more intellectualized." Although Smythe apparently attempted to satisfy the old and the young, the *Chicago Defender* still depicted Bethel as not a place where "fanatics" vented their emotions.[15] One African American Chicago minister, observed in the forties by a researcher for Drake and Cayton's *Black Metropolis*, calmed his congregation down (after having incited an explosion of emotionalism) by proclaiming, "My, I forgot where I was this morning. I musta thought I was still down between the plow-handles and not here in a Chicago pulpit. Lemme get back to this paper [manuscript]. I forgot I had these educated folks in here. But I'm not ashamed of my Jesus!"[16]

Preachers of mixed-type sermons employed several techniques designed to make allowances for emotionalism. First, as the above example shows, these sermons often made direct references to the South. In this way, the sermon evoked images of a way of life familiar to many of the listeners while at the same time suggesting a familial connection of call and response between speaker and audience. Robert Sutherland noted that in mixed-type sermons, metaphors taken from rural life were the norm. He described in his typically pejorative manner one such sermon given at a South Side church.

> The discourse was filled with anecdotes all of which were taken from rural life. His analogies were grossly drawn and he apologized for the impropriety of one—comparing a weak Christian to the runt of the litter which couldn't keep up with the sow. One story drew a moral from the antics of a donkey. Another was based on cabbage plants.[17]

Similarly, mixed-type preachers speckled the emotional portion of their sermons with vernacular speech. Used as a means to establish a rapport with the poor, less educated, or southern migrants (between whom few mainline ministers drew any distinction), the dialect speech commonly referred to aspects of urban life. They especially stressed the hardships and dislocation typically experienced by this segment of the congregation. Lastly, although mixed type preachers endeavored never to "alienate the 'educated' members," anti-intellectualism was another technique they routinely employed. Mixed-type sermons would often attribute certain sins as particular to those who were educated or intellectual. In a sermon about pride given by an African American Chicago minister in the 1940s, for example, the story of Jesus' questioning by the chief priests and Pharisees in Luke 5:27–6:10 was given a contemporary bent. After their attempt to stump Jesus with questions had failed, the minister asserted, "That fixed 'em—all those Ph.D.'s in their long robes and mortarboard hats, all puffed with their education. With all their degrees and learning, they couldn't trick the Son of the Living God!"[18]

Although mixed-type preaching as a concession to the southern folk religious sensibility became common during the Great Migration, it did not change everyone's mind about the perceived dangers of emotional worship. One Chicago preacher insisted in 1930 that the practice of "shouting," which mixed-type preaching was designed to accommodate, was a "form of insanity." Alexis de Tocqueville had made a similar claim in the early nineteenth century after witnessing the worship at a "camp meeting," asserting, "religious insanity is very common in the United States."[19] Though it appeared strange to many longtime black Chicagoans, however, "shouting" had a long history among black religionists, particularly those in the South. In southern African American rural religion, "shouting" or "holy dancing" was second only in importance to the sermon and was the centerpiece of emotionally frenzied worship. It was after having witnessed such a display of religious emotionalism that Du Bois penned his own description of "the Frenzy," calling it "the last essential of Negro religion and the one more devoutly believed in than all the rest."[20] Throughout the 1930s and 1940s, the rise of emotionalism in mainstream black Chicago churches elicited intense responses. These responses typically ranged from favorable to highly unfavorable. A few remained ambivalent. One African American pastor confessed, "I don't know how to handle it. It confuses and bothers me."[21] Even those who saw the practice as harmless worried that it was ultimately retrograde. "I think when it's sincerely done, it's alright," an interviewee proclaimed in the forties. "On the whole, though, I regard it as a turning back toward slavery days."[22] By this time, however, mixed-type preaching and emotionally frenzied worship were pervasive and characteristic of black churches across a wide denominational spectrum. It had made significant inroads even into many of the city's old-line institutions, providing identifiable spaces for the church's growing number of southern migrant congregants.

The ability to appeal to the "two classes" within most congregations became an important test for black clergy. And not every minister who recognized the need for mixed-type preaching could perform it. An African American minister in Robert Sutherland's 1930 study confessed that "I sometimes bring in some other preacher to do the emotional part and he gets results where I couldn't."[23] Ultimately, whatever ministers and churchgoers thought of mixed-type preaching or of religious enthusiasm, the presence of it in church worship reaffirmed notions essential to southern migrant religious culture. One African American pastor of a large and reputedly nondemonstrative church interviewed in the late 1930s inadvertently testified to the pervasiveness of mixed-type preaching by that time. "My preaching appeals to the better class, but it is not pedantic. We have two thousand five hundred members including ignorant people who fall in line and keep step. I believe in the preparation of sermons, in illustrations for sermons, and write my sermons down, but do not read them." With this obvious concession to the "ignorant people" of his congregation, clearly it was this minister who was falling in line and keeping step.[24]

At the same time that mixed-type preaching was reconfiguring the worship styles of many of Chicago's established black Protestant churches, black gospel emerged to replace the classical music and "Negro spirituals" that had become the most regularly performed music in these churches. As with many African American religious cultural forms, there remains an ahistorical, timeless perception about black gospel music. The genre has been so intimately associated with the black experience in the United States that the notion that black gospel emerged within a particular historical context has often been obscured. There is, however, a specific historical development to black gospel and it is intricately tied to the migration and urbanization of American blacks. Black gospel is a musical genre deeply influenced by the cadences of the South and southern religion, but it was born in the city and at its core reflects urbanization and modern life. As Mellonee Burnim stated, "when blacks migrated to urban centers in the North and South during the aftermath of World War I, they created gospel music, music which reflected their changing ideas and ideals in this new sociocultural environment."[25] Chicago was central to the historical development of black gospel, not only because it was the home of the modern gospel era, but also because black gospel provided a drastic contrast to the worship music that had become common in black Chicago churches. By the 1890s, classical music and classically trained musicians and choristers dominated the church music scene in the city's prominent black churches. The African American middle class in particular found no more appropriate way to showcase cultural refinement and respectability than with the music of their houses of worship. Churches like Grace Presbyterian, for instance, professed that they were "wide awake to the issues of the day in art and music."[26] Though churches did not entirely abandon the Negro spirituals and hymns of their evangelical heritage, it became common and expected to include the works of classical composers in the worship service. Additionally, intense vocal competitions, highly stylized concerts, and musicals were frequently staged and well attended. The sixteenth annual "Pleasant Sunday Afternoon" concert series held at Bethel AME on March 19, 1916, for example, included international folk song and dance, but the works of Grieg, Haydn, Chopin, and Tchaikovsky predominated.[27]

There was a twofold purpose for performing classical music in black churches. First, many middle-class African American pastors and their choirmasters desired to educate Chicago blacks about music of the "higher type." This motivation comprised the central mission of the Umbria Glee Club, one of the oldest such organizations in America, the R. Nathaniel Dett Club, and Chicago Choral Study Club. Under the direction of Professor Pedro Tinsley, the Chicago Choral Study Club made a commitment to doing "the most difficult pieces" in order to "create a desire for better music among Chicago Negroes." In addition to chorales by Handel, Bach, and Beethoven, the Chicago Choral Study Club also introduced to Chicago the works of the Afro-British composer Samuel Coleridge-Taylor.[28] Second, middle-class black churches that performed classical music wanted to answer charges that African Americans were limited musically. By the late nineteenth and early twentieth centuries, many whites were convinced of African Americans' "natural" musical ability but restricted that ability to "work songs," "corn field ditties," and Negro spirituals, which at their best could "only be rendered by Negroes." Such artists as Anita Patti Brown, a vocal artist of enormous popularity who regularly performed in middle-class black Chicago churches, proved that "the expression of music in the Negro could not be confined to just the Spirituals." Brown, a soprano who had developed a national reputation after graduating from Chicago Musical College, often included arias by Verdi, Donizetti, and Meyerbeer in her concerts.[29] In regular concerts rendered throughout the 1890s, she and a large number of other "Divas and Divans" helped middle-class African American churches overturn theories of the "Negro's limited musical ability."[30]

The rise of classical music performance in Chicago's middle-class black churches, however, worked as much to exaggerate social and class differences among the city's blacks as it did to educate and to dispel notions of black musical inferiority. Membership in most of the musical organizations, choruses, and choirs was strict and exclusive. With reputations to maintain for music of the highest quality, the leadership carefully monitored the groups and limited membership to the "highly refined."[31] And the performances themselves were not entirely democratic affairs. Although much of the classical music performed in churches was done as a part of the public worship service, and therefore free of charge, other performances were staged to raise funds either for the church or for the particular organization and deliberately targeted an audience of the "more cultured class." Such an audience attended Bethel AME in 1910 when "Madame" Sallie M. Jones Downs gave a concert that was "repeatedly encored by the wave of handkerchiefs." And when the Umbriai Glee Club gave its initial concert of the season that same year at Quinn Chapel AME, opening with the battle hymn from Wagner's opera, *Rienzi: Der Letzte der Tribunen* (The Last of the Tribunes), it was to "a large gathering of Chicago's best society people." The opera, set in the fourteenth century, fell outside of Wagner's Bayreuth canon and did not represent in an aesthetic sense the trajectory of his later music. The piece lacked any obvious spiritual content to suggest it as particularly apt for religious worship. It was most certainly the obscurity of the opera, therefore, that made it a prime choice for black Chicagoans keen on demonstrations of "respectability" through music. *Rienzi* would later have a tremendous influence on the young Adolph Hitler.[32]

Black gospel forged its way into this world of Eurocentric, class-based worship in Chicago African American churches by the early 1930s. Even before the modern era of black gospel, however, nascent versions of the genre were heard first among the numerous Holiness-Pentecostal churches primarily established and frequented by black southerners. While in Chicago during the First World War, Langston Hughes happened upon one of these churches and wrote that he was "entranced by their stepped-up rhythms, tambourines, handclapping, and uninhibited dynamics, rivaled only by Ma Rainey singing the blues at the Old Monogram Theater." Located on South State Street, the Monogram was one of Chicago's hottest entertainment venues, featuring the stage acts of Erskine Tate and Ethel Waters, as well as Ma Rainey. Hughes went on to say that the "music of these less formal Negro churches early took hold of me, moved me and thrilled me."[33]

Although ethnomusicologists and other scholars dispute the exact origins of black gospel, most agree that Chicago was the birthplace of the modern gospel music era.[34] And although many of these same scholars also disagree about the extent to which the evangelical hymns of nineteenth-century white Christians, African American "shout songs," Negro spirituals, and the blues influenced the genre, they all agree that each played a part in shaping it. From the onset, the music was a vernacular form, tending to address common experiences and to be imbued with an urban cosmology. It was deliberately subjective and designed to encourage an emotional response. It also necessitated an emphatic, improvisational delivery by the performer. From a thematic and theological point of view, there were important differences between black gospel and the black sacred music that preceded it. Black gospel tended to infuse God into the present, into current situations. This focus did not dispel eschatological hopes, but it did temper them with a horizontal gaze on temporal conditions. "Ain't

That Good News," a song penned in mid-1930s by "Little Lucy" Collier
and sung to choreography, captured these elements.

> Jesus is coming, coming soon
> Ain't that good news,
> It may be morning night or noon,
> Ain't that good news;
> I'm going to lay down my burden, I'm going to shoulder up my cross
> And I'm going to take it home to Jesus
> Ain't that good news.[35]

Black gospel suggested a greater intimacy with God, a God close at hand.
In contrast to Negro spirituals, the God of black gospel was present and
highly anthropomorphized. God, in the person of Jesus, did not simply
punish sin and sinners but also "talked" to his children, "wiped tears from
their eyes" and "held their hands." Many of the tunes composed in the
1930s and 1940s by Roberta Martin, who led one of the most successful
gospel ensembles in Chicago, best exemplified the intimacy and the theological immediacy of black gospel music. In one song, Martin proclaimed
"Jesus is My Only Friend"; In another, simply "Jesus Is Mine." In still another popular tune, she encouraged listeners to "Try Jesus" because "He
Satisfies."[36] The theologies of black gospel were more personal than communal and the meanings more straightforward than in Negro spirituals.
As an indigenous folk musical tradition, Negro spirituals were rooted in
the slave experience and using biblical imagery and metaphor, reflected
the cosmology of Christian slaves. Though essentially sacred in content,
Negro spirituals typically contained a double, "coded," and more subver-
sive meaning. "Go Down Moses" and "Didn't My Lord Deliver Daniel"
had as much to do with the desire for freedom and rebellion as with the
epic stories of ancient Israel. Christian slaves often used these songs to
warn of impending danger, as well as to usher runaways to freedom.
When they heard the words "Steal Away to Jesus" or "Get on Board, Little Children," escaping slaves knew the way was safe.[37] Although infused
with an urban cosmology and a decidedly this-worldly view, the lyrics of
black gospel contained no broader political implications, as had been true
for many Negro spirituals. At the same time, like Negro spirituals, black
gospel made no apology for suffering and often called for immediate
deliverance as well as ultimate salvation.

Initially, black gospel music met with sharp resistance from many
within the African American religious community. Like the complaints
about black southerners in general, some of this early resistance was
rooted in anxieties about race respectability. A daughter of one of
Chicago's African American doctors remarked that her father allowed her
to listen only to "the best kinds of music—classical and opera and the

like." "He couldn't stand the blues and the gospel songs that were becoming popular," she stated, noting that he regarded them as "nothing but a lot of shouting and were a disgrace to the race." Edward H. Boatner, a classically trained composer and arranger of Negro spirituals and anthems, recalled that when he first heard black gospel as the senior choir director at Pilgrim Baptist Church, he thought it was "degrading." "It's a desecration," he continued. "The only people who think it isn't a desecration are the people who haven't had any training, any musical training—people who haven't heard fine religious anthems, cantatas, and oratorios." Boatner, a graduate of Boston Conservatory and Chicago College of Music, committed most of his creative energy to the composition of classical works and Negro spirituals, which he hoped would have "the same status in the world of music as folk music of other races." His views about black gospel often generated palpable tensions between new migrants and longtime residents in the early days of black gospel. When Mahalia Jackson migrated from New Orleans in 1927, for example, her tendency to "start off shouting" in her performances so offended the religious sensibilities of some of the city's old-line churches that they often dismissed her from their services. Others refused to allow her in at all. Jackson found respite and welcome in many of Chicago's storefront Holiness-Pentecostal churches, where she performed regularly and was considered "a fresh wind from the down-home religion."[38] To gain the respect of the "big colored churches," Jackson said, she had to make it her "business to pack little basement-hall congregations and storefront churches." She was convinced they sat up and took notice after that. For Edward Boatner, black gospel music threatened to roll back the progress blacks had made in demonstrating race respectability through the use of classical music as worship music, a practice that had endured since the late nineteenth century. He also had doubts about the religious efficacy of black gospel. "How can something that's jazzy give a religious feeling?" Boatner inquired. This question became particularly pertinent as many became aware of the man who was most responsible for the spread of black gospel in Chicago, Thomas Andrew Dorsey.[39]

Although black gospel music first appeared in Chicago's Holiness-Pentecostal storefront churches, it was Thomas Dorsey, "the father of black gospel music," who brought the musical genre into the African American mainstream.[40] When this African American blues musician embraced and professionalized it, the genre made intractable inroads into middle-class, mainline black Protestant churches. Ironically, Dorsey helped introduce emotional worship to mainline black Chicago churches via a musical style he in large part made respectable. Acknowledging that black gospel did not originate with him, Dorsey stated in an interview conducted late in his life that he "made it beautiful, more noticeable,

Fig. 8. Thomas A. Dorsey. Dorsey pioneered the modern gospel era at Ebenezer and Pilgrim Baptist churches in Chicago during the 1930s. His song "Take My Hand, Precious Lord" remains the preeminent example of the genre. (Source: Vivian G. Harsh Collection, Carter G. Woodson Regional Branch, Chicago Public Library)

more susceptible with runs and thrills and moans in it."[41] In the process, he bridged the religious cultural worlds of southern migrants and established Chicago churches. (See figure 8.)

Before the first of two religious conversion experiences he underwent after migrating to Chicago from Georgia in 1916, Dorsey composed, recorded, and performed numerous sexually suggestive blues songs called "hokum." The most famous of these were *It's Tight Like That, Pat That Bread, You Got the Stuff,* and *It's All Worn Out. It's Tight Like That* was a masterpiece of the genre and sold nearly a million copies, inspiring additional versions by Dorsey and his writing partner, Hudson Whittaker, as well as other artists. McKinney's Cotton Pickers recorded a version in 1928 with George Thomas and Dave Wilborn on vocals. The double-entendre configuration of these songs was a winning format for Dorsey and Whittaker. Royalties from the recordings garnered a measure of success after a period of financial decline. A blues pianist of exceptional skill, "Georgia Tom," as Dorsey was called, had worked playing for Ma Rainey's band, and by 1924 was well known around Chicago's entertainment circuit. But conflicts between his life's work and his desire to return to his Baptist roots prompted Dorsey to join the Ebenezer Baptist Church in the late 1920s. It was there that he became involved with black gospel music, and within a few years his reputation as a composer and performer of black gospel began to surpass his reputation as a blues artist. But it was a gospel performance Dorsey staged in late winter of 1932, the same year he wrote "Precious Lord, Take My Hand" after the loss of his wife and child, that became a pivotal moment not only in his life and in the black churches of Chicago, but also in the history of black gospel music.[42]

A few days after Pilgrim Baptist invited Dorsey to bring his Ebenezer Baptist Gospel Chorus to the church to help celebrate J. C. Austin's sixth anniversary as pastor, Austin called Dorsey with an offer to lure him away from Ebenezer. Austin wanted Dorsey to establish a gospel chorus at Pilgrim. The request came as a surprise to Dorsey in view of Austin's reputation and the stoic order of worship he insisted on in his church. Just days before the event took place, Dorsey had been concerned about taking his chorus to Pilgrim, wondering if they should modify their usual spirited display of emotion rather than go "wild." Pilgrim Baptist, under the leadership of J. C. Austin, had been known as one of the most uncompromising among the old-line churches, refusing to adapt their worship styles in deference to southern migrants. Austin had indeed discouraged migration while a pastor in Pittsburgh, considering it "not the best thing for our people."[43] Although he would experience a complete reversal on this point, Austin made sure that Pilgrim's worship services remained some of the "most decorous" of mainline black churches. To ensure against any form of religious enthusiasm in the church, Austin went so far as to relegate preworship prayer services to the basement.[44] This all changed with one visit by Dorsey and the Ebenezer Baptist Gospel Chorus. Apparently, Dorsey, his associate Theodore Frye, and Ebenezer's pastor, J. H. Smith, decided not to change their worship style for Pilgrim, and when they had finished their musical set, "the church was all worked up and the spirit was at its highest pitch," Dorsey reported.[45]

Dorsey accepted Austin's offer and Pilgrim Baptist—not Ebenezer—became known as the birthplace of black gospel music.[46] At Pilgrim, where he stayed throughout his long career, Dorsey perfected his own black gospel style, developed a celebrated gospel chorus, and worked with some of the most renowned performers of black gospel, including Mahalia Jackson, Sallie Martin, Roberta Martin, and Rosetta Tharpe.[47] The music and worship patterns at Pilgrim changed dramatically. Black gospel allowed those members of Pilgrim Baptist who were inclined toward emotional worship to do so freely. Leola Ware Hartwell, a member of Pilgrim during the late 1930s, was proud of her rural Georgia roots and of being a member of the church's gospel chorus. "I am not like everybody else that is from Georgia that will tell that they came from Atlanta and have not ever seen Atlanta unless it was on the way," she reported. When asked what groups she participated in at Pilgrim, she responded, "I am a member of the gospel chorus. . . . Yes, I love good singing."[48] And it was not only the poor and working-class southern migrants, who were increasingly filling the church's pews, that seized this opportunity. As Dorsey recalled, many of the church's middle-class, educated professionals also learned to "clap their hands and sway their bodies and go on."[49] The introduction of black gospel into the worship at Pilgrim Baptist may even have opened the way for Pentecostal practices that were eventually observed even by J. C. Austin. Apparently, sometime during the early to mid-1930s Austin had a Pentecostal experience in California, wherein he saw a vision of angels and "received the Holy Ghost." After the experience, according to Reverend Aplin of the Sunlight Church of the Sabbath, many in the black community thought Austin and Pilgrim were "going Sanctified." It is not clear why Austin was in California, where the modern Pentecostal movement began, but "visions" and "receiving the Holy Ghost" are direct references to Pentecostal theology.[50] Depending on when exactly the experience happened (Reverend Aplin made his comments in 1938), Austin's Holy Ghost experience may help to explain a number of things. It would explain his willingness to allow black Gospel at Pilgrim in the first place and his change of heart with regard to the migration, as well as the changes in the worship practices at his church. After his California "Holy Ghost" experience, one can perhaps rightly infer that there were no more prayer services in the basement. Though gleaned from the smaller storefront and house churches that surrounded Pilgrim Baptist—many of which were Pentecostal—Dorsey's brand of black gospel spread from Pilgrim Baptist throughout the country by the late 1930s.

Austin's response to Dorsey and the Ebenezer Baptist Gospel Chorus was in some ways a mixture of awe and opportunism. He was certainly aware of the popularity of Dorsey's gospel chorus. It was the only gospel chorus in Chicago at the time and was highly sought after. Bringing the chorus to Pilgrim reflected in large part Austin's determination to observe for himself this new musical genre. Given his general concern for his congregation and his particular concern for the scores of new migrants joining it, his request that Dorsey leave Ebenezer for Pilgrim is not all that surprising. Austin witnessed the enthusiastic response his congregation gave to this indigenous musical tradition, a tradition deeply reflective of a southern ethos. Clearly, the addition of a gospel chorus at Pilgrim— already one of the most noteworthy black congregations in the city— would only enhance Austin's preaching, the church's stature, and its attraction for recent southern migrants. Austin's son, Junius C. Austin, Jr., confirmed this perspective in an interview with historian Michael Harris. "He [Austin, Sr.] was an outstanding pulpiteer, a great orator, a master preacher. Back in those days, the preacher had to have a great attraction to himself. My dad could see times changing and people desiring another type of music. He tried it [gospel music] in his church and, because of his preaching and the music, folk crowded out the church."[51]

Dorsey's motivation for leaving Ebenezer to join Pilgrim is less clear. It was not for money. He said himself that the new position "wasn't payin' nothing." It was not for prestige. He had that as the first and only gospel chorus leader in the city of Chicago. And to make sure that any prestige attached to his association with Pilgrim was not to be easily obtained, Edward H. Boatner as the head musician at Pilgrim made sure Dorsey and his gospel chorus were relegated to the back of the church. "And that's where they were until I left," Boatner confirmed years later. Boatner, a renowned composer of Negro spirituals, would always resent Dorsey for coming into his turf, bringing a musical genre he saw as "nothing but jazz, the rhythm of jazz."[52] Perhaps due to Dorsey's presence at the church, Boatner left Pilgrim in 1933 for New York, where he opened a music studio and trained Josephine Baker and Clifton Webb, among others.[53] One can only speculate that Dorsey saw in Austin a bit of himself, a kindred soul. Both men were energetic, innovative, and daring. When it came to their particular crafts, Dorsey and Austin could rightly be described as crowd-pleasing showmen. They were aware of this in themselves and in each other. Moreover, just as Austin saw in Dorsey and black gospel a courageous new current of religious expression, Dorsey saw in Austin a competitive religious leader unafraid of change as a means to church growth and social outreach. Both men were aware that they were riding a wave of change with black gospel, and Austin was perhaps even more aware of this than Dorsey. As Junius Austin said of his father: "My dad was farsighted, I think. He could see times changing and people desiring another type of music. He said, 'Dorsey's music's going to sweep the country. And I want it in Pilgrim Church!'"[54] (See figure 9.)

Black gospel's detractors and supporters alike soon realized that among all the musical influences upon the genre, the blues was perhaps the greatest. Support and disdain for black gospel met at this volatile nexus. For all those who, like Edward H. Boatner, rejected black gospel for its obvious

Fig. 9. Junius C. Austin. The invitation Austin, as pastor of Pilgrim Baptist Church, extended to Thomas A. Dorsey to join Pilgrim in 1932 is widely viewed as having launched the modern gospel era. (Source: Chicago Historical Society)

secular sound, there were many more who embraced it because of that. Of course, the blues influence in black gospel can be attributed to Dorsey, who made no attempt to alter the rhythms and cadences of his musical style. Rather, Dorsey consecrated the blues by altering the lyrical content. This is why Farah Jasmine Griffin is right to call black gospel the "sacred sister to the blues."[55] But Griffin is also right when she insists that "consideration of gospel music complicates our current understanding of working-class migrant culture as having been characterized only by the blues." For blacks in Chicago, the blues and black gospel performed similar cultural work in shaping their identity and giving expression to their quotidian experiences, concerns, fears, and hopes. Scholars have long noted the extent to which black southern migrants documented their experiences through the lyrics of the blues, often privileging the secular life of blues artists as authentic renderings of the socioeconomic process of migration and urbanization. The content of the blues has served as a lyrical map of the African American urban world, from the experiences of Big Bill Broonzy's "Keys to the Highway," "Going to Chicago," and "I'm a Southern Man" to the navigation of city life in Robert Johnson's "Sweet Home Chicago."[56] The gospel music of Chicago, however, revealed a similar lyrical map with a similar take on the African American experience in Chicago. The music of Chicago musicians like Rosetta Tharpe, Sallie Martin, Sister Calley Fancy, and Mother McCollum attempted to document city life and the confrontation of a southern religious sense with urban life in much the same way as their blues-stylist counterparts. They were just as much the new working-class orators of the black experience and of modernity, with equal authentication.

Chief among these working-class orators of modernity were two gospel artists that predated Thomas Dorsey. Recorded between 1929 and 1931, the songs of "guitar evangelists" Mother McCollum and Sister Calley Fancy demonstrated a more keen awareness of modern life than those of any other genre of black music at the time. Little is known of the two women other than that they were from the rural south, possibly the Mississippi delta, and that they recorded their songs upon their arrival to Chicago. They both were members of the Holiness-Pentecostal or "Sanctified" Church, the term that would later be used first by Zora Neale Hurston to unite all African American churches that developed from the Holiness and Pentecostal movements.[57] The instrumentation and the vernacular vocalization both women employed echoed rural southern culture, but their lyrics were rooted in modern life and possibly reflected urban existence. Though their songs were fundamentally evangelistic and apocalyptic, they made metaphoric use of the vestiges of modern life and contemporary culture to disseminate their message of salvation and warning. Both artists made repeated references to trains, train stations, automobiles, airplanes, and other relatively recent technological inventions. Mother McCollum's "Jesus Is My Aer-O-plane" and Sister Calley Fancy's "Everybody Get Your Business Right" serve as a prime examples:

"Jesus Is My Aer-O-plane"
(chorus)
Jesus is my Aer-O-plane
He holds this world in His hands
He rides over all
He don't never fall
Jesus is my Aer-O-plane.

(verse 3)
You can run to the East
Run to the West
You can't find no soul to rest
Some of these mornings He's coming again
Coming through in a Aer-O-plane.

"EVERYBODY GET YOUR BUSINESS RIGHT"

(chorus)
Everybody get your business right
Everybody get your business right
Everybody get your business right
God told me to tell you to get your business right.

(verse 1)
I'll be standing at the station
With my ticket in my hand
When the saints of God go marching in
I mean to join that band.

(verse 2)
That train that runs to glory
She runs on scheduled time
Now is your time to get your business right
Or you'll be left behind.[58]

Sister Calley Fancy, in particular, seemed to be inspired as much by the pages of the press as she was by biblical text. Many of her songs indicate that she was a keen observer of world events, domestic government, and international politics. Her song in two parts, "Death Is Riding Through the Land," is the only gospel song known to make reference to the First World War.

"DEATH IS RIDING THROUGH THE LAND"

(verse 1)
President your life is in God's hands
This message is for you Jews
And governors remember when you're sinister men
My God is watching you.

(chorus)
Death is riding through the land
He's a riding through the land
He's a riding through the land
He's bringing vengeance on beast and man.

(verse 2)
Death is bringing down your great airplanes
Overturning automobiles
He's wrecking trains causing hearts to fail
Oh, nations don't you fear?

(verse 4)
You mothers who claim to know God
God is giving you a chance
Some of you haven't prayed a heartfelt prayer
Since your son returned from France.

(verse 7)
You promised God in the World War
If He would save your land
You would change your lives and live for Christ
Now you've gone back on Him.[59]

The songs of these "guitar evangelists" may have been restricted to Sanctified churches or to performances during street preaching. Their forceful and edgy voices would suggest as much. But as a genre, black gospel music had become the church music of choice in Chicago among mainstream Protestant churches by the 1930s, reflecting southern evangelical traditions, while its emphatic delivery and subjectivity underscored the exigencies of modern city life.

Beyond churches like Ebenezer and Pilgrim Baptist, the popularity and dissemination of black gospel in Chicago can be attributed principally to the growth of black-oriented radio. By the mid-1930s, black-oriented radio became the primary mechanism for the dispersion of the new musical style, as nearly all of Chicago's radio stations either added black gospel to their regular playlists or dedicated special segments exclusively to gospel music. But more than just being a mechanism for the spread of black gospel, black-oriented radio itself became a major actor in transforming the cultural life of the city's African American population.[60] As the influx of migrants began to alter the religious culture of the city, that change was reflected in both the programming and the content of black-oriented radio. By the mid-1930s black Chicagoans could tune their radios to hear not only recordings of black gospel music but also recorded sermons and live broadcasts of emotionally demonstrative religious services. In the same way that African American mainline Protestant churches began making concessions to the religious sensibilities of southern migrants, Chicago radio stations that targeted a black audience augmented the format and personnel of their stations to appeal specifically to the tastes and concerns of lower- and working-class Chicagoans. They rightly surmised that the majority of these would be new arrivals. The clear effect of the programmatic changes implemented by black-oriented radio stations was not only the commodification of southern migrant religious inclinations but also the final triumph of a vernacular religious ethos over Chicago's African American religious culture.

In some sense, many radio stations decided to target southern migrants for practical market reasons. Literacy rates among poor and working-class southern migrants were the lowest in Chicago, suggesting that this group would be more likely to listen to radio. (By the mid-1930s more than 80 percent of American homes had radio sets.) Poor and working class blacks read the black press infrequently compared with middle-class blacks. Moreover, the black press increasingly became associated with the lifestyles and interests of the black elite and middle class, a plight many local black newspapers did not survive. Circulations declined and some African American newspapers ceased to exist, not only because of low readership, but also because they did not reflect the experiences of ordinary black Chicagoans or depict their lives in the most flattering light. Ironically, even the *Chicago Defender*, which had done so much to spark the Great Migration, declined among Chicago's newest residents and had obtained the alternate name, "The Chicago Offender."[61] Also, by the late 1920s Chicago was already a city of migrants, with the largest share of the black population having been born out of state—83 percent—and the poor and working-class portion of that population being the largest (as much as 65 percent in the decade of the 1930s).[62] So with special features, large segments of black gospel, sermons on record, and live broadcasts of spirited worship from storefront and mainline churches alike, black-oriented radio also became a harbinger of the new sacred order in black Chicago.

Religious broadcasts were not the exclusive means by which Chicago black-oriented radio stations attempted to appeal to southern migrants. Jack L. Cooper, a former lightweight boxer and vaudevillian actor turned disc jockey, utilized drama, folklore, and comedy as well as religious performances in his radio show, the *All Negro Hour*. It was one of the first such programs in the nation. Cooper, himself a southern migrant from Tennessee, came to Chicago in the late 1920s and was a regular fixture on several Chicago stations by the 1930s. Although some scholars have portrayed Cooper and his radio program as representative of the black elite with a "bourgeois perspective and uplift agenda," much of the programming cooper produced suggested his target audience was working-class black Chicagoans, particularly southern migrants. He produced three comic acts involving southern migrants that appeared frequently on his program. "Luke and Timber" was about the antics of two boys from Memphis who found themselves in the urban north. "Mush and Corinda" (also called "The Alabama Sunflowers") and "Horseradish and Fertilizer" were the names of two couples who had recently migrated to Chicago from the South.[63] These were all done in dialect and the programs became enormously popular in Chicago at a time when pejorative depictions of black life and speech done by the likes of Jack Benny's "Rochester," and Gosden and Correll's *Amos N' Andy* were hotly debated and castigated by many northern blacks.[64] Unlike these shows, Cooper's didn't simply find in southern black stereotypes rich fodder for entertainment purposes. While he was concerned that recent migrants hear black characters and experiences they could recognize, he wanted the radio to serve as a network of communication for his listeners. It was Cooper who established the *Search for Missing Persons Program* in 1938, a free service offered over the radio. By the 1950s, the popular program had reunited with their families numerous southern migrants who had lost touch with one another during the chaos of migration.[65]

Al Benson, a contemporary of Cooper's, imitated the format Cooper established and in the process also captured a huge following among Chicago's lower and working-class radio listeners. Shortly after making his radio debut on a religious broadcast from a storefront church over station WGES in 1945, Benson, a preacher whose given name was Arthur B. Learner, decided to become a disc jockey. While Cooper used dialect only in theatrical performances, Benson introduced southern vernacular to black-oriented radio in his standard radio personality. In conjunction with the "down home blues" that formed his exclusive playlist, Benson spoke in a "hukster" style and filled his speech with "black idiomatic expressions."[66] From the 1930s to the 1950s both Cooper and Benson were among a small coterie of entrepreneurial deejays who spearheaded a revolution in black-oriented radio in Chicago, making the city in the opinion of many the "black radio capital of the world."[67] But even more than that, the way in which these deejays and Chicago's black-oriented radio stations reconfigured their playlists to include religious programming, black gospel, and other special features in deference to lower-and working-class blacks further indicated the growing cultural primacy of southern migrants in Chicago during the Great Migration.

The live religious broadcast format best exemplified the primacy of black southern migrants in the religious culture of Chicago during these years. Recorded sermons, which had been popular among black Chicagoans since the 1920s, gained in popularity in the 1930s in most cities with large black populations. By the end of the 1930s, the number of African American preachers on recordings had jumped from six to seventy, and 750 sermons had been recorded by that time. In 1925, William Cook recorded a number of sermons and spirituals with his choir at Metropolitan Community Church under the direction of J. Wesley Jones for Paramount

Records, "the popular race record."[68] But live religious broadcasts brought for the first time entire worship services into the homes of Chicago's radio listening African Americans. The forerunners of this format were Reverend Clarence Cobbs and Elder Lucy Smith. Although Elder Smith pioneered religious radio in 1933, by the next year both she and Cobbs were on the air weekly on station WIND. Cobbs was able to attract to his congregation people from the ranks of the city's black middle and even elite classes because of his flashy personal style and promises of prosperity, but it was the emotionally demonstrative worship of his live radio broadcasts that made him a "mass hero" among Chicago's poor and working class.[69] Smith's broadcast, *The Glorious Church of the Air*, also generated a huge following among the city's poor and working class. Unlike Cobbs, Smith often used her radio program to make appeals for material help on the part of the city's poor. But like Cobb's broadcast, *The Glorious Church of the Air* was primarily a showcase for All Nations' highly demonstrative worship services. It also showcased Smith's "faith healing" and southern vernacular preaching style. Smith, who frequently referred to her church as one administered without regard to race or class, understood that an important basis of her appeal was that she endeavored to meet both the material and spiritual needs of Chicago's poor and working class.[70] And although many among Chicago's African American middle class reviled both Smith and Cobbs, the success of their live broadcasts demonstrated that they were both products and producers of the new religious climate. During the Great Migration, ministers such as they signified new urban religious rituals and practices in Chicago that gave priority, foremost, to the material needs and religious sensibilities of the city's lower- and working-class southern migrant population. Their live broadcasts heralded this new religious culture.

Throughout the 1940s and 1950s, Jack L. Cooper personally supported and engineered much of the live religious broadcasting in black Chicago. Program schedules from the 1940s featuring live talent, all of "a religious nature," included a number of male and mixed quartets usually hailing from the South. In many cases, their stage names indicated from where they migrated. For instance, there was no question as to the home origins of "Alabam and Georgia" and the "Arkansas Four." Also, Cooper was particularly concerned that many different types of churches fill the half-hour Sunday morning live slots on WSBC. This concern may have reflected Cooper's awareness of a widening and diversifying religious culture during the time. By the early 1950s, an eclectic array of churches broadcast their messages over the airways—churches as diverse as Greater Salem Baptist, St. Paul Church of God in Christ, and the First Church of Divine Science. Cooper responded to one complaint about the diversity of his airplay with a letter stating, "the half hour of time given to the churches of Chicago each Sunday morning is given without discrimination. . . . I have no pets. I treat them all alike and must to the best interests of the people continue to do so."[71] Although the time slots were not "given" to the churches, Cooper charged a minimal fee and personally subsidized many of these programs. Grateful acknowledgments of his financial help and support for various churches comprised a considerable portion of the correspondence he received. By the late 1940s and early 1950s, however, the word came from WSBC management that Cooper should tighten the reins on some of these churches, asking that they contribute more for the support of their own broadcasts. This was true for the Sunday morning broadcasts, as well as the late-night hour-long shows.[72] In many cases, the churches met the increasing costs; in some instances, they could not and were forced to take their programs off the air. In December 1948, Cooper wrote to Reverend Mildred R. Barnes of the First Church By the Way of the Cross Spiritual Shrine informing her that the cost of her weekly broadcast would increase in the new year. Reverend Barnes's broadcast had aired each Monday from 11:05 P.M. to midnight. She wrote back to Cooper, "Because of the financial structure of my organization I find that I will be unable to continue my radio activities with your station. . . . We regret that we have to take this action at this time but we believe it to be the best of all concerned."[73] Barnes eventually pulled her services from the air but only after Cooper had apparently done everything in his power to prevent that from happening.

A number of social and economic factors influenced the structure of some of the more prominent live late-night religious broadcasts. Elder Smith, Clarence Cobb, William Roberts of Roberts Temple Church of God in Christ, and (before her broadcast ended) Mildred Barnes conducted their services at the eleven-to-midnight hour on weeknights because it was cheaper to do so. These broadcasts went without corporate sponsorship, necessitating the many appeals made for money over the air. Every broadcast included appeals for financial support. Without the appeals, programs were in jeopardy. Smith made this point abundantly clear on more than one occasion. In a related way, these late services happened because the daytime hours were reserved for programs that could attract advertising support. Since churches carried no corporate sponsorship (and could not by law), the valuable daytime slots remained the domain of mainstream programming. Al Benson made his conversion of sorts from his original name, Reverend Arthur Learner, because WGES would not allow him to sell advertising space to support his fifteen-minute Sunday-evening preaching and gospel music slot due to the religious nature of the program. Also, many stations reduced their overall wattage at night. Indeed, live broadcasts cost less because they required less wattage. Finally, the Radio Act of 1927 did not create a favorable climate for conservative religious broadcasting generally. As Tona J. Hangen asserts, "liberal Protestants were favored by the emerging national radio networks" while "fundamentalist" programs (which characterized Chicago's African American radio programs) were relegated to the margins.[74] As a consequence of the lateness of the hour, however, many of these programs became integral parts of Chicago nightlife, as black Chicagoans on their way to or from some other entertainment venue chose to be among the live audience.

Live religious broadcasts from First Deliverance Spiritualist and All Nations Pentecostal Church, as well as the preponderance of other religious programs airing on black-oriented radio during the migration, signaled in the most expansive format available that a definite shift had taken place in the city's African American religious culture. But if the changes to Chicago's religious culture were restricted to churches like Cobb's, Smith's, and storefronts, then the profundity of the transformation of Chicago's religious culture would not be fully appreciated. It was the way many of Chicago's mainline black churches began to reconfigure their institutional priorities and worship services in deference to poor and working-class southern migrants that provided evidence of the most crucial changes. By the end of the second decade of the twentieth century, it was clear to many mainline black Protestant churches that their relevancy as religious institutions, as well as their commitment to social change would be measured by their response to the growing numbers of southern migrants around them. The alliances the churches built with social service organizations and black businesses and the adaptations they made to their worship patterns indicated their understanding of the rapidly augmenting religious culture. This new sacred order placed the concerns and spiritual inclinations of the city's growing lower-and working-class southern migrant population as the highest institutional priority. No longer would the black elite and middle class hold exclusive cultural authority over the religious culture of Chicago. Ironically, religious modernity emerged by way of an "emotional folk orality" and was disseminated by a religious diaspora of black southern migrants.[75] For churches that were less willing or less prepared to face the transformations to the city's African American religious culture, the consequences could be dire, as the story of the African Methodist Episcopal Church in Chicago will reveal.

CHAPTER FIVE

The Chicago African Methodist Episcopal Church in Crisis

> *We cannot go back to Paul, to Luther and Wesley, to Allen and Turner, to Payne, or even so late a comer as Booker T. Washington. A changed atmosphere envelops us, changed conditions surround us, new problems confront us.*
>
> —Reverdy C. Ransom

IN HIS CLASSIC BOOK of essays, *Souls of Black Folk*, W. E. B. Du Bois wrote in 1903 that the African Methodist Episcopal Church was "the greatest Negro organization in the World."[1] Though he often waxed critical of black ministers throughout his long career, Du Bois maintained respect for black churches.[2] His admiration for the AME Church was not misplaced, although that admiration was based more on perception than reality. At the turn of the century, many (like Du Bois) perceived the AME Church to be "the greatest" black organization in America largely because of its influential and publicly visible clerical leadership. In reality, other black denominations and various civic organizations by this time had gained considerable strength and prestige, enough to challenge Du Bois's depiction of the AME Church. Moreover, while the comment was not entirely hyperbolic, it was a view not widely shared beyond African American Methodist circles. The denomination did, however, have many favorable attributes. Having won complete autonomy from white Methodists in 1816, the AME Church grew in relative size and strength during the nineteenth century. It soon expanded its reach throughout the United States, Canada, Haiti, the British West Indies, and South Africa. By the beginning of the Great Migration, the church claimed more than six thousand congregations in the United States alone, with nearly half a million members. Church property was valued at just under twelve million dollars. Under the leadership of such men as Richard Allen, Daniel Alexander Payne, Henry McNeal Turner, and Benjamin Arnett, the AME Church became a site of early civil rights activism, abolitionism, and educational reform. In addition to founding numerous local churches, particularly in the South and Midwest, AME church officials established missions, benevolent societies, church journals, and colleges. Wilberforce University, founded in 1856, was the first institution of higher learning established by black Americans and became the educational center of the denomination.[3] Although by the time of Du Bois's comment a number of black institutions could vie for the reputation as the greatest black organization in the world, the AME Church was certainly among them.

By 1900, the AME denomination boasted seven churches in Chicago, each of which stood prominently in the institutional life of the African American community. Founded in 1847, Quinn Chapel was the oldest church and had the distinction of being the "first Negro church in Chicago," as well as the "mother church" of the Midwest. Quinn had hosted two American presidents—William McKinley and William Howard Taft— and the likes of George Washington Carver, Paul Lawrence Dunbar, Booker T. Washington, Rabbi Emil G. Hirsch, and Jane Addams.[4] Bethel AME, organized in 1862 as a mission of Quinn Chapel, enjoyed almost as much prestige as Quinn. In its imposing red brick structure at Thirtieth and Dearborn streets, Bethel organized public rallies and hosted black society events, including the wedding of Ida B. Wells to Ferdinand Barnett in 1895. Institutional AME Church and Social Settlement was just getting under way in 1900 but began generating a lot of attention soon after opening its doors, due largely to the unconventional approach of Reverdy C. Ransom. Although St. Steven's, St. John's, Wayman Chapel, and St. Mary's maintained smaller congregations, the influence each church held in their respective neighborhoods was just as significant as their larger sister churches. Together these seven AME congregations comprised the seat of African Methodism in the city at the dawn of the twentieth century.[5]

The AME Church in Chicago, like all northern AME congregations, owed its local and national stature to a centralized episcopal structure, carefully maintained by the general conference. That stature was due just as much, however, to a massive popular base in the South that was acquired in the decades after the Civil War. Richard Allen, a Methodist minister and former slave, had founded the AME Church in Philadelphia, but over the course of the nineteenth century the southern wing of the church grew to outnumber northern AME churches. Having considered the postwar South "an area ripe for evangelization," as Clarence Walker argued, the missionary outreach to former slaves transferred the focus of the denomination to that region. The approximate 78 percent southern membership in the AME in 1890 prompted W. S. Scarborough to conclude that the church's "greatest field is in the South." Wesley J. Gaines concurred, calling the South "the glorious center of the AME." By the late nineteenth century, Benjamin T. Tanner's 1867 pronouncement had been confirmed: "here [in the South] is to be the heart of our church, that is to throw [flow] through the whole body the vitalizing blood."[6] The first independent black denomination in the North had become a southern phenomenon. Southern ministers comprised the base of the denomination's centralized power structure, and the South, or notions of southern culture, had become integral to AME character.

Northern migration represented a formidable challenge to the AME Church's southern base, its southern character, and its tightly maintained Episcopal structure. In effect, it was the historic church's first crisis of the twentieth century. The rapid changes that were occurring in the denomination at the wake of the mass movement reached the core and destabilized the denomination's very conception of itself. The first area of concern for AME officials was the sudden and shocking decrease in southern congregations. Between 1916 and 1926, most AME churches in the South Atlantic, East South Central, and West South Central regions of the United States recorded significant losses. In South Carolina alone, the church lost a hundred congregations in that ten-year span. The AME Church was on the move, and it was moving north. As significant as the demographic shift was in itself, what it meant for the church in terms of its centralized ecclesiastical power structure was even more daunting. Northern migration initiated a process of power fragmentation and disestablishment within the AME that worked on four levels. First, the sovereignty of the bishopric and the strict adherence to church order and discipline (modeled after white Methodism) conflicted with many northern congregations that desired greater autonomy in their efforts to face the migration. Second, as the size of southern congregations decreased, southern AME ministers began to lose their base of authority within the denomination vis-à-vis northern ministers and churches. Third, the gradual shift of power within the denomination from south to north required the difficult task of reconfiguring the AME Church's mission and institutional priorities, points on which consensus was difficult to attain. Fourth, a denomination long rooted in the South and in southern, rural culture had to confront the uncertainties of northern, urban life. The great mass movement of southern migrants held grave implications, not only for demographically based fluctuations in the size of particular congregations, but also for the very soul of the historic denomination in terms of its institutional power structure and influence in the lives of black Americans.

This process of ecclesiastical decentralization among Chicago's AME churches revealed deep ironies and a religious vision that can be best described as myopic. It was ironic that the AME Church in Chicago responded ambivalently to the influx of southern migrants out of a concern that the denomination might lose its national character. That character, after all, was steeped in a southern cultural ethos. It was also ironic that the church, for the most part, resisted the very community of people most likely to help them retain the influence and stature they were losing to the city's black Baptist churches. Put simply, the Great Migration generated for Chicago AME churches a great crisis of religious vision. Traditionalists on a local and national level opposed the efforts of nontraditionalists such as Archibald J. Carey, Sr., R. R. Wright, Jr., and William D. Cook, who worked to improve the denomination's stance toward northern migration and to change its policy of limited ministerial authority. In effect, these nontraditionalists sought a radical restructuring of their church in theological, institutional, and social terms as a response to the mass movement. An ambivalence that permeated all of African Methodism with regard to the Great Migration, however, held a tight grip on the AME Church in Chicago, the outcome of which was stultifying. Throughout the migration era, the cultural influence and high stature that the AME Church in Chicago had erstwhile maintained gradually waned as the city's black Baptist churches rose in prominence. As early as the 1920s, the ambivalence of the denomination toward migration, as well as its constrained religious vision, took its toll on the city's AME churches, leading to declining numbers, increased corruption, and a palpable loss of social prestige.

IN AUGUST 1917, the executive branch of the AME Church met in Wilberforce, Ohio, to discuss the impact migration was having on its churches throughout the country. Speaking as superintendents of the entire Church, the AME Council of Bishops expressed concern about the "sudden and simultaneous departure of multitudes" from the South. They concluded that the exodus demanded attention and quick action, as thousands were leaving to "a new home under new and untried conditions." With a stoicism that undoubtedly masked their apprehension, the council recommended to all departments of the AME Church that they do their best to meet the needs of "our migrating people." They further urged all within the denomination, particularly those in northern cities, to look on the migration as a missionary endeavor. By assisting "our beloved people," the council asserted, AME churches would be acting in ways "consistent with their obligations already provided for by law and by the action of the Missionary Board." A circular written by J. W. Rankin, secretary of the AME's Board of Church Extension, was sent out to all northern AME churches, reflecting the denomination's historical missionary impulse. The questions posed in the circular revealed anxieties about the impact of migration and about migrants themselves: "How many persons, to your knowledge, have come from the South into your vicinity during the past year? To what extent are they African Methodists? From what section of the South have they come? What reasons do they give in coming to the North? Have you a Lookout Committee in your church to seek these people? If not, what organized effort is being put forth to church them?

What is the attitude of your members toward them? So far as you have seen, is the better plan, where the numbers warrant it, to establish a distinct mission for them or bring them into the already established churches?"[7]

The language of the circular indicated clearly that by 1917, AME officials were without a comprehensive strategy for handling the migration and that at least part of the delay can be attributed to the attitude of many toward southern migrants. In a March 1917 meeting of the general council in Hot Springs, Arkansas, a statement issued on "the migration question" painted the migrants themselves in the worst possible light. While first acknowledging that conditions in the South gave some legitimization to the desire to migrate, the bishops then went on to warn migrants not to leave without having a specific destination in mind and doing some investigation "before sacrificing home and belongings." Citing reports that many migrants were "a shiftless, even criminal element," the bishops suggested that southern AME pastors issue "certificates of character" for those heading north. "Letters of transmittal" became common as the migration progressed, and as Robert Gregg suggested, became "class signifiers and signaled that the bearer would 'fit in' in the North."[8]

This pejorative assessment of southern migrants was not unique to African Methodists. As early as 1918, the pioneering African American historian Carter G. Woodson complained that migrants were "treated with contempt by the native blacks of the northern cities, who consider their brethren from the South too criminal and too vicious to be tolerated."[9] In the case of the AME church, the low opinion of southern migrants, as well as the lack of a systematic approach to migration, was bound up with anxieties about the impact the movement would have on the entire denomination. The flip side of the rapid growth of AME congregations in the North was the depletion of southern AME churches and this, in turn, upset the balance of power within the denomination. As Milton Sernett asserted, "the AME Council of Bishops recognized that the Great Migration was of historical import and posed a challenge to institutional vitality."[10]

At the same time, some AME divines recognized that there would be negative consequences to any actual or perceived mistreatment of southern migrants. Ill treatment of black southerners would be a tacit reinforcement of racist notions of black ability, character, and capacity. This would lend credence to white southerners' claims that blacks were better off in the South. It would also bring into question the notion of black solidarity. A few ministers, therefore, cautioned that black southerners should be welcomed without qualification or criticism. Reverend R. R. Downs pleaded with fellow AME churches to be circumspect in their dealings with southern migrants, contending that although "they may have the crudeness of country manners," they are not "vicious or immoral." "To attempt a show of contempt to the new comers," Downs added, "would be an argument for our own belittlement and add to the scorn and derision of arrogance against us as a people who are regarded by our enemies as being inferior." The apprehension many AME churches expressed with regard to African American southern migrants, he concluded, was the product "of our own diseased imagination and our doubts of them evidence our lack of faith in the Negro and our own moral weakness." In this spirit, Bishop W. H. Heard's board of extension resolved to create a fund of $25,000 to assist in providing church homes for migrants. Heard, a former slave who had escaped from Georgia to Philadelphia in 1865 and "raised himself by his own bootstraps," knew all too well the stigma of inferiority. He also was well aware of the North's promise.[11]

Anxiety about the Great Migration reached such a high level that the movement became the primary topic of discussion at the Tri-Federation Council of Bishops meeting in Louisville in 1918. The Tri-Federation Council was the most recent attempt by the three largest independent black Methodist denominations—the AME, AMEZ, and the Colored Methodist Episcopal (CME) churches—to foster "organic union." (Black Methodists had been attempting to unify since the early nineteenth century, but deep suspicions, bitter rivalries, and refusals to relinquish control over church properties and policies always thwarted efforts.)[12] At the conference, a member of the general council gave a "strong address" on migration, which was followed by a lengthy discussion. The address was later adopted as a resolution expressing the denomination's understanding of the material causes of migration. It also revealed their ambivalence toward migrants and migration, regarding it as paradoxically both dangerous and beneficial. "We realize the dangers and evils incident to migration," the resolution began, "but we realize also the benefits derived from such movements of a race and that the danger consists not so much in the disposition to migrate as it does in the lack of disposition to make a careful study of the industrial and economic conditions of the sections to which they go and to adequately prepare themselves to meet the demands of their new environments."[13] Migration could potentially carry southern migrants from "ignorance and poverty to a state of freedom, industry and education," but migrants had to be prepared for that transition.

For most AME ministers, "the evils and dangers incident to migration" had as much to do with their apprehensions about city life and its perceived deleterious effect on religious values as with the population shift itself. As early as 1910, Bishop Levi Coppin, former *AME Review* editor, advised migrants to avoid the "tempting lure" of the North. Coppin, who had in 1908 been designated bishop over the second district, which included several southern states, was most likely attempting to halt any depletion of AME members from his new field of endeavor. He neverthe-less echoed the sentiments of a number of AMEs with misgivings about the impact of urban life on black churches, particularly AME churches. Coppin apparently held these misgivings into the 1920s. At the 1921 Ecu-menical Conference on Methodism, he read a paper titled "Drifts to and from the Church." In that paper, Coppin implicated competition from the commercial amusements, relaxed social standards, and easy mobility char-acteristic of northern cities as reasons for an apparent lack of deep com-mitment by black Methodists to their churches.[14]

Apprehension about city life was rooted in a pervasive American ambiva-lence toward industrialization and urbanization in the late nineteenth and early twentieth centuries. The world had become a very different place be-tween the Civil War and 1915. The rise of large industry, the expansion of railroads, the telephone, even the incandescent lamp transformed Ameri-can life. With massive commercial and industrial development came a host of urban maladies, including crime, vice, political corruption, poverty, slums, family disruption, and relaxing of religious values. As the Italian so-ciologist of religion S. S. Acquaviva contended at the time, "the crisis of re-ligious practice is a product of the development of an urban lifestyle . . . and of industrial civilization." The Protestant stalwart Josiah Strong pre-dicted in the 1890s that rampant industrialization and unchecked wealth would topple American civilization. In the city where there was available "everything that dazzles the eye, or tempts the appetite," he proclaimed, lay the seedbed to all that undermined "our country." For Strong and many of his contemporaries, the "perils" of immigration, Romanism, secu-larism, intemperance, socialism, and wealth all ran loose in America's cities, "where the forces of evil are massed."[15] Many AME churches were cut from this same cloth. As David Wills wrote, "the ambivalence ex-pressed toward the city was a carryover from an ascetic Protestantism among AMEs that was unable to come to terms with industrial America."[16]

The anxiety AME churches held about urbanization had an additional dimension. The apprehension many expressed toward city life and indus-trial America coincided with a notion of blacks' peculiar "fittedness" for the South. Proponents of this line of thought were usually followers of Booker T. Washington and their arguments were shot through with the "Wizard's" language and philosophy. Washington had said in 1913 that he had "never seen any part of the world where it seemed to me the masses of the Negro people would be better off than right here in these southern states." E. W. Cooke, the superintendent of an Alabama industrial school, mixed Washington's maxim with biblical imagery to declare: "this is the day for us to choose whom we will serve. As for me and my house we will serve the South." W. E. B. Du Bois, "and others of his type," Cooke further claimed, used an "abundance of hot air" in their attempts to get blacks to leave the South. Convinced that the South was the "natural home" of black Americans, Cooke admonished would-be migrants, in the words of Washington, to "cast down their buckets" where they were. The *Star of Zion*, the organ of the AMEZ, which was having its own problems systematically facing the challenges of the Great Migration, articulated the point even more clearly. "While the inducements of the North are very alluring, in the end the Negro problem must be wrought out in the South."[17]

As the movement north gained momentum, particularly in the years between 1916 and 1919, Washingtonian stalwarts and other proponents of the agrarian gospel intensified their efforts to convince migrants to "stay south." As Milton Sernett noted, agents from both Tuskegee and Hampton institutes "encouraged potential migrants to buy land, engage in diversified farming, and with the aid of expert advisers, improve their living conditions where they were." Washington's successor at Tuskegee, Robert R. Moton, went so far as to travel to France during the First World War in an attempt to "persuade black soldiers to return home and purchase farms." Clearly, Moton dreaded the negative impact migration would have on a long-established rural way of life, fears that echoed the anxieties of many late nineteenth- and early twentieth-century reformers. The eclectic group of rural reformers and Progressives under the leadership of Liberty Hyde Bailey, Gifford Pinchot, and Henry Wallace started the Country Life Movement in the early twentieth century largely in response to this perceived threat, drawing wide attention to the values of rural existence. The Country Lifers became alarmed at the decrease in farm population, deeming it a sign of the "diminished importance of rural society." Much that was good about American life would be lost, they maintained, if America became "dominated by the city." But in addition to this concern for the preservation of an agrarian ethos, Moton and other principals of southern industrial schools clearly understood that the migration threatened their educational institutions by drawing away potential students as well as white philanthropic support. As James Grossman contended, "administrations at these institutions knew that whites opposed the movement (the Great Migration) and did not want to jeopardize the fragile acceptance the schools had won."[18]

Many southern AME leaders echoed Moton's call for southern blacks to abandon their aim at venturing north in the interest of an agrarian gospel of farming, home, and the cultivation of personal values. "We beg to advise you who are still in the South to remain on the farms, and buy small or large tracts of land while you can, and practice honesty, industry, and frugality," declared Benjamin F. Lee in 1916. Lee, whose Ninth District included Tennessee and Alabama, further advised southerners to "practice the habit of saving and purchase lots and build houses." Like many AME divines, Lee acknowledged the economic and discriminatory factors fueling the mass movement and contributing to a "general 'restlessness' of the race." Yet he appealed to potential migrants to seek refuge in the AME Church rather than to leave. "It must be acknowledged," he argued, "that nothing has been more influential in remedying this restlessness than the church." "The church," he maintained, was "the magnet in every group of negroes, the great soul from whose center go the investigations for better homes, and higher degrees of honesty, intellectual development and moral character." "You are therefore urged," he concluded, "to consider and rally to the church as the Ark of Safety on this troubled sea." Appeals to a sentimental attachment to the denomination like suggestions that the South was the "natural home" of black Americans, however, did not stem the flow of migration. Neither did more bald tactics, such as suggesting that blacks could not survive cold northern winters. The *Chicago Defender* reported that a number of AME ministers attempted to discourage migration with a signed plea that urged southern blacks not to migrate to northern cities in light, foremost, of the cold weather. Although many black southern migrants made reference to their experience with the chill of Chicago's winters, there is no evidence that the city's climate deterred the exodus to any degree.[19]

Despite such cautions against the move north, migrants continued to leave the South and their AME churches in very large numbers. In the process, they disrupted the very fabric of the denomination. In a denomination that had known only steady growth in the South since 1865, any depletion to its southern bodies was cause for concern. But in most cases it was the *rate* of depletion that sent shock waves through the denomination. J. B. Carter, an AME pastor and member of the Birmingham Ministerial Alliance, reported that he knew of a church in Avondale, Alabama, that once had three hundred members. "It now has only 60. That shows how they are leaving." And Carter's example was not the most drastic. In some cases, entire congregations fled within weeks. In instances where it was clear that the majority or the entire congregation would migrate, the AME pastors of those congregations were forced to languish or to follow their members. An AME minister who lost fifty-two members of his congregation of ninety-six in only six months reported to his bishop, "I just come up here to notify you that I'm getting ready to follow my flock."[20]

While southern AME ministers sought to forestall the migration, northern AME ministers reacted to the movement with varying measures of enthusiasm, recognizing its potential to strengthen their own churches. It was clear that they also recognized its potential to release thousands of black Americans from the stranglehold of southern racism. A writer in the *Christian Recorder*, the official publication of the AME denomination, proclaimed that "indeed if a million Negroes move North and West in the next twelve months, it will be one of the greatest things for the Negro since the Emancipation Proclamation." AME Bishop C. T. Shaffer had as early as 1903 compared black migration to the flight of "the Pilgrim Fathers, who left their native land in quest of religious liberty," and "the Holland Dutch, who left the land of their birth and all their early and hallowed associations, and sought an asylum in the wilds of Africa." Shaffer, a veteran of the Civil War, believed it was no longer possible for blacks in the South to find the freedom and equality that Reconstruction had promised. In light of increased disfranchisement and discrimination in the South, where blacks were "being reduced to the most menial and least remunerative . . . employments," Shaffer was convinced that "the Negro should seek another arena upon which to play his part in the great drama of life, and build character and a place for himself and his children under conditions . . . which can never [be] obtained while we are crowded and huddled in such numbers in the South."[21]

This support did not amount to a systematic approach to handle the migration, nor did it shake northern ministers from their own ambivalence toward migrants and urban life. Despite his impassioned plea that black Americans seek another arena than the South in which to find freedom and equality, Bishop Shaffer, like many of his southern clerical brethren, was uncertain about city life. He encouraged migrants who ventured out of the South to do so "avoiding for the most part, the larger cities of the country," that is, to leave the South but not to abandon a rural way of life. Indeed, this reflected the desire of many southern migrants. Letters written to the *Chicago Defender* and the Chicago Urban League suggested that not everyone who wanted to get out of the South wanted to live in an urban area. Some migrants explicitly stated that they were "not particular about Chicago" and would rather live in a small farm, village, or town outside Chicago. Certainly for some migrants this reticence represented an intrinsic connection to the rural way of life and an inherent mistrust of cities. At least two of the letters implied that Chicago did not appeal to them because they were concerned for their children's moral upbringing and education. Others were convinced competition for jobs would be less and wages would be higher in a small town. Romantic, agrarian, and utopian, Shaffer's idea for migrating southern blacks placed them in small villages on the outskirts of large urban areas. He conclusively admonished black southern migrants to travel to the "Northern, Middle, Western and Southwestern States and Territories" where they were to form "colonies."[22]

For all these reasons, the AME Church grew slowly in most northern cities, far slower in relative proportion to the black population as a whole. Growth of AME churches in Chicago was especially slow, a situation made even more noteworthy by the rapid rate of increase among black

Baptists. To the seven AME churches that existed at the turn of the century, only five more had been added by the end of the 1920s. Trinity Mission opened in 1905 and was short-lived. Coppin Chapel and Grant Memorial were both established in 1919. Allen Temple, named after the founder of the denomination, was organized by a group of members who split off from Grant Memorial in 1923 and moved into the structure at Thirtieth and Dearborn that had once housed Bethel. Carey Temple was organized by the denomination in 1928, three years before the death of its namesake, Bishop Archibald J. Carey, Sr.[23] As significant as these gains were, the AME Church in Chicago still lagged far behind black Baptists in its ability to attract and keep new migrants, as well as in the rate of church growth. The entire denomination gained about five thousand people between 1915 and 1920, a total matched by Olivet Baptist alone.[24] Certainly, the deliberate way the denomination went about establishing churches, in contrast to the less centralized Baptist system, put it at a disadvantage. But the lag also indicated the lack of any organized effort comparable to that instituted by black Baptist churches. Observers at the time recognized that the AME Church trailed black Baptists during the years of migration. One local pundit proclaimed that the Baptists in the city had set a "fast pace," and attributed their outdistancing of the AME to the Baptist emphasis on "a more militant and practical religion."[25]

An absence of comprehensive planning was only partly responsible for Chicago AME's relative lack of success in recruiting migrants. Many migrants found the episcopal structure of the AME Church distasteful and restricting. The tight control exacted by the general conference with regard to ministerial tenure discouraged some migrants from joining the church. It prompted hundreds of others to abandon it to take part in the Community Church Movement in the early 1920s. Chicago AME churches were also the least flexible in terms of their worship practices and music. Most Chicago AME churches held very reserved worship, with music performed under the direction of trained musicians. As one AME minister asserted in the late 1930s, "the ritual of the AME church is the most beautiful of any I know." "On the other hand," he further stated, "it is now rather formal and cold." Timuel Black, a Chicago activist whose family associated with Quinn Chapel, Bethel, and St. Mary's, recalled that there was "very little shouting," if any at all, in these congregations during the years of his family's attendance. "The climate of the church," he stated, "did not lend itself to that kind of outburst."[26] Historically, the AME church had encouraged spontaneous worship and religious enthusiasm. Richard Allen revered Methodist doctrine and polity and in establishing the AME Church had adopted Methodist doctrine in its entirety, including its revivalist worship practices. Despite his personal "preoccupation with respectability and self-control," as James Campbell noted, Allen was a product of the nineteenth-century revival era, "where spontaneity and emotional outburst were the order of the day." The reforms that gradually took hold in AME preaching and worship resulted from the efforts of another AME cleric, Bishop Daniel Alexander Payne. Payne, the denomination's most prolific and vociferous theologian and spokesman in the nineteenth century, campaigned tirelessly for an "educated ministry." He also fought to "modify the extravagances in worship" he discovered in the congregations of freed people. To a greater degree than perhaps any other AME minister, Payne held ecstatic frenzy—shouting, jumping, swaying, and dancing—in utter disdain. The practitioners of such "bad habits," he maintained, were "ignorant and deluded." While some modes of worship resisted Payne's onslaught, characteristic features of AME worship had changed dramatically for the most part by the late nineteenth century.[27]

A few AME ministers in other northern cities adapted their worship styles in order to attract and to retain newcomers. Robert J. Williams of "Mother Bethel" in Philadelphia deliberately modified that church's worship services to appeal to migrants. He developed a fervent, evangelistic style of preaching and introduced music with "snap and go." As a result, black southerners joined the church in large numbers. Indeed, Williams devoted his entire tenure at Bethel to the concerns of new migrants, initially hoping to use whatever revenues they possessed to help lift the congregation out of debt. A native of Philadelphia, Williams received the call to the historic church in 1916. Finding Bethel in serious arrears, he inaugurated a plan to reduce the financial strain by increasing church membership from among new migrants. Membership had declined in recent years due to the lack of jobs in the area surrounding the church. Seizing an opportunity to steer migrating black southerners into the mother church of black Methodism, Williams sent leaflets to the South advertising the congregation and what it had to offer. A poem he wrote, "Let This Be Your Home," became the church's motto. In the poem, Williams admonished black southerners to "enter Bethel" and "never roam." Eventually, the influx of migrants into Bethel led to deep divisions within the congregation, and the older members ousted Williams, but the worship patterns he instituted made Bethel the destination for hundreds of black migrants to Philadelphia.[28] In Chicago, similar patterns of worship were more common among Baptist, Pentecostal, and Spiritualist churches.[29] AME worship deliberately catered to the percieved tastes of the black elite. By the 1930s and 1940s, many AME churches were reputed to be off-limits to ordinary black Chicagoans. WPA writers found that by 1940 Coppin Chapel, for example, established just twenty years earlier, was "the most aristocratic of the AME churches in Chicago." Reflecting on the same period, Allan Spear contended that "more sedate and formal than Olivet, Quinn Chapel soon gained a reputation as a 'swank church, not for the common herd.'"[30] With regard to church worship few Chicago AME churches followed the example set by Williams in Philadelphia.

There are important exceptions to the depiction of Chicago AME churches as ambivalent to the migration but their exceptionalism only reinforces the extent to which the denomination as a whole resisted the impact and the implications of the movement. As early as 1900, a comprehensive strategy to handle southern migrants and migration had been a central component to the work of Reverdy C. Ransom at Institutional AME Church and Social Settlement. Ransom's attempts to establish Institutional as an organization geared to meet the needs of migrants met with opposition from local AME ministers as well as from national AME officials. Partly due to apprehension about the "institutional idea" and partly due to Ransom's maverick personality (and reputed alcoholism), AME divines resisted the work at Institutional to the point of warning members not to attend the church or use its facilities. On account of Ransom's legacy in Chicago, however, a few AME divines came to recognize the migration's potential to bring positive change within the denomination. They also reconsidered the denomination's responsibility toward recent migrants. Contrary to Allan Spear's assertion that Institutional AME "declined and eventually died" not long after Ransom left Chicago for New York in 1904, many of his initiatives at the church continued. Ironically, the AME minister most responsible for continuing the outreach to southern migrants and the social gospelism of Reverdy Ransom had been one of Ransom's chief detractors, Archibald J. Carey, Sr.[31] Carey, who had come to Chicago from Atlanta in 1898, expanded Ransom's social welfare program, arranged to have prominent white and black leaders speak at the church, and, in conjunction with many black churches during the migration era, developed a "qualified staff trained as social workers."[32] Indeed, in the decade after Ransom's departure, Carey assumed the role that had once been Ransom's as the lone Chicago AME divine challenging the basic assumptions of the denomination on a local and national level.

Much of Carey's civic and church work attempted to address the problems generated by migration, namely, the material conditions of black Chicagoans, especially "strangers and southerners."[33] In addition to adding staff, including a European-trained social worker and additional "special services" at Institutional AME, Carey busied himself with activities designed to improve the lives of migrants.[34] One of his innovations was a series of special meetings held each Monday to welcome migrants as "new members into the fold." Behind Carey's efforts for the spiritual well-being of the migrating masses to Chicago's growing black enclave lay a concern for more material aims such as black civil rights, equality in housing, employment, and general social betterment.[35] Working from these concerns, Carey set up a welfare and social service agency, a kindergarten and nursery, and, with contributions from the Swift family, an employment agency. The agency placed members of Institutional in positions with the Pullman Company, the stockyards, and the Chicago public school system. Not surprisingly, it also found work for black southerners as domestics in wealthy households.[36] Although Carey's efforts to improve the material conditions of Chicago's blacks did not always meet with the approval of the general conference or his fellow Chicago AME ministers, they increased the membership rolls and decreased the financial debt of each of his ministerial charges. While at Quinn, he extinguished a thirty-thousand-dollar debt, saving the church "from the Sheriff's hammer," in the words of J. C. Caldwell, and added more than fifteen hundred members. The man many came to regard to have "a modern touch of gold" also removed the fifteen-thousand-dollar debt at Bethel, where the membership roll nearly topped three thousand people. His final charge, Institutional AME, which he assumed in 1909, grew by an additional one thousand members, a rate of increase that far outdistanced all other AME churches in the city.[37]

The experiences of Richard R. Wright, Jr., showed the AME Church's ambivalence toward southern migrants even more so than Archibald Carey's. His short Chicago tenure also showed the extent to which migration had become the central issue for the church. It had even become a focus for philosophical differences and abiding regional tensions. Wright was not as well known as Carey, but he shared the latter's belief in the social mission of black churches. Not surprisingly, the biggest influence on Wright in terms of his approach to southern migrants was Reverdy Ransom. Wright adopted his approach to church work from Ransom's program at Institutional. His involvement with southern migrants, even after he left Chicago, mirrored exactly the format set by Ransom.

The son of Major Richard Robert Wright, Sr., the nineteenth-century intellectual and scholar commonly known as "the black boy of Atlanta," Wright came to Chicago in 1900 and became assistant pastor to Reverdy Ransom at Institutional AME. From his arrival, Wright revealed a similar concern for the social welfare of black Chicagoans as well as leanings toward social gospelism. He also developed an interest in migration, which he addressed in a thesis he wrote for the sociology department at the University of Chicago in 1901. In "The Industrial Condition of the Negro in Chicago," Wright presaged the argument of many scholars of the Great Migration who would contend that southern migrants' "reasons for coming to the city are many and various." He took special note of those who came north, having been "driven from their homes" because of their views. He made mention of an "editor of a Negro newspaper in Memphis who, because of her editorials condemning lynching, was forced to leave to save her life." The editor was Ida B. Wells, someone with whom Wright likely came into contact through his association with Ransom.[38]

Bishop C. T. Shaffer gave Wright an opportunity to continue his work among southern migrants after Wright returned to Chicago from a time of study in Germany in 1904. This was an ironic gesture, since it was Shaffer who had been chief among those who maneuvered to get Ransom removed from Institutional. Shaffer had been an outspoken critic of Ransom's social settlement work and would later express disfavor with Carey's initiatives. Nevertheless, he sent Wright to Trinity Mission and Culture Center, "the smallest [AME] mission in Chicago," where Wright immediately set out to model Trinity after Institutional AME. The mission served the district above Twenty-second Street and between Michigan Avenue and Clark Street, an area composed mostly of the working poor, who were "practically shut off from all the benefits of the church." Despite its meager resources, Trinity offered a number of programs and services similar to those at Institutional. Wright, whom Bishop Shaffer considered "the best educated man I have," had declined three offers of professorships at southern black colleges to take up the work at Trinity. Because of this, he found it necessary to supplement his small salary by working as a porter, a messenger, and an "unskilled laborer." During his short-lived ministry, Wright established the Chicago College Men's Association, a bathhouse, a women's club, and a correspondence bureau "for the illiterate Negroes." Lecture series given at Trinity were often on various health issues, including "The Cause and Prevention of Tuberculosis." Though the mission church never matched the extensive programming offered at Institutional, Wright used its resources to meet the needs of the "steady flow" of southern blacks he witnessed coming to Chicago's South Side.[39]

Despite all the personal support he received from Bishop Shaffer in his work with Trinity mission, Wright remained dissatisfied with the level of support the AME denomination rendered to urban ministry among southern migrants generally. His own ministry served as an example. Never able to garner wide support from local AME churches or denomination officials, Wright was forced to close Trinity after only a few months. After the church closed, Wright left Chicago in 1905 to pursue doctoral studies at the University of Pennsylvania. The result of his time there was *The Negro in Pennsylvania: A Study in Economic History*, a book that still stands as a definitive look at black life in cities. While in Philadelphia, Wright continued his research and writing on urban issues and southern migration, producing articles that appeared in *The Annals of the Academy of Political and Social Sciences* and *Southern Workman*. He wrote

such papers as "The Extent of Negro Migration to the North," and
"Growth of the Northern Negro Population." In his written work, Wright,
a longtime champion of "practical religion" and "a more progressive approach to church work in the cities," indicted urban black churches, particularly those within the AME denomination, for their "unsystematized
charity and social work."[40]

Elected editor of the *Christian Recorder* in 1915, Wright found a national forum to critique his beloved denomination and to further propa-
gate his convictions about migration. By the time he assumed his new
post, southern migration had clearly become a mass movement, bringing
forth, as he saw it, "such changes in Negro life as have not been made
since emancipation." In an effort to steer the AME Church to respond in
concrete ways to the influx of blacks into northern cities, one of the first
things Wright did as editor was call an "ecumenical council of dark
skinned Christians" to discuss the phenomenon. No doubt drawing on his
experience as pastor of one of Chicago's AME missions, Wright urged
that mission churches be established in all northern cities to cater specifically to the needs of migrants. As one who saw the movement's potential
as greater than any difficulty it posed, Wright became an advocate of
black migration and remained so throughout his career. Foremost,
Wright believed that the influx of southern migrants would challenge the
AME Church to rethink its institutional priorities and force it to establish
and normalize a systematic approach to social service. To the question he
posed in August of 1916, "Should Negroes Come North?" he gave an af-
firmative answer. "We stand for Negro migration and throw out our arms
of welcome to every Negro who desires to come." "Get these Negroes in
your churches," he continued, "make them welcome; don't turn up your
noses and let the saloon man and his gambler do all the welcoming. Help
them buy homes, encourage them to send for their families and to put
their children in school. Welcome them, welcome them; yes bid them
thrice welcome."[41] Amid a chorus of voices within the AME denomination pleading with southern blacks to "stay south," Wright charged his
church to welcome migrants and to encourage migration. He saw southern migrants as "new blood" for the historic denomination and as possible
instigators of a revival of the church's influence. Although Wright had left
the city for Philadelphia by the time he was editing and writing for the
Christian Recorder, his impressions about migrants and the migration's
potential were shaped during his years in Chicago and by his association
with Reverdy Ransom. By 1916, both ministers agreed that the Great
Migration would be "the real challenge to Christianity" and to African
Methodists.[42]

Though far from the "thrice welcome" that R. R. Wright, Jr., had envisioned, factions within the northern branch of the AME Church began to

shift in their stance toward the Great Migration by the 1920s. A few had even begun to place a providential spin on the movement, granting to it a significance of biblical proportions. As early as 1917, for example, J. W. Rankin deemed southern migrants modern-day Israelites "bound for the promised land."[43] At the 1920 AME General Conference in St. Louis, the *Christian Recorder* noted that "the interest taken in civic and social enterprises" that year was "greater than usual." The annual address gave considerable attention to urban issues and to the labor problem, recommending the appointment of a denominational labor commission to gather information on the industrial conditions of black workers. Whatever the motivation, the redirected concern on the part of some northern AME churches for the economic plight of blacks in urban areas, and for southern migrants in particular, coincided with a striking reality. By 1926, nearly 50 percent of the entire AME constituency in the rural South had shifted to the urban North.[44]

Despite such initiatives, the AME Church in Chicago remained ambivalent and hesitant about migration throughout the 1920s and 1930s. That stance was to have dire consequences for the denomination. The first event to signal that significant troubles lay ahead took place at the annual conference of the Fourth Episcopal District, held in Des Moines, Iowa, in 1920. A controversial ministerial exchange at the conference led to a break from the denomination by the majority of the congregation of Bethel AME, Chicago's second-oldest African Methodist church. The break by Bethel demonstrated that by 1920 the Great Migration had agitated philosophical tensions within the denomination and revealed stark disagreements about tactical approaches to new migrants. As far as some reform-minded AME churches were concerned, AME officials were tightening the bureaucratic rule of the church at precisely the time when they should have shared ecclesiastical control more democratically. This would have enabled individual congregations to respond to the pressures brought on by migration. The split by Bethel and other events that took place in Chicago throughout the 1920s signaled a further fragmentation of AME power, a significant loss in numbers, and a further fraying of its cultural and religious influence. Those committed to progressive measures would have to find alternative means outside the reach of the historic church to enact them.

The split of the congregation of Bethel from the AME convention occurred when it was announced in 1920 that Dr. William Decatur Cook, who had been at Bethel in Chicago since 1916, was being sent to St. Paul AME Church in Des Moines. During his four-year tenure at Bethel, Cook had witnessed how Chicago and Bethel grew significantly because of "the greatly increased Negro population due to the Great Migration." He viewed a departure at that point not to be in the best interest of the congregation. In an unprecedented move, the "church at large" sent six delegates to the conference requesting that the bishop rescind his decision to remove Dr. Cook from Bethel. The six men took with them a petition composed of five thousand signatures and several letters from "civic organizations" and "representative citizens" appealing for the retention of Cook. A private conference held with the bishop left the men with the impression that their journey to Des Moines would be rewarded with a response in their favor. It was not. When the quadrennial appointments were announced, Dr. Cook had been assigned to St. Paul AME, and Dr. S. L. Birt had been appointed to Bethel. Word of the assignment (and of the apparent betrayal by the bishop) caused considerable dismay, and "indignation swept the entire congregation."[45] The action of the bishop confirmed for Cook and many in Bethel that the AME episcopal structure existed to the detriment of broad-based cultural and religious change. Cook, who had been an AME minister for forty-five years, bolted from the AME Church to form a new church, the Metropolitan Church and Community Center. In doing so, he aligned with a new movement in American religion, the Community Church Movement.[46] The move was a particularly notable one for Cook, whose theological and social progression came late in life. As a youthful minister with the AME Church, he had held some of the most stridently conservative views. He led the charge to rescind the pastorate of Sarah Ann Hughes in the celebrated case of 1884. In concert with the large majority of his fellow AME male clerics, Cook was inclined to believe that ministering the gospel was the special province of men. The resolution he wrote in response to the Hughes case read, "Whereas, we have in our church some female ministers who have been holding pastoral charges much to the detriment of the church; therefore be it resolved, that they are hereby prohibited from assignment to a special charge, and simply labor as evangelists."[47] Cook's affiliation with the Community Church Movement represented a rejection of such views, as the new denomination did not bar women from serving as ministers or pastors.

Cook's departure from Bethel to form Metropolitan was significant despite the prevalence of church splits among black Protestants during the 1920s. A brief look at the history of the Community Church Movement reveals that Cook chose to affiliate with a religious group he deemed best suited philosophically and programmatically to face a rapidly changing religious culture in Chicago.[48] The Community Church Movement had begun after the First World War and drew on two fundamental principles: Protestant unity and democracy. The upheavals following the end of the war prompted many institutions in the United States to reexamine their most basic tenets and to reevaluate their priorities. For Americans, this meant a turn (or return) to conservative values, including civic cooperation, personal liberty, and business efficiency, all captured under the rubric "unity."[49] The Community Church Movement rode the wave of ecumenical thought that sought to dismantle cultural and religious distinctions between Protestant denominations. David R. Piper, one of the movement's first chroniclers, defined it as "the attempt of the people . . . to apply the principles of democracy and the spirit of unity to religious organizations." "In doing this," he continued, "they have found it necessary to break down or reach across old sectarian lines of cleavage which in the past have divided Christian people in the same community."[50] Proponents of the community church idea determined that churches in the movement should be antidenominational, anticreedal, and antisectarian. Community churches were organized on "a new principle of cohesion" that dispelled denominational and theological difference. Indeed, no particular creed or theology predominated in the movement. Each church ministered to the "composite religious consciousness of the community." As a contemporary leader of the movement put it, "the constitution of this organization avowedly declares that it does not require any credal test for membership." "We welcome, therefore, into our fellowship," the constitution continued, "those from all denominations, and we as cordially dismiss our members to all denominations. We seek to promote the new Christianity which the new day requires and to discourage old sectarianism."[51]

The Community Church Movement and the churches that became a part of it were also decidedly democratic. The movement conceptualized democracy in two ways. First, it was democratic in that it sought to embrace "all classes of people irrespective of nationality, creed, or economic status." No one was turned away from a community church, and everyone had equal voice in matters of policy and administration—at least in theory. The second way community churches expressed democracy was in that each church belonging to the movement determined for itself "all matters as to doctrine, polity, and activity." Community churches, proponents maintained, "are expressions of 'self-determination.'"[52] Disdainful of "the tightening of the denominational hand," and convinced that denominationalism tended "naturally toward exploitation," community churches decided in conference with all members every aspect of church life. The movement soared in a matter of a few years. By the mid-1920s, it became obvious that "the community churches are beginning to take no mean place in the religious life of America." Largely a rural phenomenon in the years just after World War I, the Community Church Movement soon expanded to urban areas. In 1922, more than eight hundred community churches operated in the United States; by 1927 that number had increased to over twelve hundred.[53]

When the Community Church Movement spread to urban areas around the country, some African Americans from AME churches responded quickly. A group of members from First AME Church of Los Angeles joined the movement as early as 1915. They became perhaps the first group of black Protestants in America to form a community church. When Cook left the AME denomination to form the Metropolitan Community Church, Metropolitan became the first community church among African Americans in Chicago. The church got its official start when a group in "open revolt," composed of two women and eighteen men from Bethel (including the six men who were sent to Des Moines) went to the church parsonage to request that Cook become pastor of a new church.[54] After a night of prayer, Cook agreed and in a board meeting on Friday October 1, 1920, he withdrew from both Bethel and the AME conference. The following Sunday, Cook conducted the first services of the new church at Unity Hall on Indiana Avenue, a space provided by the African American congressman, Oscar DePriest. At the conclusion of those services, 585 people from the "overflow crowd," made up primarily of Bethel members, joined Cook's new church and the new movement.[55] Bethel AME was never quite the same again. In addition to the 585 that joined Cook at Metropolitan's first meeting, many others followed later. The church was compelled to sell its property on Thirtieth and Dearborn Street in 1922, and its new location at 4200 South Park was nearly destroyed by fire in 1924. After the fire, Bethel became a nomadic congregation, taking up residence at Wendell Phillips High School and sharing quarters for a time with Monumental Baptist Church on Oakwood Boulevard. The church secured a new church home and some stability at Forty-first Street and South Michigan Avenue in 1941.

By December 1920, the membership of Metropolitan, housed for a time at Wendell Philips High School, topped two thousand. The *Chicago Defender* proclaimed "never in the history of the world has such a movement met with such success as the Metropolitan Community Center." Though that claim was greatly exaggerated, it is true that never in the history of Chicago had a church or religious movement attracted so many people in so short a time. By 1927, when Metropolitan moved into the former First Presbyterian Church building with its Romanesque structure of reddish-brown raindrop stone, the church and the movement remained a major force on the South Side. A history bulletin produced by the congregation years later would proclaim that the church represented "so much to the people in this community."[56]

It has been suggested that William Cook's actual reason for severing ties with the AME conference stemmed from his frustration with having been overlooked for the position of bishop while Archibald Carey, Sr., was promoted. Both men were nominated in 1920, being equally qualified in terms of the length and distinction of their service to the church. But it was not for want of more personal power that Cook left the AME convention;

rather, it was to protest the increased tightening of control by the conference over individual churches. It was also for want of "a larger participation in the legislative councils of the church" for all black Methodists.[57]
And it was in this sense that the objectives of the Community Church
Movement and the aims of William Cook meshed. By the 1920s, the relationship between local AME churches and the general conference had
grown increasingly cold and distant. Many, like Cook and his followers,
had become "dissatisfied with treatment received from the directing and
guiding ecclesiastical forces of the African Methodist Episcopal church."
In requesting to stay at Bethel Church, despite the AME rule requiring
that he transfer after serving his four-year term, Cook expressed a desire
for more local autonomy from the national body.[58]

The example of John R. Harvey highlights the intensity of this desire
for autonomy just as clearly. Harvey had been pastor of St. Mary's AME
since 1919 and was up for transfer in 1923, but before that occurred he
left the conference to form Cosmopolitan Community Church. Though
the *Chicago Defender* lauded him for his "practical programs," they were
administered presumably without the sanction of the conference. Among
the many initiatives that raised the ire of AME officials, Harvey gave insurance policies to all "faithful" members of St. Mary's and paid substantial benefits to the sick. He established a relief fund that made donations
and loans without interest and operated a free employment agency. His
aggressive efforts to raise funds for church work, including a children's
home and a day nursery, blurred the lines between the church and the
business community. More than that, they challenged the central power
of the parent denomination at precisely the time it chose to assert that
power. Harvey found in the Community Church Movement sufficient
freedom to continue his aim of "doing something to help the members of
his church, the community and the Race."[59]

Unlike Harvey, however, Cook not only desired more local autonomy
and "self determination" for AME churches, he had also become convinced of the divisiveness of denominationalism. Considering the community church to be closer to the early church "than any other existing
form," Cook and other proponents of the Community Church Movement
deemed denominationalism, "with its complex forms and inadequate
methods of operation, a movement away from church unity." With a view
to fostering unity, antidenominationalism, anticreedalism, and antisectari-
anism, Cook met with J. A. Winters of Progressive Baptist Church (which
would become Progressive Community Church in 1925) and other ministers from Detroit and Los Angeles in 1923 to form the Biennial Council
of the People's Church of Christ and Community Centers. While the
creed of the organization simply stated that they had "no creed," the
statement of purpose was more detailed and emphatic.

The purpose of the National Council is to foster and express the substantial unity of the non-sectarian and non-denominational Community Churches in faith, polity and work. To consult upon and derive measures and maintain agencies for the promotion of their common interests, to cooperate with any non-sectarian church which may be affiliated or desire to become affiliated with The Peoples Community Churches of the United States and Elsewhere, in their National, Inter-National and Non-denominational Relations.

If the AME general conference was determined to tighten ecclesiastical control, and thereby foster disunion, denominationalism, and sectarianism at the time of the denomination's greatest crisis, Dr. Cook and Metropolitan Community Church determined to counter those forces with a community-focused church. This church would be "of the people by the people and for the people."[60] The Community Church Movement never claimed to stem from the Social Gospel, niether did Cook claim to be a Social Gospeler, but the theological liberalism the movement espoused certainly struck a chord of agreement. The institutional independence and social responsibility it encouraged was also similar to the Social Gospel. Formed out of the AME Church during the height of the Great Migration, the movement in Chicago served witness to the shortcomings of the historic church. For Cook and thousands who became a part of Chicago's three community churches, the movement best met the changing needs of a rapidly changing city. It was "the new church which the new day required."[61]

By the mid-1920s, the "dissatisfaction and unrest" that led to the formation of the city's three African American community churches ran rampant in Chicago's AME churches. And as in the case of William D. Cook, much of the disquiet continued to be rooted in ministerial transfers. The transfer of ministers had been a controversial and highly political process since the nineteenth century, eliciting varied responses from among AME clerics and laity. Many acknowledged that the system seemed especially subject to abuse. Although he argued that the transfer system was "a good thing" and largely responsible for the "growth of Methodism in the land," J. C. Caldwell confessed that favoritism played a key role in transfers. "Men are transferred from one charge to another," he claimed, "not so much for what they can do, as because they are favorites."[62] During the Great Migration, the politics of ministerial appointments became more intense. It was clear to most observers that much was at stake for the future of the church in Chicago. Bishop A. L. Gaines, who presided over the Fourth Episcopal District for most of the 1920s, initiated a series of transfers that provoked an outcry of unparalleled proportions within the church as well as among many of those outside it. It is unclear if Gaines was attempting to meet the crisis of migration by placing the best men possible in Chicago's AME churches, or if he was simply rewarding men who had supported him in Episcopal elections. But he developed a pattern of relegating local ministers (in an ironic twist) "to the country" and replacing them with his supporters. Some churches, such as Quinn Chapel, revolted, refusing to accept their new ministers. Other churches split. The transfers had even more grave consequences for a few Chicago-area AME ministers. Drs. Henderson, McCraken, and Higgins, who were sent by Bishop Gaines to Aurora, IL.; Waukegan, IL.; and rural Iowa, respectively, all died shortly after arriving at their new assignments "in the hinterlands." The Reverend William W. Lucas committed suicide by jumping out a third-floor window at Provident Hospital upon learning he was being "snatched away from his charge" at Ebenezer AME Church in Evanston, Illinois, just north of Chicago. Lucas, who had been a prominent Methodist Episcopal minister before joining the AME, had been brought to the hospital by his physician a week before the "fatal leap." The physician had found him to be in what he described as a "mentally deranged state." The *Chicago Whip*, always ready to slight black churches, editorialized that Lucas's suicide and the deaths of the three former Chicago AME ministers signified Bishop Gaines's "ruthless leadership," and that "all is not well with the Methodists in Chicago." Archibald J. Carey, who spoke at Lucas's funeral, called Lucas a "martyr-hero" and blamed the AME ministers in attendance for his "untimely death." Bishop Gaines, he declared, "was in no way responsible for the minister's death," addressing the common thought that Gaines alone had caused Lucas's suicide. "With treacherous deception," Carey contended, "you smiled in his face, then stabbed him in the back. He is now dead and you are responsible."[63]

Perhaps because of his "untimely death" and the manner of it, Lucas has never been heralded for a much larger role he played in the Great Migration. He has quite literally been excised out of one of the most recognizable icons of the Great Migration, the photo of the Arthur family. It was Lucas, in his capacity as secretary of the Co-Operative Society of America, who met the Arthur family at the Polk Street train station when they arrived in Chicago in 1920. The photo, which shows a family of eight huddled together, staring forlornly into the camera, has become synonymous with the exodus. The original photo appeared in the *Chicago Defender* on September 4, 1920, and contained an inset photo of Lucas, both taken by one of the *Defender's* staff photographers. (See figure 10.) The photo of the Arthur family has been used hundreds of times to represent a typical family of migrants from the rural south. It appeared without the inset of Lucas (or with any reference to him) in the report of the Chicago Commission on Race Relations and most famously in Allan Spear's 1967 book, *Black Chicago*.[64] The family was not identified in those works,

Fig. 10. Eight Victims of Lynch Law. (Source: *Chicago Defender*, 4 September 1920)

which has led to a few misinterpretations. Although the Arthurs were a migrant family, they were not in the strictest sense from the rural South. They were from Paris, Texas, and a tale of murder, rape, and rescue comprised the actual circumstances of their arrival to Chicago. Scott and Violet Arthur fled with what remained of their family after two of their sons, Irving and Henry, had been lynched and burned by a white mob. The two men, ages twenty-eight and nineteen, had killed J. Hodges and his son, William, the owners of the farm on which the family lived, in a dispute over money. Having fled to Valiant, Oklahoma, the men were captured and brought back to Paris, where a mob broke into the jail during the night to lynch them on the town's fairgrounds. When three of the sisters screamed as the mob passed their home with the men in chains, the women were arrested and the rest of the family retreated to the woods to escape capture. The three women were beaten and repeatedly raped by up to twenty men over several hours. Upon their release, they wandered in a swamp area for two days before reuniting with the rest of the family. Local blacks raised enough money to send the family to Chicago—the obvious destination for such a desperate situation. These same local blacks were most likely the ones who sent a message to the Chicago branch of the NAACP that the family was headed for Chicago. Reverend Lucas got a tip when the Arthurs were due to arrive and went to meet them, answering the clarion call of many black southerners to "meet me at the station." He assured them that they would be "safe in Chicago and there would be no burning here." With his help they were taken into the care of the Chicago Urban League and St. Mark's Church, organizations that worked together to find them a home. The *Chicago Defender* set up a fund for the Arthurs asking the public to give liberally to relieve the stress of the beleaguered family, whom they described as "penniless, without friends in a strange land." By 1930, the family shared a home on Federal Street, a densely populated area of the South Side. Not long after arriving in the city, they wrote the *Chicago Defender* to express thanks for aiding them in their arduous plight. However, the Arthur family faced a significant life change in Chicago. The entire family joined the swollen ranks of the black working class. The surviving son, Ennery, became a mechanic in a South Side garage and the youngest daughter, Millie, worked as a laundress.[65] The photo of the family's arrival to Chicago has become well-known, the circumstances of their arrival have not. The irony is that the photo has become an icon of the Great Migration when it most likely was arranged by Reverend Lucas, a man who would later take his own life in reaction to the AME's ambivalent response to the migration and its seemingly unfair and politicized use of ministerial transfers.

The unfavorable attention the AME Church in Chicago received from the local press and the black community at large prompted the establishment of a reform organization among the laity in 1924. The general dissatisfaction of area AME churches with church leadership was the principal motive behind the formation of the group. The laymen's organization was composed of two thousand representatives from Chicago's AME churches, and was primarily concerned with the perceived absolute power of the general conference. The group also was dismayed with the tremendous level of politicking that went into the election of bishops and ministerial transfers. The express purpose of the laymen's organization was to "reestablish the prestige of the church"—to combat the church's loss of influence and the "immorality and graft that are prevalent therein and are covered up and winked at by certain unscrupulous ministers." In the two years of its existence, the organization "quietly" investigated the conditions of the city's AME churches and followed leads on rumors and complaints, ranging from petty theft to sexual indiscretions on the part of local ministers. The organization set up a sophisticated "spy system" that operated in all AME churches. Its explicit aim was to gather information regarding the "condition of certain churches and the fitness of certain ministers, morally and otherwise to pastor them." Spies in the system found that two area ministers had "unholy love affairs with young girls" and that one of the clergymen, taken to municipal court on such charges, was released through the cunning of his "brother ministers." Episodes of this kind and the moral laxity of AME ministers became the central focus of the organization's energies. Proclaiming a demand for "the highest type of ministers," the laymen's group declared that it was time to "place the weal of the church above the personal ambition of individual, unrighteous men."[66] Disgusted with what they considered "shameful conditions" existing in the AME churches of the city, in 1926 the group appealed to Bishop Gaines for relief and "general housecleaning."[67]

Over its long history, the AME Church had endured many political battles but there existed no precedent for the type of organization established by these members of the Chicago AME laity. Their call for reformation among the clergy was an affront to a denomination accustomed to the voice of moral authority flowing downward, not from below. A petition drafted and signed by the laymen's organization signaled not only the fragmenting of African Methodism during the Great Migration, but also a relocation of moral authority within the denomination. The petition was a sober acknowledgment of a new era for the AME Church in Chicago.

> As laymen, we are proud of that history of accomplishment and achievement of the African Methodist Episcopal church: we glory in the incomparable legacy of the fathers, but we feel very keenly the loss of prestige suffered by the historic old church of Allen in the city of Chicago. And, although certain agencies and influences have constantly endeavored to deny that we have lost, not only numerically, spiritually and financially, we cannot longer delude ourselves with this glaring misstatement of facts, but as loyal African Methodists, we face a condition only too apparent and set ourselves under God, unafraid, unbiased and unprejudiced, to what we consider the heaven sent privilege and opportunity of re-establishing denominational dominance in the great city of Chicago. We realize that such a condition is not a thing of recent occurrence, but a cancerous growth due to long years of arrogant selfishness on the part of ministerial oligarchy which has entrenched itself by unholy intrigue and grown brazen and shameless by seeming immunity from punishment for any and all schemes put over at the expense of our general church.

The petition went on to say that there had been "scandal, disapproved and ugly" involving some area pastors, and that charges of immorality and graft against the denomination had swept the city, threatening it with "collapse." The laymen's organization considered the problems of the historic church to be of "sufficient gravity as to warrant Bishop Gaines' attention and immediate action in a way the general AME conference failed to acknowledge to the organization's satisfaction." And they were right about numerical loss to the denomination. Between 1926 and 1936, AME churches in Illinois decreased by about a third and by 1938 they accounted for only a small and shrinking percentage of the total number of black churches in Chicago.[68] Comparisons made of African Methodists to the numbers of black Baptists on the South Side were pathetic. A house-to-house canvass conducted by the WPA in 1938 in a relatively confined area on the South Side found that there were 231 people claiming membership in that area's AME church as compared to 2,092 who affiliated with the area's black Baptist churches. (See table 3.)

In many ways, the disruptive and chaotic ecclesiastical climate among Chicago's AMEs during the Great Migration confirmed fears and apprehensions about city life. It also suggested some justification for the denomination's ambivalence toward southern migrants and migration. Sharp disagreements about the nature and function of the AME Church and about the challenges of migration in an era of encroaching secularization underlay the conflicts between the conservative and reform factions within the church. Even those who maintained a conservative vision for their beloved denomination, who urged the AME Church to "rekindle the fires set aglow by the early fathers of the church," also acknowledged the denomination to be in desperate need of "new blood both in its spiritual and business structure." As the case of Hyde Park AME pastor Reverend Frank C. Lowry indicates, those impulses were often in conflict with one another. In 1925, the church's young and "scholarly pastor" abruptly called a moratorium on church socials and secular entertainments in the church's basement. The church had had a long history of using these means to raise money, but Lowry was convinced that the selling of "ice cream, dinners and musicales for which tickets are sold," ultimately led to "jazz and dance." "I am against them," he proclaimed, "and will be until I die. Only things spiritual should function in a church."[69] As a reformist, Lowry had hoped to point the AME denomination in new and exciting directions in terms of social outreach, clerical responsibility, and governmental structure. But, his conservative approach to the administration of his own church tended to stifle the very growth and enlargement of vision he aspired to for the denomination as a whole. The most progressive black churches in Chicago understood and embraced the ways notions of the secular and the sacred were becoming blurred, or were expanding. The black churches in Chicago that thrived during this era were those that actively and conscientiously participated in the cultural production of the city. Raising money for the purpose of meeting the administrative obligations, for example, became a viable means of introducing the arts

TABLE 3

Persons Claiming Church Membership, by Denomination: Area Wentworth to Cottage Grove between Twenty-second and Thirty-ninth Streets (1938)

Denomination	Number	Percentage
Baptist	2,092	66.6
African Methodist Episcopal	231	7.4
Methodist (unspecified) and Methodist Episcopal	174	5.5
Church of God	169	5.4
Catholic	137	4.4
Community	73	2.3
Spiritualist	66	2.1
Colored Methodist Episcopal	43	1.4
Church of Christ	31	1.0
Pentecostal	28	0.9
Episcopal	26	0.8
Presbyterian	25	0.8
Christian Science	19	0.6
Independent	13	0.4
Seventh Day Adventist	5	0.2
Congregational	4	0.1
Holiness	3	0.1
Total persons claiming membership	3,139	100.0

Source: St. Clair Drake Papers, box 57, Schomburg Center for Research in Black Culture, New York.

into the life of the church. As Drake and Cayton observed by the mid-1940s, "Bronzeville's churches are centers of entertainment as well as places of worship."[70] Quibbles with this new development in the church culture usually came from those who remained suspicious of change. As a result of Lowry's ban, many members who formerly contributed to the church stopped giving. Some left the church entirely. When a quarterly report read by the church secretary revealed that "the church is not functioning well financially, that it is considerably in arrears," the presiding elder, J. M. Henderson, wanted to know why. The church secretary proclaimed that "it's because the pastor won't lift his ban against church socials—our best avenue for raising money." The standoff between Lowry and Hyde Park AME blew over but was not resolved. By the late 1930s, lay members and officials within the denomination were still calling for "reformation," though few were clear as to what that meant.[71]

The Great Migration was a watershed moment in black American life, which generated complex social, economic, and political changes among the nation's African American citizenry. For many African American institutions, including the AME Church, the migration also generated crises in institutional identity and direction. The ambivalent and hesitant stance of African Methodists toward migration and migrants reflected a resistance to change the way of AME Church life that dated back to the early nineteenth century. It also reflected a deep fear of urbanization, of cities, and the inevitable redistribution of resources and ecclesiastical power from the South to the North. Yet, despite the concerns and warnings of AME leaders, the northward migration continued, depleting southern churches while overwhelming the resources of many existing northern churches. The shift forced the denomination to reconsider its entire structure, as migrants and migration challenged many of its time-honored policies and programs. Some within the denomination took the opportunity to call for change and for renewal. Hundreds left the church. In short, the Great Migration presented the AME Church in Chicago with its greatest crisis and an opportunity for growth and expansion that was never fully realized.[72]

CHAPTER SIX

A Woman's Work, an Urban World

> *Some people don't care for a woman pastor and some do.*
> —Lucy M. Smith

> *I am a minister and a leader of my followers who need my advice*
> *and guidance. Women preachers are important. . . . There is no*
> *doubt that we encounter a great deal of opposition, but our work*
> *is needed.*
> —Mary G. Evans

IT WAS CLEAR from the start that the migration would significantly alter the lives of African American women. Although black women in the South had been moving out of their homes to find work since the end of slavery, the vast majority remained in farm labor or domestic service. They also maintained minimal, prescribed contact with whites. In the urban North, however, more black women found themselves in greater proximity to whites on city streets and public transport. They also found themselves in a wider range of jobs. While most, particularly those recently from the rural South, worked as domestics, a number of black women found work in industry or were employed in clerical, skilled, and semiskilled jobs. Traditional family and living arrangements altered also as large numbers of single black women ventured north. Single black women were known to lodge with extended family, in rooming houses, in homes for women, or even alone. In some instances, single black women arrived in northern cities with insufficient means and no contacts, familial or otherwise. Of these "women adrift," Joanne Meyerwitz wrote, some "came to Chicago penniless and others with inadequate sums for initial room and board." She cited the example of one black woman from Alabama who came to Chicago "without money, hat, or anyone to meet her."[1] Whatever the circumstances of their arrival, black women migrants experienced significant changes in their relations with whites, in their work environments, in living arrangements, in leisure activities, and in relations between the sexes. In every way, black women migrants found in Chicago a whole new world.

The migration narratives of African American writers such as Gwendolyn Brooks and Richard Wright dramatized the trauma that migration and urbanization imposed on the psychological and familial worlds of Chicago black women. The stories they told were narratives of loss, displacement, and victimization. To these writers, city life was inherently alienating and debilitating to black women, whose former rural existence left them unequipped for urban life. In her poem "The Kitchenette Building" and in her book, *Maud Martha*, Brooks portrayed the "kitchenette"—one of the multiple small units subdivided in a large house—as a place of despair, and the lives of the women who dwelled in them as hapless and forlorn. After Maud Martha, the protagonist of the novel, realizes that her life would most likely stagnate in the damp and roach-infested apartment she and her family called home, she sees the place and its effect on her in a new way.

> She was becoming aware of an oddness in color and sound and smell about her. The color was gray, and the smell and sound had taken on a suggestion of the properties of color, and impressed one as gray too. The sobbings, the frustrations, the small hates, the large and ugly hates, the little pushing-through love, the boredom, that came to her from behind those walls . . . via speech and scream and sigh—all these were gray.[2]

The account Richard Wright gave of the life of Cleo, his southern migrant aunt, is similarly dreary. Upon his arrival to Chicago, Wright's Aunt Cleo met him at the station, and as they were traveling together by streetcar on the way to her rented room, he caught a glimpse of her. "I found Aunt Cleo aged beyond years. Her husband, a product of a southern plantation, had, like my father, gone off and left her. Why had he left? My aunt could not answer. She was beaten by the life of the city."[3] These fictionalized and semifictionalized depictions of black women's lives during the migration poignantly reflect aspects of the lived reality for thousands of black women from the rural South. They chronicle the attempts of these women to make their own way in the new and unfamiliar environment of Chicago. And, importantly, these accounts continue to have a profound impact on the popular imagination with regard to the ways we view the daily experiences of black women in cities.

Yet, for as much as these migration narratives tell us about new social relations, familial structures, and work environments for black Chicago women, they offer only a partial understanding of the experiences of these women during the migration. Both Wright and Brooks overlook or minimize evidence of personal agency and community building. They don't speak of the ways the city presented new opportunities for professional development, personal growth, and new group solidarity among black Chicago women. Certainly, we cannot burden African American novelists and poets with the task of developing a comprehensive view of black Chicago women, but aside from a few notables such as Ida B. Wells-Barnett, Madame C. J. Walker, and Irene McCoy Gaines, we know very little about the lives of migration-era black Chicago women. There remains much we have yet to understand about the experiences of black women in Chicago, whether leaders or ordinary citizens, who lived their lives in the torrent of one of the most crucial moments in United States history. How did Chicago's African American women develop and maintain notions of community among themselves? What part did ordinary black women play in institution building? How were black women's public and sexual identities formed in Chicago? How did black women navigate the class disparities developing among themselves during this era? What part did black women play in the transformation of the city's African American religious culture? The answers to these questions can best be attained through an examination of the experiences of black women within African American churches, the most vibrant female-dominated institutions extant in Chicago during the migration.

In recent years, a few scholars have given attention to the lives of women in mainstream black churches, typically either to stress the growing authority of black women in those institutions or to demonstrate the ways they subverted male authority to create autonomous female spaces.[4] Fewer scholars, however, have been concerned with the active and innovative role of black women in the reconstruction of black urban religion in both mainstream black churches and marginal religious groups. The omission has left wide gaps in twentieth-century African American history. Not only has it obscured the ways women negotiated and challenged social and cultural boundaries, but it has also occluded the gendered meanings of migration and urbanization. Most important, it has concealed the individual and collective agency of black women. The African American Protestant churches of migration-era Chicago provided arenas where black women became principal agents of change in conceptions of religious authority, worship, and social outreach. Examining two of these spaces and the women who led them, Elder Lucy Smith and Reverend Mary G. Evans, reveals much about black women's inventive influence on religion in the city and the relationships and issues around which they ordered their lives.

Like no other women in Chicago during the first half of the twentieth century, Lucy Smith and Mary Evans clearly reflected the central role black women played in developing black Chicago's new sacred order. Though they and their churches have received only scant attention by scholars, Smith and Evans profoundly influenced the black religious culture of the city. They provided new models for female urban religious leadership and extended the accepted borders of black women's church work. Within their respective churches, Smith and Evans established patterns of worship and social services that reflected a keen understanding of the conditions under which black Chicagoans lived. Not only were Smith and Evans the first women to head major churches in the city, they were also among a small number of pastors that managed to build a major church edifice from the ground up. Between them, they constructed three sanctuaries, a community center, and a retirement home. Smith assumed the role of "Overseer" of an entire General Conference of churches beginning in the 1920s, of which her All Nations Pentecostal Church became the "mother church." She pioneered religious radio, becoming the first African American minister in the Midwest to broadcast live worship over the airwaves. Her *Glorious Church of the Air* reached as far as Mexico and became the means by which many black Chicagoans first heard the voices of premier gospel artists such as Mahalia Jackson and Thomas Dorsey. Committed to the Pentecostal practice of faith healing, Smith staged weekly healing services, which became a staple of black Chicago nightlife.[5] Mary Evans, second pastor of the Cosmopolitan Community Church, became the first African American minister in Chicago to successfully maintain the operation of a church solely through "tithing," a biblical tax system based on the Old Testament text Malachi 3:10.[6] Evans became renowned for her skill at administration and debt reduction, and her church was one of the best-organized African American religious institutions in Chicago. Despite an apparent self-imposed insistence that she not speak on social issues from the pulpit, Evans staunchly supported African American civil rights. Throughout most of the early decades of the Great Migration, both women participated in the public realm at previously unimagined levels.

The little that has been written about Smith and Evans characterizes them and their churches as polar opposites. Beginning in the 1930s, this characterization drew heavily on comments made by black Chicagoans. Conducting research for various WPA and University of Chicago projects, the interviewers seemingly sought responses only from a certain segment of the African American community. This would explain, in part, the uniformity of opinion. Those interviewed were all of middle-class status and freely expressed their gender, regional, and class biases with regard to Smith and Evans. A statement by an African American social worker typified reactions. "As a rule I don't approve of 'women preachers,' but there exists a sharp difference among them. For instance, I believe M. E. [Mary Evans] is an intelligent, creditable preacher, has dignity and knows what she's talking about, but L. S. [Lucy Smith] is a disgrace." The commenter concluded, "M. E. [Mary Evans] tries to uplift church worship among our people. She is a credit to the race and to the profession." By this view, the two women pastors, whose churches stood within blocks of each other, were perceived to be worlds apart in terms of their intellect, form of worship, and contribution to racial progress.[7]

In retrospect, comparisons like these were certain to take place because of the historical tendency to "read" black women's bodies as sites of cultural and sexual inscription. Smith was very dark in complexion, stood taller than six feet, and before her health declined, weighed more than three hundred pounds. In *Black Metropolis*, St. Clair Drake and Horace Cayton described her as "elderly, corpulent, dark-skinned, and maternal."[8] In Pentecostal fashion, it was her habit to wear long white dresses made of cotton, silk, or satin, and the gold pocket watch she cherished dangled from a black chord around her neck at all times. (See figure 11.) Born in

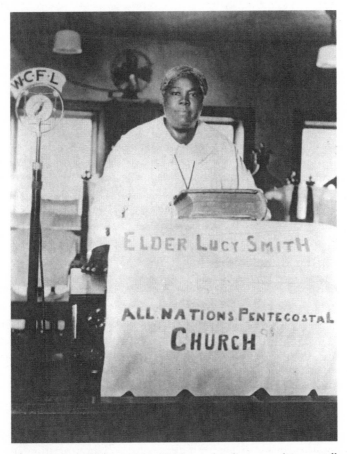

Fig. 11. Lucy Smith. A Faith Healer and radio evangelist, as well as the pastor of All Nations Pentecostal Church and "Overseer" of the All Nations Pentecostal Conference, Elder Smith pioneered live religious worship in Chicago. Her program, *The Glorious Church of the Air*, was heard for many years over station WCFL. (Source: Vivian G. Harsh Collection, Carter G. Woodson Regional Branch, Chicago Public Library)

1875, Smith possessed virtually no education, having only attended school for four months out of the year during her youth in post-Reconstruction rural Georgia. She arrived in Chicago in 1910 but retained her down-home manner of speaking, which became the signature of her sermons and radio broadcasts. Mary Evans, in contrast, was short in stature, with a very light complexion and a "stern face."[9] Known for her dignified speech and sophisticated manner, she boasted an education that surpassed many of Chicago's African American male clerics. Born in Washington, D.C., in 1891, the AME Church licensed her to exhort at age twelve.[10] Among the few sources that mention Smith and Evans, none fail to remark about the differences in physical appearance and cultural background between them.

Just as the two women differed in appearance and background, their churches operated on different theological and administrative levels. As a Pentecostal assembly, All Nations held loud, demonstrative worship services, replete with ecstatic utterances and "shouting." Services at Cosmopolitan were conducted in relative quiet. Evans displayed signs reading "silence" in various places throughout the sanctuary. Her insistence on silence before and after services was an integral part of her conception of ritual practice that extended back to her time as pastor of St. John AME in Indiana. A report on the church's activities written in the 1927 annual proceedings stated, "the decorum is to be commended." "No loud talking or laughing in the church when the services dismiss," the report further elaborated, "just a silent retiring, not even any boisterous noise is heard on the outside."[11] Church business and administration at All Nations was relegated to the "Saints," who, in the spiritual hierarchies intrinsic to Pentecostal practice, maintained a closer walk with the Divine than others of the congregation. Evans chose from among the many doctors, lawyers, and other professionals in her congregation to staff the various ecclesiastical boards and committees of the church. All Nations raised money to support its staff and programs through "free will" and "penny" offerings and by selling their "healing paper," the *Pentecostal Ensign*. Smith also made direct appeals over the radio. Evans insisted that Cosmopolitan would conduct no paid events of any kind. Church leaders were salaried and members were expected to tithe, supporting the church according to their incomes.[12] Although both All Nations and Cosmopolitan had women as pastors, there were striking differences in the administration and daily operation of these churches.

The portrayal of Smith and Evans as polar opposites, however, obscures important commonalities and more potent realities. The reality was that these women shared very similar experiences as female pastors during a time of shifting and unstable attitudes toward women in ministry. As female pastors, they were subject to levels of scrutiny and critique their male counterparts would never have tolerated. At the same time, they similarly took advantage of the new opportunities afforded black women to operate freely in the public realm. They were able to become pastors of their own churches because there were few restrictions against it in black Chicago. In the transforming African American urban religious culture of the migration era, establishing a church could be as much an entrepreneurial endeavor as a religious vocation. This new ethos provided opportunities for black women to pastor churches—particularly churches outside the established denominations—to the same degree as men. The personal freedom intrinsic to urbanization afforded new religious autonomy for black women preachers, liberating them from traditional ecclesiastical structures and restrictions. Like many African American Chicago women preachers of the time, Smith and Evans were free to construct religious institutions, practices, and theologies to their liking. More importantly, they were free to ignore those that weren't. Smith succinctly summarized this new atmosphere when she declared, "some people don't care for a woman pastor and some do."[13] It was a sentiment with which Mary Evans would have certainly agreed.

Far from experiencing constraint because of their gender in assuming historically male roles, Smith and Evans worked confidently and independently in female-dominated religious institutions. They based their authority as church leaders on their ability to provide spiritual and material sustenance to Chicago blacks. Unlike a previous generation of African American women preachers, who had to defend their work primarily on the basis of dramatic spiritual compulsion, Smith and Evans combined a sense of divine call with personal ambition and practical reasoning.[14] They justified their role as pastors on the basis of both their spiritual gifts and their administrative acumen. They shared a similar vision about what constituted the work of the church. They believed in responding to the challenges that city life presented to their different congregations by establishing charitable programs, and in orienting religious worship in ways that reflected the religious inclinations of poor and working-class black southern migrants. Using their public images and private faith to generate practical changes in the lives of black Chicagoans, Smith and Evans demonstrated that they were products of the new urban religious climate and agents of change in the new sacred order.

As pastors of large black Chicago churches, Smith and Evans were unique, but as women preachers they belonged to a long tradition of American Protestant women who had dared to proclaim a divine call to minister the gospel. For nearly two centuries, women preachers, both black and white, had claimed the right to preach and found themselves denounced as heretics and Jezebels and charged with undermining male authority. The issues of male ecclesiastical control and gender bias that bedeviled the lives of European American and African American women preachers of the eighteenth and nineteenth centuries persisted into the twentieth century, affecting in various ways the careers of Smith and Evans. Notably, the African American Protestant establishment gave less of its support to women ministers in the first decades of the twentieth century than it gave during much of the nineteenth century. Even the historically intransigent AME Church had expressed in the early nineteenth century some confidence in women's capacity for preaching. Fourth AME Bishop William Paul Quinn, for example, after hearing itinerate Rachel Evans preach, proclaimed that she had "not a superior in the western reserve." In 1817 Richard Allen changed his mind about Jarena Lee's call to ministry after hearing her give an extemporaneous sermon at Bethel Church in Philadelphia.[15] Although the AME Church instituted the full ordination of women in 1948, it maintained a culture of opposition to women in positions of church leadership during Evans's tenure in the denomination. Indeed, the opposition Evans encountered from the male membership of St. John AME in Indiana, where she served before coming to Chicago, played a part in her decision to sever connections with the AME convention. (Although, in an interview she gave in 1962, Evans stated that her official reason for leaving the AME was her conviction that the church hierarchy was not "meeting the spiritual needs of its members."[16]) Male opposition persisted even at Cosmopolitan. Former Cosmopolitan members recalled that Evans was at times opposed not only by other Chicago male ministers, but by male members of Cosmopolitan as well.[17] Lucy Smith did not face opposition from men within her church, which can be explained in part by the fact that so few men attended as members or served on church boards.

The rise in masculinist conceptions of American evangelical Christianity contributed to the regression in African American attitudes toward women preachers in the early twentieth century. A surge in masculinist sentiment within mainline denominations, which sought to reverse the feminization of American religion, framed the discussion about women ministers not in terms of naturally predetermined gender spheres but more simply in terms of proper gender work roles.[18] African American men had a greater stake in retaining the ministry as the exclusive work of the male sex because in the twentieth century the ministry remained one of the few arenas available to black men to assert public authority in the wider world. Though twentieth-century African American women preachers were not accused of being actual men, as a few of their nineteenth-century counterparts had been, they faced charges that they were usurping positions that rightfully belonged to men. When young Mary Evans first mounted the pulpit of her Baptist church to deliver an extemporaneous sermon, her shocked parents reprimanded her. Preaching was "man's work" they said.[19] This masculinist conception of ministry, which insisted that black preachers must be not only male but stereotypically "manly," renewed opposition to women preachers. As an element of the movement that some scholars have called "muscular Christianity," masculinist conceptions of African American ministry locked the debate in a masculine-feminine binary. As one black Chicagoan asserted in 1940, "preaching is a calling for a man." It constituted work not fitting for females. In a reversal of nineteenth-century thought regarding gendered spheres of public and private life, men became caretakers of the soul in the home and in the church. Conceived of in terms of physical robustness, not just the male sphere, manliness became the template by which to judge black preachers—male and female.

The masculinist conception of ministry, and the discourse of "masculine" and "feminine" so intrinsic to it, drew attention to black women preachers' bodies and invited speculation about their sexuality. The terms used to express objection to black women preachers during the migration era typically focused on their bodies. A wide range of sources from the 1930s characterized them as "plain," "buxom," "plump and brown," and "homely." Many commented on the unusually "deep voices" of Chicago black women preachers. A WPA worker who witnessed Lucy Smith's assistant pastor, Rebecca Porter, preach in 1938 remarked: "she was a very emotional speaker with a strong husky male voice. Her movements were likewise very masculine." One of the African American "informants" to the study done by Samuel Strong in 1940 concluded that "women preachers are somewhat mannish, overweight, and hoarse." Another added that they are "usually of a mannish type and imitate men preachers." Still another succinctly claimed, "women preachers are usually lesbian."[20] These depictions remained fairly consistent throughout the migration era, indicating clearly that the debate about black women preachers centered on a gendered reading of their physical appearances. They also indicated that many black Chicagoans perceived something particularly provocative in a sexual or bodily sense about women in positions of ministerial leadership.

Chicago black women preachers developed complex and inventive strategies designed to deflect attention away from their bodies while paradoxically subverting gender norms and working within a set of what Elaine Lawless has called "confused gender expectations."[21] Some denied their gender while assuming the "gender" of the Holy Spirit or claimed that they had transcended gender altogether. "Mrs. Williams," the pastor of a small Pentecostal storefront church called the Royal Prayer Band, told a WPA worker, A. N. Canon, in the late 1930s that when she comes under the influence of the Holy Spirit her gender is changed and such is the basis of her authority to preach. "The spirit of the Holy Ghost is a male spirit," she contended, "but when a woman receives the spirit she is no longer a woman—then she has the right to perform the duties of a man—like preaching. (Until then she should only do missionary work and teaching work.) She further argued that ("The word of God is a 'he' and women are the flesh of the world,") and that there are people who are devoted to God in such a way that "they don't have time to think about sex and the things of the world."[22] Given the limited access blacks had to educational resources in the rural South during the first half of the twentieth century, it is unlikely that Williams was aware by means of formal study that her statement reflected certain currents in medieval theology. Intuitively, however, she could have been aware that other female theological thinkers—such as Hildegard of Bingen, the first woman theologian—shared her contrast of men/spirit and women/flesh. Like Bingen's assertion that "woman is to man as flesh is to spirit," Williams's comment inadvertently placed men in a spiritually superior position to women and male ministers in a desexualized category.

With regard to the apparent transformation of her gender implicit in Williams's comment, there was precedent for such a claim in the history of American women preachers.[23] An eighteenth-century white woman preacher, Jemima Wilkinson, "occasioned much talk" in the city of Philadelphia when she declared that she had literally died and been resurrected not as a woman but as a genderless spirit. After a bout with typhus, the Rhode Island farmer's daughter declared that she had "dropt the dying flesh and yielded up the Ghost," that her soul had ascended and her body was possessed by the "Spirit of Life." She, in effect, was no longer a "she."[24] More commonly, however, Chicago black women preachers aimed to detract attention from their bodies, sex, and sexuality not by denying their gender but by rendering themselves sexually ambiguous or by complicating the notion of "femaleness." They seized control of their self-representation as women and as ministers by manipulating a set of confused gender expectations that required that they be both maternal (nurturing) and pragmatic (rational). This often involved embracing "motherliness" while rejecting conventional domesticity and conscientiously performing "mannishness."

The rumors circulating among black Chicagoans that Mary Evans was lesbian, for example, sprang from her relationship choices. She never married but maintained two long-term relationships with other women. Her first relationship, with Harriet Kelley, was carried out while she was a young preacher in Indiana. The second, with Edna Cook, the daughter of William D. Cook, lasted for much of the remainder of her life in Chicago. Known as a private person, Evans never spoke of the nature of her relationship with Kelley. When questioned by U.S. census takers in 1930, Evans indicated Kelley as her "sister." If it was an effort to shield the nature of the relationship, the guise was not foolproof. It was clear the two women were not related. The same census record showed that Evans's parents had

[margin handwritten note: motherly but mannish]

been born in Virginia. Kelley's parents were from Illinois and Kentucky respectively. Evans was equally silent or evasive about her relationship with Edna Cook. The two women lived their lives quietly together, apparently without comment or explanation. Evans's personal demeanor fueled the gay rumors. She dressed austerely—for years in the same "shiny black suit," refusing to buy new clothes until the church had made progress in raising money for one of its building projects. She was also known to wear a "severe hairstyle" and "no makeup." With her strict leadership style, ambitious building projects, and involvement in the public realm, Evan exceeded what black Chicagoans would likely have expected from a single woman preacher.[25]

Whether Mary Evans was actually a lesbian, however, is in many ways beside the point. She apparently never made a public proclamation of her sexual orientation and perhaps would have been disinclined to do so on account of the reserved climate of the time regarding matters of sex and sexuality. At the same time, the relationships with Kelley and Cook, in particular, would seem to suggest that Evans could at least be accurately described as "womanist," as Alice Walker has coined.[26] The long length of time in which Evans and Cook lived together and the apparent closeness of the two women suggests a relationship that was emotionally intimate and likely physically intimate as well. It must have been obvious to many that the two women understood themselves to be in a nonconventional relationship that mirrored heteronormativity. At the very least, it was a "romantic friendship" similar to that of women of the late nineteenth-century who were, in the words of John D'Emilio and Estelle Freedman, "passionately attached to each other and committed to a lifetime together."[27] More to the point is that Evans carefully manipulated her public image as "motherly" and "mannish." She manipulated both images in order to set the terms for her own self-presentation, to navigate a confused set of gender expectations for black women preachers with the idea of deflecting attention off her body and her sexuality.[28] This last aim was ironic in her case because it was unlikely that a woman living in a long-term relationship with another woman could escape speculation about her sexuality. But Evans had historical precedent for this strategy. When the African American Shaker Rebecca Cox Jackson joined the celibate religious sect in 1836 and later engaged in a lifelong relationship with fellow Shaker Rebeccah Perot, it was because Jackson wanted to relinquish sex with her husband. She held to the view that sexual relations, even with a married partner, were incompatible with a spiritual life. Even so, the relationship she maintained with Perot continues to generate assertions by some scholars that the women were lesbian. We will probably never know for certain whether any of these women were actually lesbian in sexual orientation. And while it is more likely that Evans was lesbian and Jackson was not, what is more important is the way Evans exploited "motherly" and "mannish" images of herself in order to attract attention to her skills as a minister and away from her body and sexuality.

African American women preachers in black urban churches were expected to "mother" their congregations. Indeed, their ability to mother their congregations was one of the ways women preachers authenticated their calls to ministry. Mary Evans utilized the mother typology to great effect, accomplishing this in a variety of ways. Most particularly, she asserted herself as the primary matriarchal figure in the church. She also took pragmatic steps to ensure her mother status and on occasion addressed her congregation as "children." Former members of Cosmopolitan, for example, recalled that Evans sent birthday cards to each of her members on their "natal days" and they, in turn, "minded her just like we were children." Evans was known to have a particular fondness for children, even considering one of the children of the congregation her "adopted daughter." This fondness for children perhaps served as the primary motivation to have the Martha Carter Playground constructed near Cosmopolitan. It was said to be equipped "with everything a young heart could wish for." Evans's sermons were known to possess a maternal quality. While at one point she could be "sharp like a two-edged sword," she would then become "kind and entreative [sic]."[29]

But there was a larger aim and effect to Evans's appropriation of a mother image. The mothering of her congregation effectively desexualized her, derailing any attention that would otherwise focus on her body or the nature of her relationships. This was precisely the ironic power held by the mother image. It presented the best way for black women preachers to de-emphasize the body, sex, and sexuality. Similarly, her "mannishness" seemed a self-conscious display or "performance" of gender ambiguity. Numerous photos of Evans, taken mostly later in her career, suggest first that she was a woman particularly interested in controlling her public image.[30] All done in clerical garb and some in profile, where the body and often not even the face were emphasized, the photos were evocative in the way that on the one hand they do not explicitly suggest a particular gender but on the other hand could be viewed as "masculine." (See figure 12.) The latter photos contrast strikingly to descriptions from her early career, where she was once declared "the bobbed haired evangelist" whose voice was "mellowed with a touch of sweetness that makes it thoroughly feminine."[31] If WPA workers found Mary Evans to be businesslike and the church to reflect business efficiency, it was due, in part, to Evans's strict style of leadership and the ambitious building projects that dominated her career, as well as her involvement in the public realm of civic culture and politics, arenas deemed to be the province of the city's male clerical leadership. So, whether motherly or mannish, lesbian

Fig. 12. Mary G. Evans. Mary Evans left the AME Church in the early 1930s to join the Community Church Movement in Chicago and became the pastor of Cosmopolitan Community Church. The change in affiliation allowed her to extend the reach of her church into various local and national civic causes. A woman seemingly concerned with her public image, Evans sat for numerous photos throughout her long career. Most were done in clerical garb and at the church's podium. (Source: Vivian G. Harsh Collection, Carter G. Woodson Regional Branch, Chicago Public Library)

had to be [handwritten annotation]

strictly business [handwritten annotation]

or not, the message she sent was clear. She was in that neutral category of "minister" that did not invite speculation about the body, femaleness, or sexuality.

Elder Lucy Smith faced the same challenges as Mary Evans but dealt even more emphatically with the paradox of being a black woman and a preacher. Ultimately, the aim was the same: to deflect emphasis away from her body and toward her ministry. But Smith's physical stature made that task more difficult, and she seemingly felt compelled to remark about her

[margin notes: public's obsession with black women preachers appearance]

[margin notes: rejection of traditional women employment]

size in every interview. When responding to one of the many inquiries about her weight, she told an interviewer in 1935 that she had once been "small," but since becoming a pastor God had taken her "out of the kitchen" and "fleshened her up."[32] The statement richly implicated Smith's rejection of domesticity. Like Evans, Smith exploited the maternal expectations placed on black women preachers of the era. Indeed, "Mother Smith" was one of the many ways people addressed her. She, too, was known to "mother" her congregation, and contemporary observers recognized this, dubbing her "mother-image to the drifting black masses."[33] But Smith constantly constructed her public presentation between the mother image and the masculinist term "Overseer," her official church title. In a further attempt to deflect attention from her sexuality and her body, Smith veiled her husband from public view. She told her biographer in one of two unpublished biographies that her husband abandoned her in Georgia, leaving her to migrate alone to Chicago in 1910 with her children. "My husband left his family," she said, "and went to another city. I had to work to keep the children from starving and going naked."[34] Though the abandonment narrative made for compelling drama, William Smith joined Lucy Smith a short while later and stayed in Chicago until his death in 1938.[35] Whether he had planned to do so all along is not certain. Nor is it clear if and how long he lived in the same residence with her. What is clear is that Mr. Smith reunited with Lucy Smith and the union produced two additional children. The only surviving record that clearly identified him as her husband, however, is his obituary, in which he was praised for his help with the first of her two churches. The biographies made scant and oblique mention of him as "brother Smith," "brother S," or simply "William Smith."[36]

Though "mother-image to the drifting black masses," Smith adamantly rejected a characterization of herself as "Mrs. William Smith." The reason she veiled her husband from public view could be deeply embedded in the particulars of that relationship—and beyond our grasp. Or, it could be that she considered the biography her story, not his. This could have been a way to exert some control over her life, some control over how her life was remembered. Smith would not be the first African American woman to realize the significance of the self in the act of telling her story. Since William Smith was not a Christian, perhaps she didn't want to besmirch the testimony of the work of God with an account that centralized the role of an ungodly husband. Each of these possibilities is likely. It is just as likely, however, that the deliberate augmentation of her life's narrative had as much to do with an aim to deflect attention away from her body and sex. By portraying herself as a woman preacher seemingly without a husband, Smith mitigated such speculation. But if Mary Evans was attempting to render herself sexually ambiguous, Smith was reconfiguring femaleness altogether. Her strategy of being both mother and Overseer included a rejection of domesticity and a reconfiguration of woman's place in the public and private realms. The inference of her statement that since she became a pastor God had "taken her out of the kitchen" suggests that she was doing God's work, not "woman's work," or that "woman's work" was God's work. Her role as a pastor took precedence over her role as wife. And for Smith, this familial restructuring had some roots in her Pentecostal faith. It was clear from the inception of the modern Pentecostal movement that it tended to confirm gender norms and to subvert them at the same time.[37] This modern-day revival on the one hand supported the fundamental order of God, home and family, man and woman. At the same time, however, the tradition decentralized the home, instilling a new order of priority that placed Jesus first, the institution of the church second, and family last. Pentecostalism's effect in the life of Lucy Smith was a reconfiguration of traditional gender norms broadly speaking and of gender relations specifically. The Pentecostal tradition allowed her, in practice, to subvert conventional notions of gender norms while in theory working well within them—as an Overseer who is also motherly.

This subversion of femaleness characterized Smith's private and professional life. Privately she lived in a world of women, each assigned particular tasks to facilitate her work as pastor of the church. Smith's main contacts were her surviving daughters (several children preceded her in death); her personal secretary, Anna Johnson; her dressmaker, Mrs. Sutton; the "subleader" of the church, Rebecca Porter; and her granddaughter, "Little Lucy." By 1930, many of these women were living in residence with Smith on Langley Avenue. (Smith's church was a female sacred world, containing a membership ratio that was 4 to 1 female to male.[38] Although most of the women were married, presumably their husbands did not attend the church. Various photos taken by photographers working for the FSA in the 1940s bear witness that the relatively few male members of the church existed literally on the margins of the congregation. Smith's strategy, then, at undermining speculations about her body and about sex, was similar to Evans's in the sense that she, too, manipulated her image in the performance of a self that shifted within the gendered expectations of her as a woman and preacher. Smith also, however, complicated the very notion of what it meant to be female.

As African American women preachers, Smith and Evans took part in a long tradition of black women who, because of their ministries, had to confront the interrelated issues of gender bias, speculation about their sexualities, and the objective gaze on their bodies. The specter of sex and even sexual impropriety had lingered as a subtext to black women preachers' activities since the early nineteenth century. The rage that Zilpha Elaw saw in the eyes of an "unusually stout and ferocious looking man" who taunted and circled her as she preached was shot through with sexual tension and aggression.[39] Addressing claims that she was actually "a man dressed in female clothes," the freeborn AME preacher Jarena Lee declared in her 1836 autobiography that she was a "true woman." Indeed, the very title of the narrative, *The Life and Religious Experiences of Mrs. Jarena Lee, A Coloured Lady*, disputed claims that Lee was not a true woman or womanly.[40] Despite donning a simple bonnet and shawl (which covered her entire body) throughout her preaching career, charges that she was a "Jezebel" persisted.[41] There were, however, important differences between Smith and Evans and their predecessors, differences that bespoke broad religious and social change. Lucy Smith and Mary Evans were not only women preachers; they were also independent pastors of their own congregations. And this significant difference from their eighteenth- and nineteenth-century "sisters of the spirit" factored into why they did not base their authority as preaching women solely on divine commission or feel compelled to restrict their church work because of their gender.[42] Smith and Evans based their authority as black women preachers primarily on their ability as leaders to meet the needs black Chicagoans faced in the urban context. In this way, the city itself played a role in the way they authenticated themselves as church leaders. Instead of being barred by their sex from pastoral leadership, Smith and Evans were liberated by the openness of city life, which offered an apt arena for their particular ministerial and administrative gifts.

It is no coincidence, however, that both Smith and Evans established and administered churches outside the historical denominations. At the time they began their ministries in Chicago, no mainline African American church allowed women to occupy the pastorate with full ordination. The AME Zion Church maintained the most progressive stance among African Methodists toward women in church leadership, having ordained women to ministry as early as 1891. But it did not allow women full pastoral privileges. The Church of God in Christ, the largest African American Pentecostal denomination in the country, barred women from positions of leadership. The decentralized structure of black Baptist churches rendered a consistent policy on women and leadership difficult to maintain, but even here "the general climate has not been supportive of women preaching and pastoring churches."[43] Yet, while established denominations continued to discriminate against women as ministers, it was increasingly common for independent religious organizations to ordain women as clergy, pastors, and supreme officers, and even to allow self-ordination by the 1920s.[44]

Having been raised a Baptist, Lucy Smith affiliated first with Olivet Baptist Church when she reached Chicago before moving to Ebenezer Baptist. Although it is not clear that she left these churches because of their policies against ordaining women pastors, considering the church with which she next affiliated, it is a distinct possibility. The Stone Church, a predominately white Pentecostal assembly on Thirty-seventh and Indiana, maintained a liberal policy toward preaching women, allowing its women congregants to preach and inviting such nationally known figures as the faith healer Maria Woodworth Etter to render "special meetings."[45] William H. Piper had founded the church in 1906 after becoming associated with the Pentecostal movement. As an early exponent of the "Latter Rain," a term coined to refer to the "outpouring" of the Holy Spirit at Azusa, Piper emphasized the second coming of Christ, divine healing, and the manifestation of the Holy Spirit, particularly "speaking in tongues." Healing, however, was of particular importance.[46] After receiving her "call" in 1914, Smith left the Stone Church and founded All Nations Pentecostal Church and General Conference.[47] There are many uncertainties about how Smith's founding of the All Nations Pentecostal General Conference came about. Most likely after having witnessed the success of All Nations Church and its broadcast, churches approached Smith about forming a conference of All Nations Pentecostal churches with her own church as the head church. Exactly when this happened the records do not show. What is certain is that the General Conference's minimal requirements for membership and its guaranty of local church autonomy reflected the liberty with which Smith operated. It also resonated with her particular sense of calling. Any church desiring to affiliate with the General Conference needed at least six members and a starting fee of twenty-five dollars. Additionally, convention rule eight stated that "each church is to own its own property and call its own pastor." By the late 1930s, the All Nations General Conference included principal churches in Nebraska, Florida, and Alabama.[48]

During the time that Mary Evans had been pastor at St. John AME in Indiana, she did not possess the full clerical authority enjoyed by her male counterparts. Although throughout the nineteenth century the AME Church made gradual concessions to the demands of women in the church for preaching licenses, the male leadership stopped short of fully ordaining women ministers. A group of women calling themselves the Daughters of Zion petitioned the general conference in defense of women's ordination several times over an eight-year period beginning in 1844, but each time they were defeated with arguments about domesticity.[49] Under consistent pressure from women within the denomination, however, church leaders capitulated in 1868, instituting the office of "stewardess." They capitulated again in 1884 and 1900, instituting preaching licenses to women and extending to them the office of "deacon," both without full ordination. The lack of full ordination did not prevent Evans from becoming one of the most active ministers in the AME conference, but the level of involvement she was allowed indicated clearly the conference's gendered notion of women's activities. The proceedings from the 1927 annual conference listed her as "evangelist," a title reserved exclusively for the women preachers of the AME. She was also a trustee of Wilberforce University, her alma mater, served on the standing committee of the Women's Mite Missionary Society, and was elected as lay delegate to the general conference.[50]

Clearly, from Smith's own testimony, her call indicated not simply a commission to preach in a church but a call to assume the leadership of a church. It is also clear from the path she took in establishing All Nations Church and Conference that she recognized both the need and the opportunity to operate independently. Like many black churches in Chicago, Smith's All Nations Pentecostal Church began as a prayer meeting held by a small gathering of women. In 1916, two years after leaving the Stone Church, Smith started conducting prayer meetings in her home on Langley Avenue. After a few years and the addition of other members to the prayer group, Smith announced her desire to start a church, soliciting the support of the women in the group. They agreed, and for several years the small band of Pentecostal believers occupied a few locations around the South Side, including a tent church and the infamous Pekin Theater, until they built the church on Langley. Like the black women preachers who preceded her, Smith attributed her calling to divine injunction and laced her recollection of it with biblical language. Describing her calling in an autobiography, Smith recalled a vision where she heard the voice of God say, "I have called you, I have chosen you, I am ready for you to take the field." This call was a calling to leadership. "Then one Sunday morning at 3636 Cottage Grove Avenue the Lord said, 'I want you to be the pastor . . . will you be a leader for my people?'"[51]

In Pentecostal fashion, Lucy Smith declared that she was a "raised up pastor by the mighty hands of God," a statement by which she evoked all the seemingly primitivist metaphysicality characteristic of early Pentecostals.[52] But other statements and particular actions also revealed pragmatic motivations that at times seemed to counter Pentecostal theology and church custom. In other words, for all the "otherworldliness" expected of her, the focus of her church work was inspired by temporal conditions. Beginning in the 1930s, Smith incorporated a system of charitable distribution into the weekly program of All Nations. Every Thursday, the charitable outreach effort distributed food and clothing out of the church basement. By the height of the Depression, people were "lining up daily." Remembering particularly the winter and spring of 1932, Smith recalled that she and her staff of female workers "fed as high as 90 people a day for mighty near six months." The charitable distributions continued during the latter

1930s when "quite a few" of her members went on direct relief. As someone considered to possess a "fair knowledge of social and political problems," Smith was acutely aware of the economic devastation's most likely sufferers and made savvy use of her radio program to solicit funds and materials to be distributed. She informed a University of Chicago student in 1935, "we does a lot of charity work here—especially since the radio peoples sends us things to give out to the needy."[53] But Smith's work during the Depression grew from a basic conviction about the necessities of daily life. "We need bread, meat and clothing. We really can't do without them." And at least in one instance, this conviction prompted her to relax her fundamentalist Pentecostal theology. When asked what she thought of allegations that members of her congregation participated in the policy game, Smith replied, "I don't hold it against the people if they play policy numbers, so long as they don't deny themselves the necessities of life. I know that this is often unavoidable . . . what else can the people do? Conditions here are not good."[54] Maintaining that "the politicians and business people" were doing nothing for Chicago's poor, Smith drew her authority primarily from the "mighty power of God," but she also rooted that authority in her capacity to meet the material needs of black Chicagoans.[55]

Little information is available on Mary Evans's call to ministry. What the available information reveals is a woman who, like Smith, based her ministerial authority as much on her own leadership ability as on divine commission. When Evans was licensed to preach by a "Rev. Timothy" in 1905, Chicago-area AME churches were stolid places that promoted classical music and decorous religious worship. Her induction into the ministry by AME officials at age fourteen, however, suggests that her call was nothing short of dramatic. Although later in life she was known to render "brief meaningful sermons," those preached in her youth were long, fiery, and unsparing. A sermon she gave at Institutional AME in 1922, titled "The Wages of Sin Is Death," received an endorsement in the *Chicago Defender*, with the writer calling Evans "fearless, uncompromising and courageous." Hypocritical church members and male ministers were her particular target: "You live double lives, you church hypocrites. You men with two living wives and you women with two living husbands! A man with a wife and a woman friend on the side—a woman with a husband and a man friend on the side. Your lives are filthy, you live in adultery, but you are in the church and because you are in it, it is unclean. But you members are not by yourselves; your male preachers are just as immoral, just as filthy as you."[56] For the many black Chicagoans who heard Evans during her evangelistic preaching tours throughout the city in the early years of her ministry, sermons like this were proof enough of her divine call.

The drama and evangelical fervor of her early ministry notwithstanding, Evans rarely spoke of her call as supernatural in origin. Nor did she seem particularly troubled by extant debates (theological or otherwise) among African Americans regarding women preachers and pastors. Evans seemed settled on the issue as a practical matter, as indicated by a statement she made in 1940: ("women preachers are important. . . . there is no doubt that we encounter a great deal of opposition, but our work is needed.") Rather, her entry into church leadership appears to have happened primarily because she understood herself to possess special gifts for leadership and administration. Such self-awareness could account, in part, for the transformation she underwent from the fiery evangelist of her youth to the near-methodical officer of the church she became in later life. It was this special gift for leadership and administration that the AME conference recognized when they commissioned Evans to take charge of Wayman Chapel AME in Indianapolis when she was only twenty-four years old. Her skill at administration and her proven record at church debt reduction led John Harvey, the founder of Cosmopolitan Community Church, to request that she leave the AME conference to take the mantle at Cosmopolitan. Long active in the Chicago AME conference, Harvey had left it during the exodus of AME ministers out of the denomination in the early 1920s. He had founded Cosmopolitan but was leaving the church to pursue other interests. Harvey was confident that Evans would be able to handle the "business as well as the spiritual side" of the church.[57] WPA workers were equally convinced. After a visit to Cosmopolitan in the late 1930s to overlook its facilities (apparently to assess its capacity to hold WPA classes), Hortense Bratten concluded that the church was run by a "very complete and efficient management." Another worker writing in 1936 reported that after visiting Cosmopolitan and meeting Evans her impression of the woman pastor was "not only gratifying but profound."[58] Members of Cosmopolitan and associates of Mary Evans also concurred about her administrative abilities, recalling that she was "extraordinarily well organized" and that she "dotted every i and crossed every t."[59]

Like many black Chicago ministers during the migration era, Evans concerned herself particularly with debt reduction. Few were as skilled at reducing church debt as she, which is apparently why she was assigned to the debt-ridden St. John after Wayman Chapel. An AME official stated that a "spirit of success and prosperity" abounded at the church and its debt was being "gradually reduced" in just four years after Evans took charge. When Evans assumed the pastorate at Cosmopolitan in 1931, it was also in "grave financial distress," burdened with a debt of $36,000. At the height of the Depression, when her small congregation was just as affected by the national economic downturn as most black Chicago churches,

Class? or very good Services/worth it

Evans managed to uphold a system of giving that required members to offer 10 percent of their income to the church. Those who refused were reprimanded, and 98 percent of the congregation gave in this manner by 1936. A fervent believer in what the *Chicago Defender* dubbed "the Biblical method of finance," Evans guided Cosmopolitan out of debt, burning its mortgage papers at a time when Chicago's black churches were among the most debt-ridden of all black churches in the urban North and Midwest.[60] By comparison, Lucy Smith, who broke ground for the second All Nations Pentecostal Church building on Oakwood Boulevard in 1937—incurring an initial $50,000 debt—had made no substantial reduction of the financial burden by the early 1950s. Evans's campaigns to make Cosmopolitan a "singing, praying, tithing" church reaped rewards in congregational growth, prosperity, and confidence. While Lizabeth Cohen's general analysis may be correct that the Great Depression threatened "patterns of loyalty" to traditional institutions, the example of Mary Evans and Cosmopolitan Community Church demonstrates an instance where financial support and loyalty during the Depression continued unabated.[61]

Unlike the case with Lucy Smith, not much in the way of reflections by Mary Evans on her ministry in Chicago exists, or has yet surfaced. But an examination of programs she inaugurated at Cosmopolitan reveal concerns beyond "brilliant administration" and debt reduction. Later in her life, when she was asked what qualifications anyone who assumed leadership after her would have to possess, Evans replied, "all that is required is that he or she have the interest of the people at heart."[62] She remained committed to ameliorating the conditions of those in her congregation and those in the extended community of black Chicago. Although Evans rarely spoke on social issues in sermons, her involvement in community and civic action was unmistakable. Like many other African American churches during the migration era, Cosmopolitan developed a focus on professional social work, forming a Social Service Department that devoted its time to discussions of the "fundamentals of social work."[63] Like Smith, Evans instituted a program of charitable giving, which operated out of the church basement, and distributed food and clothing to the needy every Thursday. Indeed, it is very likely that Evans modeled her Thursday charitable work on Smith's program. Cosmopolitan also hosted WPA educational classes as well as maintaining a rent fund. Dr. William M. Jones, a member of the church, ran a free medical clinic on the church premises. In association with the Juvenile Protection Association and the Church Federation of Chicago, Evans involved Cosmopolitan in the wider struggle to curb juvenile delinquency and poverty. Her support for the NAACP was equally well known and motivated by her abhorrence of lynching. In 1942, at one of her annual campaigns in support of the

NAACP, Evans persuaded seven hundred members from among her congregation of 826 to sign pledge cards, calling them to the church altar to do so. "If three Negroes can be lynched in one week in Mississippi," she contended, "we Negroes should on our knees join the one organization that is fighting lynching." The next year she was installed as a member of the executive committee of the Chicago branch of the NAACP, and twenty years later Evans was leading "every other minister in the nation in the solicitation of memberships" for the civil rights organization. As a WPA worker observed, "the entire South Side public recognizes that Mary G. Evans is a consecrated woman preacher who is giving her life for a good cause for her people."[64]

In the same way that Mary Evans acted on her stated conviction to have "the interest of the people at heart" in matters of civic and social concern, she also extended that approach to spiritual matters.[65] Her belief in faith healing showed that she, like Smith, developed the programs of her church to reflect the needs and inclinations of the congregation and surrounding community. Embraced in varying degrees by Protestant orthodoxy since the first century, the practice of faith healing has been central to the theologies of many religious dissenters and sects. There is at least one account of faith healing in the Old Testament and several in the New Testament, most performed by Jesus. By the first decades of the twentieth century, "faith healing" among African American churches was associated almost entirely with Pentecostal and Holiness denominations. As a community church pastor and former AME minister, therefore, Evans's belief in faith healing breached a theological divide.[66] Evans's particular approach to faith healing, however, was devoid of some of its more metaphysical aspects such as the "laying on of hands." She did not believe that she or anyone else was a faith healer, that is, she rejected the notion that anyone could be a physical conduit of healing. Evans's conversion to the doctrine apparently grew from personal experience. In the late 1930s she was involved in a serious rail accident that left her nearly paralyzed. When word of the accident reached Cosmopolitan, members staged an "all night vigil," after which Evans declared, "I was completely healed." "Since then," she told a University of Chicago sociology student, "healing has become a major part of my program."[67] Healing services at Cosmopolitan were simple affairs that involved only prayer and soft music. There was no physical contact and no one among the congregation claimed to have the "gift of healing," a special blessing from God to physically heal people. The healing services, called "the Quiet Hour," were held every Friday and were well attended.

More so than traditional Pentecostal understandings of divine healing, Evans's approach to the practice reflected the philosophy of "New Thought." New Thought philosophy, from which various psychotherapeutic approaches to American religion developed in the late nineteenth century, held that physical healing was an act of the mind. Disease was of mental origin, and sickness resulted from the failure to realize God as the ultimate reality and the failure to acknowledge one's unity with God. Correct thinking ultimately led to physical healing, and correct thinking required quiet meditation. Mary Evans's description of the services was clear on this point. "The church is open all day, and people drop in three times a day. They sit in quietness and either pray or meditate and then get up and feel better."[68] In New Thought philosophy, healing does not involve the interruption of physical laws but places spiritual ones into operation. Healing takes place when the mind embraces a new reality. Physical and mental healing takes place with prayer and change of belief. Christian Scientists, Mormons, and Jehovah's Witnesses all practice a variant of faith healing that emphasizes the importance of a change in thinking in order to enjoy a change in physical or mental health. Evans's belief in New Thought philosophy apparently lasted her entire life. As late as 1950, a sermon Evans rendered at an Ash Wednesday service at Cosmopolitan reflected the tradition. Each person "must know thyself," she asserted. "[L]ife means not what happens to us but the attitude that we take about it. We can change our lives."[69]

The institution of faith healing services increased Cosmopolitan's membership and diversified the church's composition from an almost entirely middle-class congregation to a congregation composed of some poor and working-class blacks. This seems to have been a key intent of Evans. Although located within the Black Belt, Cosmopolitan was on Wabash Avenue, in a neighborhood one WPA worker described as a "large quiet residential section which is unmolested by the clang of passing street cars, the noise of railroad trains, the exciting traffic of the boulevard, and the turmoil that might come by the rush to or from business houses."[70] The middle-class congregation of Cosmopolitan Community Church reflected the surrounding quiet residential neighborhood. It did not, however, reflect the highest aims of the Community Church Movement. Although community churches maintained no creed, their philosophy was that each church be "non-sectarian, broadly humanitarian, serving all the people."[71] And unlike its sister church, Metropolitan Community Church, on South Park Boulevard, Cosmopolitan was not representative of "all the people." The institution of the Quiet Hour began to change that. Not only did church membership increase in the late 1930s, but more of the city's poor found their way to the church. And the contention by Evans that the new "poorer people" of her church were not like those drawn to Lucy Smith's church was more likely a pejorative judgment than a statement of fact. Presumably, the poor congregants of Cosmopolitan Community church were similarly poor to those members of All Nations Pentecostal, with similar worship tastes. That would help explain why they were attracted to the two ostensibly different churches. Also, Mary Evans, like so many other black ministers during the migration era, made programmatic changes both to attract new migrants and to reflect the social changes happening as a consequence of the migration. Evans realized the imperative of outreach to poor and working-class blacks during these years and the extent to which the religious culture had become dominated by their needs and religious sensibilities. (Although she was a woman of "refined" emotional display, she imputed certain programmatic changes deemed necessary to attract a "following made from every walk of life.") Though the format that faith healing took at Cosmopolitan Community Church may have differed from what many poor and working-class blacks would have been used to, they would have recognized the belief in faith healing as an aspect of their own religious tradition.[72]

The distinction Mary Evans made between her practice of faith healing for the kind of poor people who attended her church and the practice of faith healing offered to those who attended Smith's church raises some important questions about the two women and their pastorates. To what extent were Smith and Evans aware of each other? Did they view themselves to be in competition? In what ways did each distinguish her ministry from the other's? How did they see themselves in relation to other women ministers of the day? On this last point, one thing is clear. (Although Chicago claimed other women preachers and a few women pastors other than Smith and Evans, the two women were by far the most prominent.) Other black women preachers were either local evangelists, including Reverend Dorothy Sutton Branch and Reverend Evelyn Hooks, or traveling evangelists and pastors of smaller "cult" bodies. A former actress, Reverend Pauline J. Coffee, held numerous revival services in Chicago in the 1930s and 1940s. An evangelist and associate of Aimee Semple-McPherson, the Los Angeles-based founder of the International Church of the Four Square Gospel, Coffee preached to large crowds in churches of differing denominations.[73] Bishop M. W. Hall (a woman) maintained a church on South State Street. Reverend Sadie B. Owens and Mother Naomi Bagby attracted small followings also on the South Side.[74] But Smith, as one WPA worker confirmed, was "the most widely known of all women pastors in Chicago," and clearly Evans felt some rivalry with her. Comments both women made regarding each other's programs of faith healing certainly suggest a level of uneasiness between them. "I don't think she is healing," Smith declared. "[H]er kind of services are altogether different, and my people would not understand her nor feel comfortable there." Evans's response was just as sharp. "L. S. [Lucy Smith] is a good woman, but she is ignorant—terribly ignorant and superstitious." She stated further, however, that Elder Smith deserved credit for "reaching a group of people that none of us can get to."[75]

rivalry

These comments belied a more amicable relationship between these women but show how Smith and Evans engaged in a type of theological and class analysis of their congregations. And in a curious way, the women agreed with each other's conclusions. Smith was convinced that her followers would not understand the educated Evans. Evans was convinced that Smith, with her vernacular style and southern ways, could reach a constituency few others could. Both perhaps overstated their cases in that the migration was rendering just this type of congregational class typology untenable, but it is important to recognize the extent to which both women responded in similar ways to the same process of social and demographic change. Their comments about each other demonstrated the degree of specificity with which each understood and attempted to reach their respective congregations.

Lucy Smith's doubts about Mary Evans's practice of faith healing centered primarily on its limited format, not on the practice itself or on Evans's intentions. The distinction she drew between Evans's practice and what she was doing at All Nations Pentecostal underscored an understanding that her approach to faith healing was a more complex phenomenon. Mary Evans offered healing services as a way primarily to increase her congregation and to diversify its class composition. Although Wednesday afternoon healing services attracted large crowds to All Nations, increasing attendance and membership was not the primary intent. More important, unlike Evans's approach to faith healing, which relied on thought to change perception of reality, Smith's belief in faith healing was rooted in the Pentecostal tradition. As a Pentecostal, she believed healing to be miraculous—a supernatural act of God. Further, instead of quiet reflection, divine healing at All Nations church required physical contact, *intimate* the "laying on of hands," according to the Scriptures. With this approach Smith claimed to heal the deaf, the blind, and "all sorts of lung trouble." She claimed to have healed more than two hundred thousand people in her lifetime. The basement of All Nations contained a "trophy room," which stored the canes and crutches of those who allegedly regained their ability to walk after Smith's touch (See figure 13.). She undoubtedly learned this tactic from the Stone Church, because William Piper was known to have a similar room.[76] But, for all the metaphysicality of Smith's approach to faith healing, her own testimony and testimonies from those who claimed recovery, suggest that—like Mary Evans's approach—it had its pragmatic element. It was ultimately an attempt to address and to ameliorate the real-world conditions of black Chicagoans.

Numerous interviews with Lucy Smith and observations of All Nations Pentecostal taken by WPA workers give a fairly exhaustive look into the life of the church. They detail the healing and other worship services, the membership, and the church's organizational structure. These sources

Fig. 13. All Nations Pentecostal Church. Women "saints" attend to church business in the sanctuary of the second All Nations Church on Oakwood Boulevard. The canes and crutches were abandoned by those who had been healed during one of the church's weekly healing services. Additional canes and crutches were kept in a place in the church basement called "the trophy room." (Source: Library of Congress)

have also divulged a wealth of information about the contribution of Smith and All Nations Church to the city's developing religious culture with regard to patterns of worship and music. The WPA workers seemed particularly fascinated with the divine healing services and provided accounts rich in detail. By all accounts, Wednesday night healing services began around 8:00 P.M. The choir of about one hundred mostly female voices sang about four songs, each "a little more infectious than the last," accompanied by piano and drum. After a brief message by Smith, those who had come for healing were called forward, where Smith and her all-female "co-workers," robed in white, attended to them, rubbing ailing spots with olive oil and praying audibly. As in most Pentecostal worship, the emotional tone of the services escalated to the point of frenzy. While the healing was taking place, the pianist, Edgar G. Holly, resumed what Fenton Johnson called "his jazzy hymn playing."[77] This served to further increase the intensity of the atmosphere. A WPA worker, Robert Lucas, vividly described the emotional climax.

The interminable number of verses and choruses was accompanied first by the patting of feet, the clapping of hands, and then ecstatic shouts, shoulders twitching and bodies swaying . . . following a crescendo of music and voices, the members leaped to their feet, threw both hands high over their heads and shouted "Thank you Jesus" over and over.

Lucas left this particular healing service with a promise to Smith that he would return. Other WPA workers were not so inclined. After witnessing a healing service in 1937, Dorothy Jones reported, "I left in a hurry—the All Nations Pentecostal Church was upsetting my equilibrium."[78]

Although WPA workers may have registered disquiet, those who regularly attended Smith's healing services or listened to her broadcasts were familiar with the emotional frenzy, ecstatic utterances, and exuberant music of All Nations by the late 1930s. Clearly, some people attended the healing services out of novelty, attracted to its spectacle, as in the case of a group of young white couples Robert Lucas observed, who took no part in the service "except financially," or the African-American woman who "calmly shelled and ate peanuts while she knelt (in prayer)." A wide range of Chicago citizens, however, irrespective of race or class, sought Smith's help in the apparent belief in her ability to help. WPA workers verified Smith's claim that "even poor whites" and immigrants came to receive help from her.[79] A man of Ukrainian descent made repeated trips to All Nations seeking relief from a ringing in his ear. When questioned by WPA workers on one of those occasions, he reported that he felt "some what better" but would return yet again. Asked how he learned of the church, he said that a "Swede" who told him that the faith healer had "made him okay" had recommended Smith to him. A white man known to attend healing services at All Nations regularly proclaimed to workers that Smith was "a wonderful woman," whose prayers for him had "helped some." Like many who consulted doctors before resorting to Smith, a young man about age twenty reported his healing to WPA workers, saying, "I had kidney trouble and I don't know, it got worse. The doctors said I didn't have a chance, but I didn't believe them."[80] These accounts testify to the high level of belief many Chicagoans had in Lucy Smith's ability to heal, and they were predicated on her unflinching belief in her own ability. Admonishing Samuel Strong during his series of interviews with her in the late 1930s, Smith asserted, "you should come to my church more often and witness how many hundreds of men and women I heal. All kinds of sores and pains of the body and of the mind. I heal with prayers. I just lay my hand on the troubled place and pray and it all goes away." The declaration reflected the impression Herbert Smith (no relation) penned a few years earlier, proclaiming Smith to be a "woman with deep human sympathies, who believes absolutely in her own power to help and to heal other people."[81]

Lucy Smith appealed to whites and ethnic minorities not only because of her offers of spiritual and material help but also because of her explicit interracialism. Smith first witnessed interracial worship when she joined the Stone Church in 1914. Presumably the rural Baptist church where she was "justified" at the age of twelve was exclusively African American, as were both Olivet and Ebenezer Baptist when she briefly affiliated with them between 1910 and 1912. She recalled that when she first walked into the Stone Church and saw blacks and whites worshiping together, it surprised her. Also, seeing that "everyone seemed happy," she concluded, "there must be something to it." The scene so impressed Smith that it served as the inspiration for her to name the church "All Nations."[82] In the same way that interracial worship was central to early Pentecostalism, interracialism became as predominant a theme in the life of All Nations as faith healing. In nearly all the interviews conducted with Smith throughout the late 1930s, the topic surfaced and sometimes with extended commentary. In 1935, Herbert Smith recorded what would become a mantra for Elder Lucy Smith: "This is not a colored church, but a church for all nations. . . . we has all kinds of people who comes here regularly. Swedes, Polish, Italians, just plain white folks, and Jews. . . . Everybody is welcome," she insisted.[83] Indeed, All Nations was actually even more racially and ethnically diverse than Elder Smith intimated. When Herbert Smith walked through the church for his research he also recognized what he thought to be Filipinos, Haitians, and two "full blooded American Indians." Cosmopolitan Community Church, by contrast, was predominately African American, with only a "few whites" as members. Although Smith's views on whites and ethnic minorities did not always reflect a high level of racial sophistication—she called whites "the other nation" and believed "Jews own everything"—she asserted that the racial mix of her church was "the only hope for Christianity."[84] One casual attendee of All Nations confirmed this view to WPA workers, "I think that they [All Nations Church] are interested chiefly in the integration of all races and religions."[85]

However, poor and working-class blacks, particularly southern migrants greatly outnumbered whites and ethnic minorities at All Nations. Smith's vernacular speech, her preaching style, and the church's frenzied worship services all struck a responsive chord. A migrant herself, Smith preceded the mass exodus out of the south by only a few years and started the All Nations Pentecostal Church at precisely the moment in Chicago when scores of fellow rural southerners began trekking to Chicago, bringing their southern religious sensibilities with them. Many southern migrants who joined All Nations were former Baptists like Smith, and they recognized her and her church as one of their own. As most members of All Nations were southerners, Smith evoked her own southern heritage on occasion as a source of both her popularity and her piety.[86] She also contrasted her own southern approachable style to other ministers in Chicago who, in her words, were "stuck up and live separated from the people." The healing services demonstrated that a wide range of Chicagoans were attracted to Smith and All Nations Pentecostal Church. But it was the growing numbers of black southern migrants, drawn by her vibrant religious worship and "easy informality" in language and manner, that made All Nations what Samuel Strong called "a legend on the South Side."[87]

inviting, non-elitist church

African American women provided the leadership in all major departments of All Nations Pentecostal Church, constituting what amounted to a female sacred world. Clear lines of authority and succession were defining aspects of this world. Smith functioned as sole pastor of All Nations Church and as "Overseer" of the All Nations General Convention. Her white-garbed women "Saints" served as her closest ministerial and administrative companions. She operated without an assistant pastor until she appointed her daughter Ardella as her successor in the late 1940s. Rebecca Porter, a family associate from Alabama was elevated to "subleader" by Smith largely because of Porter's remarkable preaching skills (See figure 14.). Although there were some male ushers, it is not clear if any of the male members of the church served as ministers during Smith's lifetime. Only upon her death, under the direction of Ardella, did men forthrightly assume clerical duties at All Nations. The highest-ranked male at All Nations was the minister of music, Edgar G. Holly, a Haitian who had left Tuskegee Institute for Chicago. ("I didn't want to study agriculture, I wanted to study art," he explained.) Elder Smith's twelve-year-old granddaughter, "Little Lucy," however, later replaced Holly. According to a survey taken at All Nations by WPA workers in the late 1930s, about 90 percent of All Nations women were married. "Quite a few," the report added, were between the ages of 50 and 60. Most, characteristically, were employed in domestic service. Smith's All Nations Pentecostal Church was, as Herbert Smith noted, "overwhelmingly feminine."[88]

Although Mary Evans apparently attempted to strike some gender balance at Cosmopolitan Community Church, the church under her leadership also constituted a female sacred world. The administration was drawn largely from a membership that was primarily female. All church stewards were male, the board of managers and the usher board at Cosmopolitan were divided evenly between men and women, and all other departments had at least one officer that was a woman.[89] Evans did not have an assistant pastor, which tended to substantiate the charge that she "ruled with an iron hand."[90] But she chose as her closest ministerial companions a number of other women preachers active in the city at the time, among them Evelyn Hooks, Noel Collins, and Dorothy Sutton

Fig. 14. Rebecca Porter and "Little Lucy." Although "sub-leader" to Elder Lucy Smith, Rebecca Porter was the primary preacher at All Nations Pentecostal Church. "Little Lucy" became the head musician at the church after Edgar G. Holly. She was also the pianist for the Lucy Smith Singers and a prominent member of the famed Roberta Martin Singers. (Source: Vivian G. Harsh Collection, Carter G. Woodson Regional Branch, Chicago Public Library)

Branch. A few of these women associates were expected to succeed Evans, but Evans never chose a successor. Although it is not clear to what extent the female sacred world Evans cultivated at Cosmopolitan also comprised poor and working-class women from the South, Evans's explicit outreach to southern migrants ensured that some would choose to join the church. Cosmopolitan Community Church was not "overwhelmingly feminine" in the same manner as All Nations Pentecostal, but it too was a place where women comprised the majority authority structure and developed a community that addressed women's particular concerns.

If poor and working-class black southern migrants were attracted to Smith because of her easy informality, southern roots, and vernacular preaching style, the associations Smith developed with middle-class blacks and ministers from mainline black Protestant churches attest to how pervasive Pentecostal-type worship became in Chicago during the migration era. These associations also show how complicated class had become in black Chicago churches, as well as the fluidity of church membership. A pastor of a middle-class black church told Miles Mark Fisher in the late 1930s, "If you want to see my folks (members) on a Sunday night, go to Elder Lucy Smith's."[91] Allan Spear's assertion that Smith gathered her congregation from "the back streets of Chicago" and Drake and Cayton's contention that she acquired the "intense hostility of the higher status members of the community" overstate the case.[92] Smith did have her detractors, including one railroad worker who called her a "damn nuisance."[93] But by the time Smith and her congregation were ensconced in their "modernistic" building on Oakwood Boulevard, the faith healer and radio preacher counted some of the city's most prominent ministers and citizens among her friends and supporters. Regular guests at annual banquets and special services at All Nations included Clarence Cobbs of First Church of Deliverance Spiritualist, Joseph H. Branham of Olivet Baptist, E. R. Williams of South Park Baptist, Louis Bodie of Greater Harvest Baptist, and Marjorie Stewart Joyner, a leading dignitary in black Chicago and a member of Cosmopolitan. Joyner, who presided over the Chicago Defender Charities for most of her long life, became one of All Nations Pentecostal's chief supporters, taking time from her responsibilities at Cosmopolitan and the *Chicago Defender* to aid in the work of Smith's church. She, along with alderman William L. Dawson (later a congressman), funeral director W. T. Brown, and Major Adam Patterson, a representative of Mayor Edward J. Kelley, assisted Smith at the ground breaking for the second All Nations Pentecostal building on Oakwood Boulevard.[94]

Contrary to depictions of black Chicago churches as divided by static class and denominational barriers, there was a fair amount of exchange between Lucy Smith, Mary Evans, and various congregations in black

Chicago. Reverend Joseph Evans (no relation) of Metropolitan Community Church (successor to William D. Cook) and J. C. Austin of Pilgrim Baptist, for example, made repeated visits to All Nations throughout the late 1930s and 1940s. Austin's friendship with Smith and her family grew to the extent that he was called on to deliver the eulogy for Smith's son, William, Jr., in 1952.[95] Many of these same ministers also developed relationships of church exchange with Mary Evans. And although written accounts of church exchange between All Nations and Cosmopolitan have yet to surface, it is not untenable. As "Little Lucy" Smith Collier contended about the two women pastors, perhaps slightly overstating the case, "they were good friends." Lucy Smith summarized her relationship with mainline Protestant churches to Herbert Smith as early as 1935. Explaining first that the "kicks" had come from the "Holiness People" who "don't care for a woman leading a work," Lucy Smith proclaimed, "I been to mighty near all de churches. Dem few I ain't been to—it's because I been busy, not because they haven't asked me. They all recognizes me."[96]

Many middle-class blacks and ministers of mainline black Protestant churches that recognized Lucy Smith did so in acknowledgment of the pervasive power and mass appeal of her congregation's frenzied emotional worship style. But by the late 1930s, Smith's popularity by way of her radio program, *The Glorious Church of the Air*, would have made her difficult to avoid. Black preachers had been on the radio since 1924, but beginning in 1933, Smith was the first black Chicago preacher to broadcast live worship over the radio.[97] Reverend Clarence Cobbs of First Deliverance Spiritualist Church followed with his own broadcast within a short time. But it was Smith who held undisputed rule over the airwaves for two decades, using three different stations: WIND, WSBC, and WGES.[98]

Although it would be difficult to establish a direct causal link between the time of Smith's broadcast, her exceeding popularity among black Chicagoans, and the phenomenal growth of her church, it is clear that there is at least some relationship among these factors. When *The Glorious Church of the Air* first appeared in 1933, the migration of southern blacks had swelled Chicago's black population to nearly a quarter million. Though illiteracy among southern migrants fell precipitously throughout the 1930s, many southern migrants remained illiterate and turned to radio rather than print media. Radio ownership (and presumably listenership) skyrocketed during the 1930s. By 1936, one in four Chicago southern migrant families owned a radio, compared with one in fifty families in the South. The black press did not do so well. Indeed, a number of longstanding Chicago African American newspapers were forced to cease publication, and even the vaunted *Chicago Defender* lost circulation. The perception that radio was for the poor and working-class whereas newspapers were a middle-class indulgence affected sales and readership.[99] When many of

Chicago's newest citizens first heard Lucy Smith's "unschooled speech," claims to heal, and the lively worship of All Nations, they recognized something familiar. Smith, for her part, appropriated radio's potential to further her ministry and social programs. She made requests over the air not only for the financial support of the broadcast itself, but also for the church's new building and for the Thursday charitable distributions. Like her mainstream counterparts, Smith developed relationships with area black businesses, calling on them specifically for contributions of food and clothing.[100] By the late 1930s, the midnight broadcasts of *The Glorious Church of the Air* were a Bronzeville staple, and a cavalcade of "saints," "seekers" and sightseers made their way to Oakwood Boulevard to take part. As the *Chicago Defender* columnist and Mississippi native Earl Calloway remembered, "it was the thing to do."[101]

In addition to broadcasting a southern religious worship style over the radio, *The Glorious Church of the Air* provided a principal means by which black gospel was spread to a mass audience in Chicago. Having been introduced to mainline African American churches by Thomas A. Dorsey just a year before Elder Smith's program first aired, black gospel music had already begun to alter the tone of religious worship in black churches throughout Chicago. Smith's radio worship promoted the new style of black sacred music, and many radio listeners, as a 1952 news release claimed, "kept up with the latest song hits from Sister Lucy's church just as they did with juke box favorites." With a choir of one hundred voices, various soloists, and ensembles like the Lucy Smith Singers, by the late 1930s "the church [was] known all over the city for its singing." As Lucy Smith herself contended, the music of All Nations had "swing to it."[102] All Nations' music actually raised as much curiosity and response from University of Chicago students and WPA workers as the frenzied worship and "divine healing" services. Reactions, though, were mixed. "One of the most interesting features about this church is the band," one worker wrote, "the music has all the earmarks of a jazz band." Herbert Smith dismissed the black gospel he heard at All Nations as "jazz, savage and imperious," at a time when jazz music had not reached legitimacy as a musical genre nor was it deemed the music of "respectable" people. After his initial visit to the church and in response to the broadcast, the African American poet Fenton Johnson, however, simply exclaimed, "what music!" Johnson, a native of Chicago, found work with the WPA after his early success as a writer and magazine editor had begun to fade. (He would later disparage his time with the program in a poem entitled, "The W.P.A. Worker"). Born in 1888 to a prominent family on State Street, Fenton had shown all the marks of a member of Chicago's "Negro elite," even becoming one of the first black youths to own an automobile. Religion, however, emerged, as a central theme in many of Johnson's early poems, and he seemed to hold a particular fondness for rural religion. He celebrated this fondness in a poem called "The Banjo Player," the first line of which reads "There is music in me, the music of a peasant people."[103] In the same way that she understood the potential of radio to bolster her own programs, Lucy Smith recognized the power of radio to reach the masses. When told by Samuel Strong that he had recently heard her broadcast over the radio, Smith interrupted, "my services are getting to be known among all people, all over."[104]

Like other aspects of All Nations Pentecostal Church, the proliferation of live broadcasts of Pentecostal worship and of black gospel radio were barometers of religious transformation. (They were signal features of a new sacred order, and in many ways Lucy Smith was just as much a product of that religious transformation as she was an agent of it.) The liberty afforded her by the new openness of the urban environment and a democratized religious culture allowed her to work as a woman in what many in the established denominations still considered men's work. Primarily this work involved establishing church programs designed to help poor black Chicagoans in particular face the challenges of urban life. Though Mary Evans maintained a different theological persuasion, the cultural dominance of a southern black religious sensibility compelled her to respond in similar ways to the same process of social and demographic change. The great differences between their congregational sizes indicate that Lucy Smith resonated with black Chicagoans in a way that Mary Evans did not. Smith's congregation peaked at five thousand by the late 1940s, whereas Cosmopolitan Community Church retained a membership of eight hundred to a thousand in 1949. But the way that Mary Evans instituted faith healing, charitable outreach to the poor, and (much later) black gospel music into the programs of Cosmopolitan acknowledged the necessary shift in institutional priorities faced by many black Chicago churches during the migration era.

Lucy Smith and Mary Evans predicated the relevance of the female sacred worlds they constructed on the degree to which they incorporated the religious inclinations of poor and working-class blacks into the worship of their respective congregations. Faced with the challenges posed by the broad demographic and social changes of the migration era, they also sought to address the practical needs of black southerners. Their efforts constituted the signature features of black Chicago's new sacred order, indicating the important role of black preaching women in the reconfiguration of the African American religious culture. Working unrestrained by their gender, both women rooted their authority as pastors in their capacity for leadership and in an increasingly open and diverse urban religious culture in black Chicago.

AFTER ELDER LUCY SMITH died in her home on South Parkway following a brief illness in 1952, her funeral became one of the largest in the history of black Chicago. It was nothing short of phenomenal. Arguably, not since the race riots of 1919 had an event captivated the minds of so many black Chicagoans and elicited such an outpouring of emotion. Sixty thousand people made their way to view the body, which lay in state for two days at the A. A. Rayner Chapel on Cottage Grove Avenue. Four hundred policemen had been assigned by the city to maintain order at the funeral home. The All Nations Pentecostal Church, where the funeral services were held, was filled to capacity. Many thousands more mourners spilled onto the streets in the surrounding neighborhood on Oakwood Boulevard. Elder Smith's three surviving children, Ardella, John, and Henry received more than four thousand letters of condolence, including ones from Governor Adlai Stevenson, Mayor Martin H. Kennelly, and Congressman William L. Dawson. The honorary pallbearer list read like a who's who of black Chicago's politicians and civic leaders. Among the twenty-eight listed were Wendell Green, Duke Slater, Ralph Metcalfe, Claude A. Barnett, Earl B. Dickerson, Kinzie Bueitt, and Corneal Davis. Most of the city's prominent black ministers attended the services. In addition to Reverend Archibald J. Carey, Jr., those in attendance included the Reverend Joseph H. Branham of Olivet Baptist, Reverend Clarence Cobbs of First Church of Deliverance, Reverend Mary G. Evans of Cosmopolitan Community Church, and Reverend Louis Bodie of Greater Harvest Baptist. Mahalia Jackson, who had sung on numerous occasions at Smith's church and on her broadcast, *The Glorious Church of the Air*, rendered a favorite of Smith's, "It's My Desire." The tune had been written by Thomas A. Dorsey, another frequent visitor to Smith's church. After the services, a one-hundred-year-old handmade horse-drawn hearse carried the black and gold casket to its interment at Lincoln Cemetery. The two white drivers of the hearse were dressed in high hats and frock coats. The processional was estimated at between seventy-five and one hundred and sixty-five cars long, including three flower limousines and eleven buses. All along the route, an estimated fifty thousand people lined the streets to pay final respects. Overcome by heat and emotion, several mourners fainted, requiring the attention of the dozens of nurses on duty. Others proclaimed their devotion, crying out Smith's name, as the cortege made its journey down South Parkway. (See figure 15.) At the gravesite, where cemetery workers broke a two-week strike to handle the burial, the

Fig. 15. Funeral of Lucy Smith. More than a hundred thousand Chicagoans, including some of the city's most prominent black citizens, attended Elder Smith's wake and funeral. It became the largest funeral in black Chicago history. (Source: Vivian G. Harsh Collection, Carter G. Woodson Regional Branch, Chicago Public Library)

Georgia native who had been so fundamentally a part of black Chicago's religious culture was laid to rest. Bedecked in white satin robes, kid slippers, and the open-face watch she cherished, Smith was placed beside the graves of her husband and several of her children who had preceded her in death.[1]

The death and funeral of Elder Lucy Smith signaled the apex of black Chicago's new sacred order. In the simplest terms, what happened on the occasion of her death would not have happened and could not have happened during the previous generation. And it was not merely because pre-migration-era Chicago did not have the population to stage such a massive scene. The response to Smith's passing indicated that tremendous changes had taken place among the black churches of the city during the first decades of the Great Migration. It was an acknowledgment across a vast cross-section of black Chicagoans that the city's African American religious culture had been dramatically transformed and that Smith had been a key figure in that transformation. Spectacular funerals for African American ministers were not uncommon even during Smith's lifetime. Lacey Kirk Williams's funeral in 1940 following his death in an airplane crash, for example, attracted a record-breaking crowd at Olivet Baptist. (It was also accompanied by a mysterious fire that broke out during the services. A few days after the conflagration, Harlem's Adam Clayton Powell, Jr., proclaimed that the fire had signaled God's retribution for Williams's alleged involvement in the murder of a Baptist colleague in 1930.)[2] But a significant part of the spectacle of Smith's funeral can be attributed to who she was and what she had become during her time in Chicago. The vast cross-section of citizens and civic leaders, which included representatives from local and state government, turned out to pay their respects to a simple woman with humble origins. Smith had claimed no education, not to mention a theological degree. She had actually disparaged higher education and made no pretense to theological astuteness. Her daughter, Ardella, asserted at the time of Smith's passing that Smith "preached faith without any theological definition or reasoning."[3] Smith was not from a prominent family. Although she amassed several properties over the years and was known to own a "big car," the South Side preacher did not possess great wealth. Rather, Elder Lucy Smith was the pastor of a Pentecostal church, a radio evangelist and faith healer from rural Georgia. From her pulpit she spoke in a down-home vernacular manner about simple matters of faith and trust. Her gospel was a puritanical one that divided the world into classes of saints and sinners. The working poor, primarily but not exclusively African American southern migrant women, populated the Pentecostal church she founded. "Divine healing" services were the heart of the church's ministry, and the music of All Nations was revivifying black gospel, sung at a fever pitch to evoke a frenzied emotional response. The grand display given on the occasion of Smith's funeral acknowledged her centrality in black Chicago church life and the cultural dominance of the working-class religion—the new sacred order that she had played a key role in instigating and that she had fully embodied.

As the life of Elder Lucy Smith attests, the Great Migration prompted the development of new urban religious practices and traditions among black Protestants that reflected both black southern religion and city life. These practices and traditions—particularly in the areas of music, worship, preaching, and social outreach—were rooted in the rural, folk culture of the South but became the very expression of modern African American religion in the urban North. Many African American southern migrants such as Lucy Smith established their own churches to reflect their folk religious sensibility. The vast majority of migrants, however, chose to affiliate with already-established Protestant churches and to infuse them with their own sense of religious worship and values. Indeed, the phenomenal growth, as well as the institutional and ritual transformation of mainstream African American Protestant churches to reflect a southern religious ethos, was the truest barometer of change during these years. Most Protestant churches exerted great effort in meeting the institutional challenges posed by the influx of black southerners. Those who did not sacrificed not only potential congregational growth but also prestige and relevancy. The African Methodist Episcopal Church in Chicago failed to come to terms with the degree to which black Protestant churches creatively and unambiguously responded to the needs of black southern migrants. With a few important exceptions, black Chicago AME churches resisted indications that a new dynamic religious culture had emerged and failed to understand that a church's interest in social change and its vitality as a religious institution depended on a systematic and positive response to it. The congregational growth of AME churches, therefore, paled in comparison with Baptist churches during the same period. By and large, most African American Protestant churches across denominational lines became a part of this new sacred order, contributing to a richly dynamic and pluralistic religious culture. In the tension between southern and northern, rural and urban, past and present emerged a reconception of the very notion of black religion.

The first and most obvious change to the African American religious scene in Chicago was the phenomenal growth of Protestant congregations. Many of these churches across a wide spectrum of denominations experienced previously unimaginable growth. Although not all of these churches fully jettisoned prejudicial ideas about the South and black southerners, they developed programs that appealed to migrants and, in the case of Olivet Baptist, actively recruited new arrivals. The increased membership often taxed the resources of these congregations, most of which were still able to offer a full range of social and ministerial services including day care, kindergarten, literacy programs, employment bureaus, and housing services. Social service became so integral to the work of many of these churches that they employed full-time professional social workers, usually single black women from middle-class families. The churches most likely to take this step were also those that were inclined to develop close relationships with black businesses in the effort to encourage self-help among all black Chicago citizens.

The transformation did not stop at congregational growth. Black southern migrants, who for the most part insisted on a frenzied emotionality in church services, significantly altered worship patterns that had been in place among black Chicago churches since the late nineteenth century. By the 1880s and 1890s, most of Chicago's twelve or so African American churches were decidedly middle-class and led exclusively by men, usually those who possessed a high level of theological education. Most of the congregational resources were devoted to erecting large impressive buildings and to undermining notions of black inferiority. Countering these notions became a critical concern for many blacks in the late nineteenth century in light of the spread of scientific racism. Emotional worship was abandoned for the way it reflected "African" traditions. In its place, Europeanized classical music became the most regularly performed music of most mainstream black Chicago churches. An influential religious establishment of middle-class professionals led the churches and crafted in their wake a homogeneous religious culture. By 1915, however, the influx of black southerners shifted the cultural influence in black Protestant churches to lower and working-class southern migrants. Some southern migrants started their own churches, usually highly innovative storefronts, but the vast majority aligned with mainstream congregations, complicating the way class and status operated in these churches. The diverse religious culture that emerged from the influx contrasted sharply with the African American ecclesial scene of the previous century.

Black southern migrants also insisted on sustaining their southern identities in Chicago, an insistence that underscored their status as a religious diaspora. Though residing in the urban North, few southern migrants lost touch with their home church communities; rather, they maintained close connections with their former congregations by way of letters, visits, and monetary support. A key aspect to the alienation many migrants registered with regard to Chicago's mainstream black churches reflected their sense of dispersion from churches in the rural South. This sense of dispersion generated a collectivity among southern migrants. It was not uncommon for migrants to join a particular church because the members were primarily from the same area in the South. Not only did churches migrate en masse, those who had migrated separately often gravitated toward churches populated by those from their hometown or state. In the same way that southern migrants were prone to affiliate with churches populated by those from their former areas, ministers used their regional identities to attract potential members to the churches they established. Many of the interviews recorded by WPA workers in the late 1930s and early 1940s indicate that black southerners considered southern churches superior to the ones they found in Chicago. With a striking regularity, black southerners compared Chicago's black churches with those from their home communities, finding the Chicago churches wanting. The perennial tension between southernness and urban life, or between southern identity and northern identity, underlay this discussion. As far as black southerners were concerned, Chicago churches could not match the social and spiritual intimacy of the South. Longtime Chicago residents, on the other hand, considered a southern identity as one of the primary deterrents to the development of what Richard Wright considered the "critical consciousness" necessary for urban existence.[4]

The interplay between black southern migrants and longtime Chicago residents comprised a key component to the city's new African American sacred order. That interplay, however, was only the surface expression of the deeper tensions between North and South, rural and urban, modern and premodern that characterized black religious culture during the migration era. Indeed, the new sacred order emerged from the nexus of those tensions. The larger implication drawn from the story of migration-era black Chicago churches is that there is a close, inextricable relationship between migration, urbanization, and religious change. And the process is reciprocal. City life had a profound impact on the development of black religion in Chicago, and black religion altered many aspects of the city. Storefront churches, for example, greatly altered the physical landscape of black Chicago. Located usually in commercial districts, these small churches infused the most ordinary city scenes with a bit of the transcendent. Another larger implication drawn from this story is that African Americans construct their religious expressions contextually, through social engagement and in relationship to shifting contexts. This understanding should complicate and expand the ways in which we conceptualize black religion. African American religion is perhaps the only part of the mosaic of American religion that is routinely locked tight into ahistorical abstractions—beyond human volition, agency, and social context. Seemingly, it just is and always has been. From this ahistoricism have emerged many false notions, including the "natural religiosity" of black people and the ethereal quality of black religion. It is seen as useful only to protest against or judge the moral lapses of white Christianity, or to serve as a retreat into private spirituality and escapism. However, what the story of migration-era black Chicago tells us is that institutional or "public religion" and even notions of the sacred were products of the adherents' own making. Indeed, this is partly what Lacey Kirk Williams had in mind when in 1929 he called for black churches that were "passionately human, but no less divine."[5]

An emphasis on human agency in the construction of black religion has been missing from many historical accounts of African American Protestant Christianity. That is due primarily to a pervasive resistance to a conception of African American religion that requires the active participation of its adherents in the shaping of religious traditions and ritual practices. Black religion has been seen as something that just happens, not something that is made and responsive to human action and social conditions. It is as if a conception of African American religion that centralizes human agency and social context would undermine its spiritual quality. Historical investigation into other areas of black American life, however, have not slighted human agency. Indeed, black agency in every epoch of African

American history, from slavery to the Great Migration, has been the analytical focus of black studies since the 1960s. It has been easier to notice the active participation of black Americans in the development of their social, cultural, and political lives than in their religious lives. But the story of migration-era black religion in Chicago shows that blacks were just as active in the self-conscious construction of their religious lives as they were in other areas. And one of the great advantages to recognizing the primacy of human agency in the construction of black religion in Chicago is that it challenges notions of otherworldliness. Few black Chicago churches during the migration era could have been rightfully characterized as otherworldly. A this-worldly focus predominated, even in churches where one would least expect it, because of the temporal demands of the mass movement. The material and spiritual needs of poor and working-class black Chicagoans, and the actions of those working in their favor, comprised the core of black Chicago's new sacred order. This religious pragmatism or neo–Social Gospelism signaled a reconception of black religion, born from the self-conscious action of thousands of black Chicagoans.

Recognizing the role of black religion in Chicago as a significant factor in the city's "cultural production" serves as another key advantage to emphasizing the primacy of social context and human agency. This cultural production was a key aspect of the working-class culture rooted in the experiences and expectations of ordinary black Chicagoans. During the first decades of the twentieth century, the very notion of blackness or black culture was being made—produced and commodified. It was taking shape in the areas of art, music, fashion, literature, politics, and enterprise. All along the corridors of State, Michigan, Dearborn, and South Parkway a dizzying array of black-owned commercial and cultural enterprises testified to the emergence of "black Chicago." Banks, insurance companies, newspapers, recording studios, literary clubs, grocery stores, nightclubs, barbershops, and beauty salons thrived on the South Side, making many of their proprietors wealthy. Madame C. J. Walker and Robert S. Abbott, for example, became two of the nation's premier African American millionaires. These establishments also earmarked the South Side as an identifiable, semiautonomous black space. Organizations such as Anthony Overton's Hygienic Manufacturing Company, Jesse Binga's bank, Supreme Liberty Life Insurance, Madame C. J. Walker's Cosmetics Company, Poro Beauty Products, Decca Records, and the Regal Theater rivaled Harlem's institutions for the way they gave shape to black cultural expression from the 1920s to 1940s.

Chicago's black churches emerged as major producers of this African American working-class culture. The incalculably large numbers of churches of every size and architectural configuration became an irrepressible part of the urban landscape. As Drake and Cayton declared,

"Sunday morning in Bronzeville [was] a colorful occasion."[6] Clustered primarily (but not exclusively) in poorer sections of the South Side, storefront churches in particular came to typify black churches in the city. The haggard handwritten signs, eclectic religious symbolism, even the crisp white dresses worn by the female "saints" represented black urban religion. Many of these churches displayed an unusual mixture of Catholic, Protestant, Eastern Orthodox, and Jewish iconography. Pictures of "Jesus of the Sacred Heart," the Virgin Mary, and the Star of David could be found in some congregations. In numerous photos taken by the FSA during the 1940s, Roberts Temple COGIC displayed a diverse array of religious iconography. Flashing red crosses lighted during services came into vogue and served as an example of how black Chicagoans literally appropriated aspects of modern life for ritual purposes. Churches as diverse as First Church of Deliverance, All Nations Pentecostal, and Cosmopolitan Community Church featured these crosses.[7]

The cult of personality surrounding some of the ministers of migration-era churches added to this eclectic mien of black urban religion and to its contribution to black cultural production. Many churches were known to operate as centers of entertainment as much as of worship. Former members of the First Church of Deliverance on Wabash Avenue remembered it as a major stop on the gay nightlife circuit in the 1930s and 1940s. The church welcomed gay people and Reverend Clarence Cobbs, along with many of his staff, was rumored to be gay. An African American gay male recalled that one prominent staff person was a "celebrity" during his years with Cobbs's church. "The fact that he worked for Rev. Cobbs," the man continued, "he was like a diva. He wore these fur coats." After attending the live broadcast at the church, which ran from 11:00 P.M. to midnight, club goers would simply walk from First Church of Deliverance to one of the area nightspots, usually the Kitty Kat Club, the Parkside, or the 430.[8] Many of these men were young and from the South and apparently drew little distinction between what occurred in First Church of Deliverance and what took place in the local gay clubs. Both were deemed safe (perhaps even sacred) spaces from which they received inspiration, community, and social acceptance.[9] Cobbs's acceptance of gays and his own apparent homosexuality confirm what George Chauncey has argued about New York during the same time. In the working-class world of the South Side, African American male homosexuals in Chicago—at least those associated with First Church of Deliverance—created a flourishing, conspicuous, and lively subculture long before the era of gay rights in the 1960s. It was a subculture practiced and "performed" in public, coded but public.[10]

The first code was silence. The fact that there is no record of Cobbs ever verbally claiming a homosexual identity serves as a key to understanding why he was able to be simultaneously obvious and invisible. Also, unlike his even more flamboyant Detroit contemporary, Prophet Jones, Cobbs never compromised his social standing; Jones was arrested (and acquitted) on morals charges in 1956. The extent to which we can argue that both men were closeted homosexuals, living veiled yet open lives, may suggest something crucial about working-class African American culture prior to the 1960s. As Tim Retzloff recently queried, "were middle-class African Americans more homophobic than working-class African Americans?" The answer is probably. Not only is homophobia a relatively recent development in African American culture, it also most likely emanated originally from among the black middle class, not the black working class, during the era of the 1960s.[11] In the context of a dynamic working-class African American urban religious culture, Cobbs and others who espoused nonconventional sexualities operated freely, seemingly with little rebuke or condemnation. His apparent silence about his sexual identity, however, was the price he paid for his high stature.

Many of the characteristic features of black gospel music, a key aspect of black Chicago's new sacred order, were developed in churches like Cobbs's First Church of Deliverance. Indeed, Cobbs has not been rightly appreciated for his role in significantly changing the sound of black gospel music. In addition to offering the largest choir in the city, First Church of Deliverance premiered the first Hammond organ, which went on to revolutionize black gospel all around the country in 1939.[12] Cobbs purchased it for his minister of music, Kenneth Morris, who would later claim, " I introduced the Hammond organ to Chicago and the world. . . . People came from all over just to hear me play that organ." Along with his duties as music minister at First Church of Deliverance, Morris composed, arranged, and published numerous gospel songs, which in turn contributed substantially to the popularity of Cobbs. Teaming with the gospel great Sallie Martin—a frequent visitor to Cobb's church—Morris formed the Martin and Morris Music Company in 1940, with Cobbs supplying the financial backing. The successful company published the works of many gospel artists such as Sam Cooke, William Brewster, Lucie Campbell, Raymond Rasberry, and Alex Bradford. Morris recalled in an interview conducted late in his life that several of his songs written in the 1940s put him and Martin "on the map." Their company garnered revenues and royalties of up to two hundred thousand dollars a year by the mid 1950s.[13]

The participation of black Chicago churches in the city's cultural production and the subsequent commodification of black religion bothered few people. Although not everyone would entirely agree with Cobbs that "the church is something like a business," there seemed to be an understanding that churches could participate in the market and that what emanated from the church could be marketed.[14] A realization that the "sacred" was a production contributed to this marketing of black religion. This was the vantage point from which Morris worked and Thomas Dorsey before him. Dorsey was the first gospel artist who took to the streets to sell the songs he had written. Both men built commercial empires from the production, performance, and sale of black gospel music. By 1948, Mahalia Jackson was the top-selling gospel artist in the country, having catapulted to stardom with a song composed by William Brewster, "Move On Up a Little Higher." With Morris on the Hammond organ, it sold more than fifty thousand copies in Chicago alone. It went on to sell over two million nationally and become the first of three million-selling recordings for Jackson in a two-year period.[15] Her success attracted the attention of secular artists who repeatedly (and unsuccessfully) wooed her to sing their songs and led to a popular radio and television show.[16] Jackson's career stood out far above the rest, but she was accompanied by dozens of soloists, choral groups, quartets, and gospel choirs who made a major impact on the cultural life of Chicago during the migration era. The work of these artists, along with the showmanship of such preachers as Lacey Kirk Williams, William D. Cook, J. C. Austin, Clarence Cobbs, and Rebecca Porter was so significant and influential as to suggest that the modern era of African American religion began in Chicago during the migration period.

The modern era of African American religion was forged in the complex nexus of North and South, rural and urban, and modern and premodern. Black southern migrants' confrontation with the urban North generated new expressions of black religion. These expressions came by way of their own initiatives and from the response rendered by many mainstream Protestant churches. With regard to the practice, representation, and performance of African American religion in Chicago, the Great Migration shifted the balance of cultural influence in favor of the thousands of poor and working-class migrants. Ralph Ellison's astute observation that "geography is fate" implies that geographic mobility leaves no person, group, institution, or cultural expression unchanged by that mobility. Indeed, the very expectation of a change in place can have a significant impact on an individual or group, as well as on the cultural institutions to which they belong. The Great Migration profoundly shaped the religious culture of black Chicago. Drawn from the tenacious elements of a religious expression born in the rural South, black southern migrants in participation with established, mainline Protestant churches created a uniquely urban religious culture. Geography is fate, and the city made all the difference. The demands and the challenges of the urban North prompted a reconceptualization of black faith during the migration era. St. Clair Drake captured the spirit of those times when he declared, "the city is a world of rapid change. . . . Such a tempo of life affects even religious behavior profoundly."[17]

Epilogue

THE CHURCH that I for many years called my home church still sits outside Washington, D.C. In recent years, it has built a larger and much grander edifice that literally adorns the lower-middle-class neighborhood in which it is situated. Because of its many years of service to the surrounding community, the church maintains a high status. The pastor, who as a boy conducted funerals for the dead animals on his family's farm, has also increased in stature. Not only is he a dominant force in the Free Will Baptist Conference, local officials and civic leaders also seek his sanction and support for their initiatives. Countless men and women have become ministers under his direction, and many of those have started their own churches. His seemingly endless responsibilities as General Bishop of the Free Will Baptist Conference and head pastor of two large churches afford him little time for rest. He has become an important and busy man.

The congregation of Faith Temple No. 2 has changed in many ways. Although poor and working-class folks still comprise the majority, a greater number of middle- and professional-class blacks have become members. Although the congregation is still not rich, the fine apparel on display during the parade to the offering plate more accurately reflects the economic status of many of them. Some of these are the second- and third-generation progeny of the original migrant congregation. Many of the original members still attend the church, including the woman with the "diamond shoes." Some have joined a wave of outmigration back to the South. Others have died. The second and third generation have less direct experience with their southern heritage, but the southern ethos in the church has remained strong. Many in the congregation continue to embrace a southern identity, and the reciprocal relationships with congregations in the South have only intensified. The church thrives and the memory of the South still lingers among a people who left it for the urban Upper South decades ago.

The years have not been so kind to many migration-era black Chicago churches. Since the high point of the 1950s, their stories have been one of declension: decreased membership, physical decay, and demolition. Olivet Baptist, once hailed as "the largest Protestant church of any race in the world," claims an aging congregation of a few hundred. Pilgrim Baptist has become popular on the tourist circuit because of its pivotal role in developing black gospel music, but it too maintains a small congregation of mostly elderly members. The tour buses that bring dozens of people each week—many of them foreign nationals visiting the U.S.—to sit in the balcony and watch the services are a sad reminder of a time gone by. Although registered as a historic landmark, Quinn Chapel has been all but abandoned in an area of the South Side that is seemingly populated by more vacant lots than people. The oldest black church in Chicago—from whose pulpit spoke the likes of Booker T. Washington, Rabbi Emil G. Hirsch, Jane Addams, and American presidents William McKinley, Theodore Roosevelt, and Howard Taft—sits in physical decay. A plaque outside the church commemorating a visit by Martin Luther King, Jr., in the 1960s is also emblematic of a bygone era, and both Olivet and Quinn appear mere shells of their former grandeur.

Many of the churches have been razed and others have been threatened with that fate. The original Olivet building at Twenty-seventh and Dearborn, designed by J. M. Higginbotham, was demolished in 1941 and the lot remains vacant. A few blocks away at Thirtieth and Dearborn, Allen Temple AME Church has also been bulldozed. As the original Bethel AME Church building, the church hosted numerous important events during the late nineteenth and early twentieth centuries: Ida B. Wells and Claude A. Barnett married there in 1895. Theodore Roosevelt spoke to a packed house in 1912 on the eve of his defeat for the Republican presidential nomination. Frederick Douglass, Amanda Smith Berry, and the explorer Matt Henson complete a list of black notables who also addressed the congregation. Following two years of bitter infighting by the congregation, the east wall of All Nations Pentecostal Church mysteriously collapsed. A subsequent inspection found nothing faulty in the church's construction and could not explain the mishap. Since the congregation had split over disagreements with Elder Lucy Smith's successor, Ardella Smith, the building was torn down. Only a mound of earth and a few bricks where the front stairs had been remain as reminders of the Pentecostal empire Smith built.

Depopulation and racial transitioning are key factors in the decline of many migration-era black churches. Beginning with the land-clearance initiative of the late 1930s, the decreased housing stock on the South Side has scattered the black community, including many of those who had been members of various local churches. The decision to build public housing projects in areas that had once contained a thriving commercial base also had a deleterious impact on local religious institutions. The wave of blacks who have relocated to the Chicago suburbs in the past two decades has also decreased church membership. And the rise of black congregations in those suburbs has made it difficult, if not impossible, for former members of the flagship congregations to remain faithful to the historic churches. Many of these churches sit as fading, yet glorious reminders of a time of dynamic religious transformation in black Chicago.

A new generation of post-1950s black churches has emerged to take their place. This new generation of black churches belongs to a new era of black religion in Chicago, an era that deserves its own study. It is an era that has been more explicitly committed to civil rights, community action, black power, and Afrocentrism. Reverend Clay Evans founded the Fellowship Baptist Church in 1958, and in 1965 he helped Jesse Jackson start Operation PUSH. He and his church have long been on the forefront of civil rights in Chicago and around the nation. Reverend Dr. Johnnie Coleman is reminiscent of both Mary G. Evans and Elder Lucy Smith. Like Evans, Coleman espouses New Thought philosophy, believing that changing one's thoughts can change one's life. She has devoted her entire ministry to teaching people how to live better lives. Like Smith, Coleman heads a large and vibrant congregation. Christ Universal Temple, which she founded in 1956, reportedly has nearly twenty thousand members. Dr. Arthur M. Brazier serves a church almost as large as Coleman's. His Apostolic Church of God has more than eighteen thousand members. In addition to his duties as pastor, Brazier heads the Woodlawn Organization and the Fund for Community Redevelopment and Revitalization. Reverend Dr. Jeremiah A. Wright has been pastor of Trinity Church of Christ since the early 1970s. A community leader and activist, Wright has presided over a phenomenal growth in the congregation's size. His belief that black churches should be Afrocentric is reflected in Trinity's motto: "Unashamedly Black and Unapologetically Christian."

The music in the churches of the new generation is the same revivifying black gospel. The sermons are usually conducted in the African American tradition of call-and-response. Many black Chicago preachers still rely on the "mixed-type" format, combining text with the extemporaneous. And even though the institutional priorities have changed to reflect the changing times, social service is deemed central to the work of these churches. The worship patterns and the civic involvement of black Chicago churches is now historic. One only hopes that this new generation realizes that it was built on the foundation of a new sacred order that was established during the Great Migration.

Notes

PREFACE

1. John A. Davis and Cornelius L. Golightly, "Negro Employment in the Federal Government," *Phylon* 6 (4th Qtr. 1945): 337–346; John Hope II and Edward E. Shelton, "The Negro in the Federal Government," *Journal of Negro Education* 32 (Autumn 1963): 367–374; August Meier and Elliott Rudwick, "The Rise of Segregation in the Federal Bureaucracy, 1900–1930, *Phylon* 28 (2 Qtr. 1967): 178–184.
2. Limmie Nathaniel Forbes, General Bishop of the Free Will Baptist Conference, Pastor of Faith Temple Nos. 1 and 2 Freewill Baptist Churches, telephone interview with author Harvard University, 19 December 2003.

INTRODUCTION

1. John Hope Franklin and Alfred A. Moss, Jr., *From Slavery to Freedom: A History of Negro Americans*, 6th ed. (New York: McGraw-Hill, 1988), 53; Ira Berlin, *Many Thousands Gone: The First Two Centuries of Slavery in North America* (Cambridge, Mass.: Harvard University Press, 1998), 29: Eugene G. Genovese, *Roll Jordon Roll: The World the Slaves Made* (New York: Vintage Books, 1972); Orlando Patterson, *Rituals of Blood: The Consequence of Slavery in Two American Centuries* (Washington, D.C.: Civitas/Counter Point, 1998); James Oakes, *Slavery and Freedom: An Interpretation of the Old South* (New York: Vintage, 1991).
2. Albert J. Raboteau, "African-Americans, Exodus, and the American Israel," in *A Fire in the Bones: Reflections on African American Religious History* (Boston: Beacon, 1995), 17–36; Albert J. Raboteau, *Slave Religion: The 'Invisible Institution' in the Antebellum South* (New York: Oxford University Press, 1978), 312; Eddie S. Glaude, Jr., *Exodus! Religion, Race, and Nation in Early Nineteenth-Century Black America* (Chicago: University of Chicago Press, 2000).
3. Richard Wright, *12 Million Black Voices* (reprint, New York: Thunder's Mouth, 1988), 93.
4. Ralph Ellison, *Going to the Territory* (New York: Random House, 1980), 133.
5. The most definitive works on the Great Migration remain those that were written during the 1980s. They include James R. Grossman, *Land of Hope: Chicago, Black Southerners and the Great Migration* (Chicago: University of Chicago Press, 1989); Carol Marks, *Farewell—We're Good and Gone: The Great Black Migration* (Bloomington: Indiana University Press, 1989); Peter Gottlieb, *Making Their Own Way: Southern Blacks' Migration to Pittsburgh, 1916–1930* (Urbana: University of Illinois Press, 1987); Joe William Trotter, Jr., *Black Milwaukee: The Making of an Industrial Proletariat, 1915–1945* (Urbana: University of Illinois Press, 1985). The excellent exhibit, "Field to Factory," developed by the Smithsonian Institution in

Washington, D.C., made its first appearance in 1987. Studies that have appeared since the 1990s include Nicholas Lemann, *The Promised Land: The Great Black Migration and How It Changed America* (New York: Knopf, 1991); Joe William Trotter, Jr., ed., *The Great Migration in Historical Perspective: New Dimensions in Race, Class, and Gender* (Bloomington: Indiana University Press, 1991); Victoria W. Wolcott, *Remaking Respectability: African American Women in Interwar Detroit* (Chapel Hill: University of North Carolina Press, 2001); Kimberley L. Phillips, *AlabamaNorth: African-American Migrants, Community, and Working-Class Activism in Cleveland, 1915–1945* (Urbana: University of Illinois Press, 1999). A few of the best documentary films done on the Great Migration have been: *The Promised Land*, (Morgan Freeman and Nicholas Lemann, 1995); *By River, by Rail*, (Terry Tadesco, Maya Angelou, Jacob Lawrence, et al. 1994); *Moving North to Chicago* (Felice McGlincy, 1991); and *Up South: African-American Migration in the Era of the Great War* (Andrea Ades Vosquez, Pennee Bondee and Joshua Brown, 1996).

6. I am aware that notions of "the folk," as Robin D. G. Kelley has brilliantly explained, are "socially constructed and contingent." There is nothing self-evident about the folk, nor does it represent some unreconstructed notion of that which is authentic about black life. I am, however, using the term both to work within its contingent nature and to subvert the same. As Kelley claims, "'folk' and 'modern' are both mutually dependent concepts embedded in unstable historically and socially constituted systems of classification. In other words, 'folk' has no meaning without 'modern.'" On the one hand the mutual contingency of the terms "folk" and "modern" does not deprive them of all meaning in themselves. On the other hand, given a particular context and ideological point of origin, the distinction between the two could be fuzzy at best. See Robin D. G. Kelley, "Notes on Deconstructing 'The Folk,'" *American Historical Review* 97 (December 1992): 1400–1408.

7. Mircea Eliade, *The Sacred and the Profane: The Nature of Religion* (1957; reprint, New York: Harcourt, Brace, 1987), 10–11. For other analyses of Eliade's view of the sacred and profane, see Randall Studestill, "Eliade, Phenomenology, and the Sacred," *Religious Studies* 36 (June 2000): 177–194; William W. Quinn, "Mircea Eliade and the Sacred Tradition (A Personal Account)," *Nova-Religio* 3 (October 1999): 147–153; and Bryan S. Rennie, *Reconstructing Eliade: Making Sense of Religion* (Albany, N.Y.: SUNY Press, 1996).

8. Emile Durkheim, *The Elementary Forms of Religious Life*, Joseph Ward Swain, trans. (1915; reprint, New York: Free Press, 1965), 52–54. For discussions of Durkheim's philosophy of religion, his notion of the sacred, and *Elementary Forms*, see Donald A. Nielsen, "Transformations of Society and the Sacred in Durkheim's Religious Sociology," *Blackwell Companion to Sociology of Religion* (Oxford, U.K. and Malden, Mass.: Blackwell, 2001): 120–132; W. S. F. Pickering, Willie Watts-Miller, and N. J. Allen, *On Durkheim's Elementary Forms of Religious Life* (London: Routledge, 1998); William E. Paden, "Before 'the Sacred' Became Theological: Rereading the Durkheim Legacy," *Method and Theory in the Study of Religion* 3 (1991): 10–23; Robert A. Segal, "Interpreting and Explaining Religion: Gertz and Durkheim, *Soundings* 71 (Spring 1998): 29–52.

9. Karen E. Fields, "Translator's Introduction: Religion as an Eminently Social Thing," in Emile Durkheim, *Elementary Forms of Religious Life*, Karen E. Fields, trans. (1915; reprint, New York: Free Press, 1995), xlvi.

10. Arthur H. Fauset, *Black Gods of the Metropolis: Negro Cults of the Urban North* (Philadelphia: University of Pennsylvania Press, 1944); Joseph R. Washington, *Black Cults and Sects* (Garden City, N.Y.: Doubleday, 1972); Erdmann Doane Beynon, "The Voodoo Cult among Negro Migrants in Detroit," *American Journal of Sociology* 43 (May 1938): 894–907; Ira de A. Reid, "Let Us Prey," *Opportunity* 4 (September 1926): 274–278; Miles Mark Fisher, "Organized Religion and the Cults," *Crisis* 44 (January 1937): 8–10, 29–30.

11. Two historians, Lawrence Levine and Evelyn Brooks Higginbotham, have written about African American religious modernity in a similar way. Lawrence Levine, *Black Culture and Black Consciousness: Afro-American Folk Thought from Slavery to Freedom* (New York: Oxford University Press, 1978), 179–180; Evelyn Brooks Higginbotham, "'Out of the Age of Voice': The Black Church and Discourses of Modernity" (a paper delivered at the Conference on the Black Public Sphere in the Era of Reagan and Bush, University of Chicago, October 14, 1993); Evelyn Books Higginbotham, "Rethinking Vernacular Culture: Black Religion and Race Records in the 1920s and 1930s," in Wahneema Lubiano, ed., *The House that Race Built* (New York: Vintage, 1998), 165. See also Houston A. Baker, Jr., *Blues Ideology, and Afro-American Literature: A Vernacular Theory* (Chicago: University of Chicago Press, 1984); Henry Louis Gates, Jr., *The Signifying Monkey: A Theory of African American Literary Criticism* (New York: Oxford University Press, 1988).

12. Levine, *Black Culture and Black Consciousness*, 5.

13. St. Clair Drake, "Churches and Voluntary Associations in the Chicago Negro Community" (report of Official Project 465-54-3-386, conducted under the auspices of the Works Progress Administration, Chicago, December, 1940), 6–7.

14. Although the concept of "otherworldly" black churches reaches back to scholarship of the nineteenth century, the depiction began in earnest with the work of Benjamin Mays and Joseph W. Nicholson in the 1930s. Mays and Nicholson concluded that the worship and preaching in most black churches in both the North and South tended to be of an otherworldly nature. These churches were concerned with the hereafter—so much so that "practical aspects of life are secondary or submerged." More emphasis was placed on the mysterious, the magical, and heaven than on "daily living." They found that more than 50 percent of the sermons they documented were otherworldly, where as by contrast only 6 percent even mentioned the extant Depression. See Benjamin E. Mays and Joseph Nicholson, *The Negro's Church* (New York: Institute of Social and Religious Research, 1933), 59.

15. Walter Rauschenbusch, *A Theology for the Social Gospel* (New York: Abingdon, 1960); Washington Gladden, *Applied Christianity: Moral Aspects of Social Questions* (New York: Arno, 1976); Social Salvation (Hickville, N.Y.: Regina, 1975); Donald K. Gorrell, *The Age of Social Responsibility: The Social Gospel in the Progressive Era, 1900–1920* (Macon, Ga.: Mercer University Press, 1988); Ronald C. White and C. Howard Hopkins, *The Social Gospel: Religion and Reform in Changing America* (Philadelphia: Temple University Press, 1976); Charles Howard Hopkins, *The Rise of the Social Gospel in American Protestantism, 1865–1915* (New Haven: Yale University Press, 1967); Robert T. Handy, ed., *The Social Gospel in America, 1870–1920* (New York: Oxford University Press, 1966).

16. Norman W. Spaulding, "The History of Black Oriented Radio in Chicago, 1929–1963" (Ph. D. diss., University of Illinois, 1981), 10. See also Curt Johnson and R. Craig Sautter, *Wicked City of Chicago: From Kenna to Capone* (Chicago: December, 1994); Donald L. Miller, *City of the Century: The Epic of Chicago and the Making of America* (New York: Simon and Schuster, 1996); A. T. Andreas, *History of Chicago* (New York: Arno, 1975); Bessie Pierce, *A History of Chicago* (New York: Knopf, 1937); William Kenney, "Chicago's 'Black and Tans'" *Chicago History* 26 (1997): 4–31; Claudia Cassidy "The Years of Splendor: Chicago's Music and Theater," *Chicago History* 2 (1972): 4–13; Ralph Pugh, "Chicago's Theater," *Chicago History* 30 (2001): 36–59; Mark H. Haller, "Policy Gambling, Entertainment, and the Emergence of Black Politics: Chicago from 1900–1940," *Journal of Social History* 24 (1991): 719–739; Lewis A. Erenberg, "Ain't We Got Fun?" *Chicago History* 14 (1985–1986): 4–21; Thomas J. Schlereth "A Robin's Egg Renaissance: Chicago Culture, 1893–1933," *Chicago History* 8 (1979): 144–155.

17. *Mahalia: The Power and the Glory*, Scheftel/Taylor Productions, 1997; Timuel Black, telephone interview with author Princeton University, 20 March 2003; Gayle Wald, "From Spirituals to Swing: Sister Rosetta Tharpe and Gospel Crossover," *American Quarterly* 55 (September 2003); Daniel Wolff, S. R. Crain, Clifton white, and G. David Tenenbaum, *You Send Me: The Life and Times of Sam Cooke* (New York: William Morrow, 1995).

18. Spaulding, "History of Black Oriented Radio," 106.

19. St. Clair Drake quoted C. Luther Fry, who in his report on religion to a committee on social trends stated, "since 1900 the church has been forced to compete more and more with an ever increasing number of secular agencies and activities." Drake affirmed this statement, suggesting that secularization was a natural consequence of urban life and that the categories of "sacred" and "secular" were reified in the urban context. He drew his thinking from Robert Park and his theory on rationality and the city. See Drake, "Churches and Voluntary Associations," 11.

20. W. E. B. Du Bois, *The Souls of Black Folk* (New York: New American Library, 1969), xi. Du Bois quote found in Mason Stokes, "Someone's in the Garden with Eve: Race, Religion, and the American Fall," *American Quarterly* 50 (1998): 718.

21. Allan H. Spear, *Black Chicago: The Making of a Negro Ghetto, 1890–1920* (Chicago: University of Chicago Press, 1967); St. Clair Drake and Horace Cayton, *Black Metropolis: A Study of Negro Life in a Northern City* (reprint, Chicago: University of Chicago Press, 1993), 430. In 1929 the *Chicago Whip* started a similar campaign, "don't spend your money where you can't work."

22. Drake, "Churches and Voluntary Associations," 163.

23. Neil R. McMillen, *Dark Journey: Black Mississippians in the Age of Jim Crow* (Urbana: University of Illinois Press, 1990), 259; Simon Kuznets, and Dorothy Swaine Thomas Thomas, *Population Redistribution and Economic Growth, United States, 1870–1950*, vol. 1 (Philadelphia: American Philosophical Society, 1957), 74–90; Spear, *Black Chicago*, 139.

24. Richard S. Hobbs, *The Cayton Legacy: An African American Family* (Pullman: Washington State University Press, 2002), 114; *Bulletin of the Society for Social Research*; Horace Cayton, Statement to the U.S. Congressional Committee on Interstate Migration, Chicago Hearing, August 1940, box 34, folder 8, Special Collections, University of Chicago.

25. Drake, "Churches and Voluntary Associations," 25.

26. By the early 1990s only one study, Robert Gregg's *Sparks from the Anvil of Oppression: Philadelphia's African Methodists and Southern Migrants, 1890–1940*, centered its analysis on the effect of the phenomenon of migration on black churches and black religion. Working from some of the assumptions about race, class, and "ghettoization" held by scholars of the Great Migration during the 1960s and 1970s, Gregg found that Philadelphia's black churches became "battlegrounds for power and prestige." They were irrevocably divided into warring classes due to racial and spatial restrictions. During the migration, he concluded, Philadelphia's black churches "began to be associated with class groups more directly than ever before." Perhaps the most important contribution Gregg's study has made is to complicate our understanding of black southern migrants. Insisting that black southerners who migrated to Philadelphia not be viewed as an "unindifferenciated mass," Gregg argued that there was "diversity within the migrant population." More recently, a general study of migration and African American churches was made available. In *Bound for the Promised Land: African American Religion and the Great Migration*, Milton C. Sernett explored "the impact of the Great Migration on churches in the North and in the South." His central assertion, and perhaps his most significant contribution, has been to show the ways black southerners viewed the Great Migration as a "second emancipation." In the final analysis, Sernett was concerned with the shaping and reshaping of the "internal life" of African American churches as places where "matters of ultimate meaning" are confronted. With these studies, after three decades of careful attention to the Great Migration, scholars have begun to focus on arguably the most important cultural institution in black life, the church, to determine the ways African American religion was reshaped by the mass movement of blacks from the rural South to the urban North. See Robert Gregg, *Sparks for the Anvil of Oppression: Philadelphia's African Methodists and Southern Migrants, 1890–1940* (Philadelphia: Temple University Press, 1993); and Milton C. Sernett, *Bound for the Promised Land: African American Religion and the Great Migration* (Durham, N.C.: Duke University Press, 1997).

27. Drake and Cayton, *Black Metropolis*: 677–678; Brett Williams, "The South in the City," *Journal of Popular Culture* 16 (1982): 30–41; Farah Jasmine Griffin, *Who Set You Flowin'? The African American Migration Narrative* (New York: Oxford University Press, 1995); Sernett, *Bound for the Promised Land*, 7.

28. Scholars of the migration have been speaking of the motivations for the exodus in terms of "push and pull" since the 1930s. A book by Edward E. Lewis was one of the first to refer to the concept of push and pull. See Edward E. Lewis, *The Mobility of the Negro* (1931; reprint, New York: AMS Press, 1969), 12–20; McMillen, *Dark Journey*, 264.

29. The first scholarly examination of the Great Migration was produced by the U.S. Department of Labor. *Negro Migration in 1916–1917* was published in 1919 under the auspices of the DOL's Division of Negro Economics and was conducted by James H. Dillard. Other studies followed up until the 1930s. They include: Carter G. Woodson, *A Century of Negro Migration* (1918; reprint, New York: Russell and Russell, 1969); Thomas J. Woofter, *Negro Migration: Changes in Rural Organization and Population of the Cotton Belt* (1920; reprint, New York: Negro Universities Press, 1969); Charles S. Johnson (Chicago Commission on Race

Relations), *The Negro in Chicago: A Study of Race Relations and the Race Riot of 1919* (1922; reprint, New York: Arno, 1968); Louise V. Kennedy, *The Negro Peasant Turns Cityward: Effects of Recent Migrations to Northern Cities* (New York: Columbia University Press, 1930); Lewis, *Mobility of the Negro*; Clyde V. Kiser, *Sea Island to City: A Study of St. Helena Islanders in Harlem and Other Urban Centers* (New York: Columbia University Press, 1932).

30. Grant Wacker has produced a fascinating account of early Pentecostals, their theology, and their culture. See Grant Wacker, *Heaven Below: Early Pentecostals and American Culture* (Cambridge, Mass.: Harvard University Press, 2001). For a description of the "sanctified" church, see Zora Neale Hurston, *The Sanctified Church* (New York: Marlowe, 1997); and Cheryl J. Sanders, *Saints in Exile: The Holiness-Pentecostal Experience in African American Religion and Culture* (New York: Oxford University Press, 1996).

CHAPTER I

1. *Chicago Tribune*, 13 January 1929.

2. The phrase "square deal" was undoubtedly influenced by Theodore Roosevelt, who made it famous in the early 1900s. African Americans were known later to incorporate this language into "New Deal" discourse during the 1930s. See, for example, Jesse O. Thomas, "Will the New Deal Be a Square Deal for the Negro?" *Opportunity* 11 (October 1933): 308–315.

3. *Chicago Tribune*, 13 January 1929; *Chicago Whip*, 17 March 1920; 3 April 1920.

4. The piece has recently been published in a collection of primary sources on African American religion. See Milton C. Sernett, ed., *African American Religious History: A Documentary Witness*, 2nd ed. (Durham, N.C.: Duke University Press, 1999), 372–375.

5. Having been a Republican partisan newspaper since it was founded, the *Chicago Tribune* had a history of being pro-black. It unabashedly supported Abraham Lincoln during the Civil War, editorialized about the perils of slavery and about the need for African American civil rights. See Mark M Krug, "Lincoln, the Republican Party, and the Emancipation Proclamation," *History Teacher* 7 (November 1973); L. E. Murphy, "The Civil Rights Law of 1875," *Journal of Negro History* 12 (April 1927); Jacque Voegeli, "The Northwest and the Race Issue, 1861–1862, *Mississippi Valley Historical Review* 50 (September 1963); Noel P. Gist, "The Negro in the Daily Press," *Social Forces* 10 (March 1932).

6. *Chicago Whip*, 10 January 1920; *Chicago Whip*, 17 January 1920.

7. *The Light and Heebie Geebies*, 2 June 1928; "Prohibition Issue Will Defeat Democrats, Says Dr. L. K. Williams, Pres. Nat'l. B. Convention," Claude A. Barnett Papers, box 385, folder 5, Chicago Historical Society; *Chicago Defender*, 29 January 1955.

8. "Resolution Offered to the 52nd Annual Session of the National Baptist Convention of America," 1932, Claude A. Barnett Papers, box 385, folder 5, Chicago Historical Society; Wallace Best, "The Chicago Defender and the Realignment of Black Chicago," *Chicago History* 24 (1995).

9. The phrase "documentary witness" is taken from Milton Sernett's book by that name.

10. Williston Walker, *A History of the Christian Church* (New York: Charles Scribner's Sons, 1949), 121–123; Bernhard Lohse, *A Short History of Christian Doctrine: From the First Century to the Present*, F. Ernest Stoeffler, trans., rev. ed. (Philadelphia: Fortress, 1985), 52–56; Walter Lowe, "Christ and Salvation," in Peter C. Hodgson and Robert H. King, eds., *Christian Theology: An Introduction to Its Traditions and Tasks*, 2nd ed. (Philadelphia: Fortress, 1985), 226–228.

11. *Chicago Tribune*, 13 January 1929.

12. Ibid.

13. James Grossman, *Land of Hope: Chicago, Black Southerners and the Great Migration* (Chicago: University of Chicago Press, 1989), 127; Allan Spear, *Black Chicago: The Making of a Negro Ghetto, 1890–1920* (Chicago: University of Chicago Press, 1967), 12; St. Clair Drake and Horace Cayton, Jr., *Black Metropolis: A Study of Negro Life in a Northern City* (reprint, Chicago: University of Chicago Press, 1993), 8.

14. Lizabeth Cohen, *Making a New Deal: Industrial Workers in Chicago, 1919–1939* (New York: Cambridge University Press, 1990), 28, 165–166; Drake and Cayton, *Black Metropolis*, 229.

15. Drake and Cayton, *Black Metropolis*, 233; Carol Marks, *Farewell—We're Good and Gone: The Great Black Migration* (Bloomington: Indiana University Press, 1989), 121; Elizabeth Ross Haynes, *Unsung Heroes; The Black Boy of Atlanta; Negroes in Domestic Service in the United States* (reprint, New York: G. K. Hall; London: Prentice Hall International, 1997).

16. William M. Tuttle, Jr., *Race Riot: Chicago and the Red Summer of 1919* (New York: Atheneum, 1970), 157–183; Walter White, "Chicago and Its Eight Reasons," *Crisis* (October 1919): 293–297.

17. Harold Gosnell, *Negro Politicians: The Rise of Negro Politics in Chicago* (Chicago: University of Chicago, 1935); Charles R. Branham, "The Transformation of Black Political Leadership in Chicago, 1864–1942" (Ph.D. diss., University of Chicago, 1981); William J. Grimshaw, *Bitter Fruit: Black Politics and the Chicago Machine, 1931–1991* (Chicago: University of Chicago Press, 1992); Christopher E. Manning, "Ties That Bind: The Congressional Career of William L. Dawson and the Limits of Black Electoral Power, 1942–1970," (Ph.D. diss., Northwestern University, 2003).

18. Spear, *Black Chicago*, 183; Carl R. Osthaus, "The Rise and Fall of Jesse Binga, Black Financier," *Journal of Negro History* 58 (January 1973): 39–60; an "Achievements of Liberty Life," *Messenger* (December 1923): 910–911; *Chicago Defender*, 17 January 1920; Robert Christian Puth, "Supreme Life: The History of a Negro Life Insurance Company" (Ph.D. diss., Northwestern University, 1967).

19. St. Clair Drake, "Profiles: Chicago," *Journal of Educational Sociology* 17 (January 1944), 265.

20. Richard Brent Turner, *Islam in the African American Experience* (Bloomington: Indiana University Press, 1997), 92–108; Arthur Huff Fauset, *Black Gods of the Metropolis: Negro Religious Cults on the Urban North* (reprint, Philadelphia: University of Pennsylvania Press, 2003), 42.

21. St. Clair Drake, "Churches and Voluntary Associations in the Chicago Negro Community" (report of Official Project 465-54-3-386, conducted under the auspices of the Works Progress Administration, Chicago, December 1940), 234–235; Drake and Cayton, *Black Metropolis*, 388.

22. Grossman, *Land of Hope*, 4.

23. Charles S. Johnson, "These Colored United States, Chicago: Mecca of the Migrant Mob," *Messenger* (December 1923), 928.

24. Emmett J. Scott, "Additional Letters of Negro Migrants," *Journal of Negro History* 4 (October 1919): 459; *Chicago Tribune*, 12 February 1995; Jerry W. Ward, Jr., "Sterling D. Plumpp: A Son of the Blues," *Southern Quarterly* 29 (1991): 5–36.

25. Bessie Smith, *The Complete Recordings, vol. 1*, Roots and Blues Series, Columbia Records, 1991. See also Michelle Renee Scott, "The Realm of a Blues Empress: Blues Culture and Bessie Smith in Black Chattanooga, Tennessee, 1880–1923 (Ph.D. diss., Cornell University, 2002); Hazel V. Carby, "It Just Be's That Way Sometime: The Sexual Politics of Women's Blues," *Radical America* 20 (1986): 9–22.

26. Robert Johnson, *King of the Delta Blues*, MoJo Working Series, Columbia Records, 1997. See also Elijah Wald, *Escaping the Delta: Robert Johnson and the Invention of the Blues* (New York: Amistad, 2004); Marybeth Hamilton, "Sexuality, Authenticity and the Making of the Blues Tradition," *Past and Present* 169 (2000): 132–160; Samuel Charles, "Seeking the Greatest Bluesman," *American Heritage* 42 (1991): 50–60.

27. Neil R. McMillen, *Dark Journey: Black Mississippians in the Age of Jim Crow* (Urbana: University of Illinois Press, 1990), 264; Paul Oliver, *Blues Fell This Morning: Meaning in the Blues* (New York: Cambridge University Press, 1960), 46; William Barlow, *Looking Up at Down: The Emergence of Blues Culture* (Philadelphia: Temple University Press, 1989), 199, 294–297.

28. Emmett J. Scott, "Letters of Negro Migrants of 1916–1918," *Journal of Negro History* 4 (July 1919): 299; Emmett J. Scott, "Additional Letters of Negro Migrants of 1916–1918," *Journal of Negro History* 4 (October 1919): 430; Scott, "Letters," 309.

29. Victoria W. Wolcott, *Remaking Respectability: African American Women in Interwar Detroit* (Chapel Hill: University of North Carolina Press, 2001); Scott, "Additional Letters," 428.

30. Milton C. Sernett, *Bound for the Promised Land: African American Religion and the Great Migration* (Durham, N.C.: Duke University Press, 1997), 56.

31. Sernett, *Bound for the Promised Land*, 6; Daniel Wolff, *You Send Me: The Life and Times of Same Cooke* (New York: William Morrow, 1995), 23. Sam Cooke added the "e" to his name when he launched his professional singing career.

32. Marks, *Farewell—We're Good and Gone*, 2; George Edmund Haynes, *Negro Migration in 1916–1917* (Washington, D.C.: Government Printing Office, 1919), 12.

33. "The Migration of Negroes," *Crisis*, June 1917; James Grossman, *Land of Hope*, 90; Alaine Locke, *The New Negro* (1925; reprint, New York: Atheneum, 1992), 7; Milton C. Sernett, "If Not Moses, Then Joshua: African American Methodists and the Great Migration of 1916–1918" (Unpublished paper in possession of author), 6.

34. Miles Mark Fisher, "The Negro Church and the World War," *Journal of Religion* 5 (September 1925): 485.

35. Harold M. Kingsley, *The Negro in Chicago: A Spiritual Interpretation of an Economic Problem* (Chicago: Chicago Congregational Missionary and Extension Society, 1933), 2.

36. Trotter asserts that the "race relations model" within black urban history rose at the turn of the twentieth century and lasting until the early 1930s. It was followed by

the "ghetto model" in the 1960s and 1970s, which was concerned with the relationship between migration and ghetto formation. The third model he dubbed "proletarian," as it concentrated on the rise of a working class and class formation. See Joe William Trotter, Jr., ed., *Great Migration in Historical Perspective: New Dimensions in Race, Class, and Gender* (Bloomington: Indiana University Press, 1991), 1–21.

37. Nell Irvin Painter, in Trotter, ed., *Great Migration in Historical Perspective*, xx.

38. Commission on Race Relations, *The Negro in Chicago: A Study of Race Relations and a Race Riot in 1919* (reprint, New York: Arno, 1968), 1 and 142.

39. Ibid., 144.

40. Martin Bulmer, "Charles S. Johnson, Robert E. Park and the Research Methods of the Chicago Commission on Race Relations, 1919–1922: An Early Experiment in Applied Social Research," *Ethnic and Racial Studies* 4 (1981): 289–306; Ralph L. Pearson, "Charles S. Johnson and the Commission on Race Relations," *Illinois Historical Journal* 81 (1988): 211–220.

41. Robert Lee Sutherland, "An Analysis of Negro Churches in Chicago" (Ph.D. diss., University of Chicago, 1930), 44. Sutherland continued his interest in race and urban culture at the University of Texas. While there he wrote articles on educational psychology and comparisons between the mental health of blacks and whites. The American Youth Council commissioned his only book. It was an exploration of many of the themes he found interesting as a graduate student at Chicago. The book also employed a similar method to that used in his doctoral dissertation. See Robert L. Sutherland, *Color, Class and Personality* (Washington, D.C.: American Council on Education, 1942).

42. Sutherland, "Analysis of Negro Churches," 96, 100.

43. Sutherland, "Analysis of Negro Churches," 44.

44. Robert E. Park, "The City: Suggestions for the Investigation of Human Behavior in the City Environment," *American Journal of Sociology* 20 (March 1915): 577–612; Robert E. Park, "Human Migration and the Marginal Man," *American Journal of Sociology* 33 (May 1928); 881–843; Robert E. Park, "Human Ecology," *American Journal of Sociology* 42 (July 1936): 1–15; Robert E. Park, "The City: Suggestions for the Investigation of Human Behavior in the City Environment," *American Journal of Sociology* 20 (March 1915): 577–612; Park, "Human Migration" Paul J. Baker, "The Life Histories of W. I. Thomas and Robert E. Park," *American Journal of Sociology* 79 (September 1973): 258.

45. Over the past two decades, scholars have begun to question whether there was actually a Chicago school of sociology. Martin Bulmer, for example, has argued that the Chicago school was never unified ideologically. It did not exist as a school of thought. Rather, there was a high level of methodological diversity being practiced by the various sociologists working out of the sociology department at the University of Chicago. I hold, however, that the diversity of thought and method Bulmer recognized did not extend to black life. Also, when it came to black Americans, the thinking of Robert Park was pervasive. See Martin Bulmer, *The Chicago School of Sociology: Institutionalization, Diversity and the Rise of Sociological Research* (Chicago: University of Chicago Press, 1984). See also Fred H. Matthews, *Quest for an American Sociology: Robert Park and the Chicago School* (Montreal: McGill-Queens University Press, 1977). Daniel Breslau, "The Scientific Appropriation of Social Research: Robert Park's Human Ecology and American Society," *Theory*

and Society 19 (1990): 417–446; and Rolf Lindner, *The Reportage of Urban Culture: Robert Park and the Chicago School* (New York: Cambridge University Press, 1996).

46. Vattel Elbert Daniel, "Ritual in Chicago's South Side Churches for Negroes" (Ph.D. diss., University of Chicago, 1940), 11. Daniel accepted a position at Wiley College in Marshall, Texas, where his written work stayed close to the interests he developed as a student at Chicago. See Vattel E. Daniel, "Ritual and Stratification in Chicago Negro Churches," *American Sociological Review* 7 (June 1942): 352–361; "Negro Classes and Life in the Church," *Journal of Negro Education* 13 (Winter 1944): 19–29.

47. Daniel, "Ritual in Chicago's South Side Churches for Negroes," 12.

48. Ibid., 99.

49. Fannie Barrier Williams, "Social Bonds in the 'Black Belt' of Chicago," *Charities* 15 (October 7, 1905): 40–44; Thomas L. Philpott, *The Slum and the Ghetto: Neighborhood Deterioration and Middle-Class Reform in Chicago, 1880–1930* (New York: Oxford University Press, 1978), 119–121.

50. Samuel M. Strong, "Social Types in the Negro Community of Chicago: An Example of the Social Type Method" (Ph.D. diss., University of Chicago, 1940), 203. Perhaps the most successful student of the Chicago School, Strong taught at Macalester College and held a position at the *American Journal of Sociology*, for which he wrote several important articles. His notion of "social types" became influential in the field, attracting both admirers and detractors. See Samuel M. Strong, "Social Types in a Minority Group: Formulation of a Method," *American Journal of Sociology* 48 (March 1943); Samuel M. Strong, "Observations on the Possibility of Attitude Modification: A Case Study of Nationality and Racial Group interaction in Wartime," *Social Forces* 22 (March 1944); Samuel M. Strong, "Negro-White Relations as Reflected in Social Types," *American Journal of Sociology* 55 (July 1946): 23–30.

51. Strong, "Social Types in the Negro Community of Chicago," 218.

52. D. S. Howard, *WPA and Federal Relief* (New York: Russell Sage, 1943).

53. St. Clair Drake, "Churches and Voluntary Associations," 11, 150–151.

54. Drake and Cayton, *Black Metropolis*, 526–715. See also Davarian L. Baldwin, "Chicago's New Negroes: Race, Class and Respectability in the Midwestern Metropolis, 1915–1935" (Ph.D. diss., New York University, 2002); Ira De A. Reid, "Sargasso of Racial Oppression," *Phylon* 7 (1946): 92–93.

55. In *Souls of Black Folk*, congruent with his discussion of "double consciousness," Du Bois asserted that African American religionists faced an "unenviable dilemma" having always to face the "Negro Problem" in context to their religious faith. "Such a double life," he further claimed, "with double thoughts, double duties, and double social classes, must give rise to double words, double ideals, and tempt the mind to pretence or revolt, to hypocrisy or radicalism." For Du Bois, this binary element to black religion was intrinsic. It ran deep and was "tingeing and changing" black Christianity. All black religionists existed between the "two great and hardly reconcilable extremes." The dialectical model of African American religion as posited by Du Bois has been tremendously influential over most of the twentieth century. C. Eric Lincoln and Lawrence Mamiya, in their 1990 study, attempted to nuance the dialectical model of black religion by suggesting that the binarisms were not rigid, but rather that black religion has historically held "polar

opposites in tension, constantly shifting between polarities in historical time." Anthropologists, Hans Baer and Merrill Singer have posited a similar model suggesting that there are "varieties of protest and accommodation," and that there have
historically been contradictory and conflicting responses within African American
religion depending on context. Evelyn Brooks Higginbotham in her study of
women in the black Baptist church sought to reshape the model even further.
While largely in accord with Lincoln and Mamiya, Higginbotham characterized
black churches and black religion as a "dialogic model" rather than a dialectical
one, underscoring "dynamic tension" in a multiplicity of meanings within black
faith that are not framed in discrete polarities. See W. E. B. Du Bois, *Souls of Black
Folk*, (New York: New American Library, 1969), 221–222; C. Eric Lincoln and
Lawrence Mamiya, *The Black Church in the African American Experience* (Durham,
N.C.: Duke University Press, 1990), 11; Hans A. Baer and Merrill Singer, *African
American Religion in the Twentieth Century: Varieties of Protest and Accommodation*
(Knoxville: University of Tennessee Press, 1992), ix–xxiii; Evelyn Brooks Higgin-
botham, *Righteous Discontent: The Women's Movement in the Black Baptist Church,
1880–1920* (Cambridge, Mass.: Harvard University Press, 1993), 18.

56. Richard Wright, *Native Son* (reprint, New York: HarperPerennial, 1993);
Richard Wright, *American Hunger*, reprint (Harper and Row Publishers, 1977);
Richard Wright, *12 Million Black Voices* (reprint, New York: Thunder's Mouth,
1988). See also John M. Reilly, "Richard Wright Preaches the Nation: 12 Million
Black Voices," *Black American Literary Forum* 16 (Autumn 1982): 116–119.

57. Farah Jasmine Griffin, *"Who Set You Flowin'?" The African American Migration
Narrative* (New York: Oxford University Press, 1995), 71.

58. Griffin, *"Who Set You Flowin',"* 131 and 79, respectively; Wright, *12 Million
Black Voices*, 127.

59. Wright, *12 Million Black Voices*, 135.

60. Drake, "Churches and Voluntary Associations," 234; Walter Lippmann, *A
Preface to Morals* (New York: Macmillan, 1929).

61. Clifford Geertz, *The Interpretation of Cultures: Selected Essays* (New York: Basic
Books, 1973), 126–127.

CHAPTER 2

1. "All Chicago Mourns the Death of Julius Avendorph," *Chicago Defender*, 12
May 1923; Helen Buckler, *Doctor Dan: Pioneer in American Surgery* (Boston: Little,
Brown, 1954), 157; Junius B. Wood, *The Negro in Chicago: How He and His Race
Kindred Came to Dwell in Great Numbers in a Northern City; How He Lives and
Works; His Successes and Failures; His Political Outlook* (reprint, Chicago: Chicago
Daily News, 1916), 20; "An Anniversary Party Invitation," Booker T. Washington
Papers, container 7, reel 7, Library of Congress; "Six Major Negro Churches,"
Federal Writers' Project, WPA Files, container A125, folder: "Illinois Religion,"
Library of Congress.

2. Junius N. Avendorph, "Chicago's Social Condition Today and Twenty Years Ago,"
Chicago Defender 6 (October 1917). Hazel Carby employs the term "moral panic" to
describe the anxiety on the part of some blacks in the urban North during the

migration over what they considered "uncontrolled black women." Such women, it was believed, threatened the "progress of the race." See Hazel V. Carby, "Policing the Black Woman's Body in the Urban Context," *Critical Inquiry* 18 (Summer 1992): 741.

3. Allan Spear, *Black Chicago: The Making of a Negro Ghetto, 1890–1920* (Chicago: University of Chicago Press, 1967), 109; *Chicago Whip*, 6 July 1919; *Chicago Defender*, 26 June 1920.

4. "Music (Chicago South Side)," Federal Writers' Project, WPA files, container A876, Library of Congress; *Chicago Defender*, 10 May 1910.

5. Willard B. Gatewood, *Aristocrats of Color: The Black Elite, 1880–1920* (Bloomington: Indiana University Press, 1990), 232; *New York Age*, 24 September 1905; 25 July 1907.

6. *Christian Times*, 2 September 1857; Miles M. Fisher, "History of the Olivet Baptist, Church of Chicago" (M.A. Thesis, University of Chicago, 1922), 8; *Times*, 8 and 15 August 1860; Lenwood G. Davis, "Miles Mark Fisher: Minister, Historian and Cultural Philosopher," *Negro History Bulletin* 36 (January-February-March 1983): 19–21; Bessie Louise Pierce, *A History of Chicago: The Beginning of a City, 1673–1848*, vol. 1 (New York: Knopf, 1937), 234, 244–245; Henry Justin Smith and Lloyd Lewis, *Chicago: A History of Its Reputation* (New York: Harcourt, Brace, 1929), 87.

7. Carol Marks, *Farewell—We're Good and Gone: The Great Black Migration* (Bloomington: Indiana University Press, 1989), 1–3; Spear, *Black Chicago*, 12; Commission on Race Relations, *The Negro in Chicago: A Study of Race Relations and a Race Riot in 1919* (reprint, New York: Arno, 1968), 602.

8. The term "South in the City" is borrowed from Brett Williams. See "The South in the City," *Journal of Popular Culture* 16 (1982): 30–41.

9. Spear, *Black Chicago*, 143–144; U.S. Census, 1790–1915; U.S. Census, 1920 (fourteenth), Library of Congress.

10. James Grossman, *Land of Hope: Chicago, Black Southerners and the Great Migration* (Chicago: University of Chicago Press, 1989), 155; Richard Wright, *Black Boy: A Record of Childhood and Youth* (New York: Harper and Row, 1996), 228. See also Jeff Karem, "'I Could Never Really Leave the South': Regionalism and the Transformation of Richard Wright's American Hunger," *American Literary History* 13 (2001): 694–715.

11 *Chicago Defender*, 17 May 1919; 2 April 1921.

12. *Chicago Whip*, 23 October 1920.

13. Robert Bone, "Richard Wright and the Chicago Renaissance," *Callaloo* 0 (Summer 1986): 455; Barbara Ballis Lal, "Black and Blue in Chicago," *British Journal of Sociology* 38 (December 1987): 550; Park Dixon Goist, "City and Community; The Urban Theory of Robert Park," *American Quarterly* 23 (Spring 1971): 46–49.

14. Grossman, *Land of Hope*, 154; *Chicago Whip*, 23 October 1920; 4 March 1922; "Things that Should Be Considered," *Chicago Defender*, 20 October 1917; *Chicago Defender*, 24 February 1917; Spear, *Black Chicago*, 65–66. Samuel Ward McAllister was a nineteenth-century arbiter of the New York aristocracy. A San Francisco lawyer who married a New York millionaire's daughter in 1852, McAllister is famous for compiling a list of 400 people he deemed true members of New York society. It was a highly exclusive list used by the likes of Mrs. William Astor and others to order their social worlds in the 1890s. See Ward McAllister, *Society as I Have*

Found It (New York: Cassell, 1890); and Eric Homberger, *Mrs. Astor's New York: Money and Social Power in a Gilded Age* (New Haven: Yale University Press, 2002).

15. Pat Abrams, Sr. Warden of St. Thomas Episcopal, telephone interview with author, Princeton University, 19 March 2003.

16. *Chicago Tribune*, 19 November 1893.

17. "Six Major Negro Churches," 3; Gatewood, *Aristocrats of Color*, 283; *New York Age*, 21 March 1907.

18. "Mrs. Georgia Avendorph, Pioneer Chicagoan, Dies," *Chicago Defender*, 30 May 1925.

19. C. Eric Lincoln and Lawrence H. Mamiya, *The Black Church in the African American Experience* (Durham, N.C.: Duke University Press, 1990), 117; St. Clair Drake and Horace R. Cayton, *Black Metropolis: A Study of Negro Life in a Northern City* (New York: Harper Torchbooks, 1945); E. Franklin Frazier, *Black Bourgeoisie: The Rise a New Middle Class in the United States* (New York: Collier, 1957); Joe William Trotter, Jr., *Black Milwaukee: The Making of an Industrial Proletariat, 1915–1945* (Urbana: University of Illinois Press, 1985); Peter Gottlieb, *Making Their Own Way: Southern Blacks' Migration to Pittsburgh, 1916–1930* (Urbana: University of Illinois Press, 1987).

20. *Chicago Defender*, 12 May 1923; Spear, *Black Chicago*, 65–66; *Chicago City Directory*, 1910 and 1920, Newberry Library, Chicago, IL. According to E. Franklin Frazier, headwaiters and valets were considered Chicago's "society" leaders in the 1890s, followed by Pullman porters, and barbers. See E. Franklin Frazier, *The Negro Family in Chicago* (Chicago: University of Chicago Press, 1932), 9.

21. Gatewood, *Aristocrats of Color*, 275.

22. "The First Church of Deliverance (Spiritualist)," Federal Writers' Project, WPA Files, container A124, folder: "Illinois Religion"; "And Churches," Illinois Writers' Project Files, "Negro in Illinois," box 45, folder 1, Vivian Harsh Collection, Carter G. Woodson Regional Branch, Chicago Public Library.

23. "The First Church of Deliverance (Spiritualist)," Federal Writers' Project; Rev. Otto Houston, Pastor of First Church of Deliverance, telephone interview with author Princeton University, 18 March 2003; "Interview: Rev. Cobbs," box 187, folder: "First Church of Deliverance [ed. Copy 1]," Federal Writers' Project Files, Illinois Historical Library, Springfield; "500 Honor Rev. Cobbs At Testimonial Banquet," *Chicago Defender*, 15 February 1941.

24. NAACP Letterhead, 1946, NAACP Papers, box C44, "Chicago, IL., 1946" folder, Library of Congress; Timuel Black, telephone interview with author, Princeton University, 26 March 2003.

25. Rev. Otto Houston, telephone interview.

26. Drake and Cayton, *Black Metropolis*, 645–646. The *Chicago Bee* newspaper popularized the term "Bronzeville" in the 1930s to replace the term "Black Belt," which had fallen into disfavor with a number of black Chicagoans. See St. Clair Drake and Horace Cayton, "Bronzeville," *Holiday* (May 1962): 5.

27. *Chicago Tribune*, 13 January 1929; Michael W. Harris, *The Rise of the Gospel Blues: The Music of Thomas Andrew Dorsey in the Urban Church* (New York: Oxford University Press, 1992), 118; Grossman, *Land of Hope*, 156; Fisher, "History of Olivet Baptist"; Spear, Black Chicago, *142, 178*.

28. Arthur E. Holt, "Religion," *American Journal of Sociology* 34 (July 1928): 175.

29. *New York Age*, 21 March 1907.

30. Spear, *Black Chicago*, 91, 178; "St. Thomas Church Dedicated," *New York Age*, 4 July 1907; Miles Mark Fisher, "The Negro Church and the World War," *Journal of Religion* 5 (September 1925): 5; Grossman, *Land of Hope*, 131; Charles S. Johnson, "These Colored United States, Chicago: Mecca of the Migrant Mob," *Messenger* (December 1923): 928; Robert Lee Sutherland, "An Analysis of Negro Churches in Chicago" (Ph.D. diss., University of Chicago, 1930), 44.

31. "Greater Bethesda Baptist Church," Illinois Writers' Project, box 18, Carter G. Woodson Regional Library, Chicago; "Bethesda Baptist Church," Works Progress Administration, Federal Writers' Project files, container A124, folder: "Illinois Religion," Library of Congress; "Bomb Baptist Church; Loss $250,000," Claude A. Barnett Papers, box 385, folder 1, Chicago Historical Society; "Law Hot on Trail of Church Bombers," *Chicago Defender*, 24 October 1925; "Rebuilding Bethesda," *Chicago Defender*, 12 December 1925; "A History of Greater Bethesda Missionary Baptist Church, Chicago Illinois, 1882–1982," booklet produced by Greater Bethesda at 100th anniversary (copy in possession of author).

32. "Ebenezer Baptist Church," Illinois Writers' Project, box 18, Vivian Harsh Collection, Carter G. Woodson Regional Library, Chicago Public Library; "Ebenezer Baptist Church (Colored-Chicago)," Works Progress Administration, Federal Writers' Project, container A876, Library of Congress; "Ebenezer Baptist Church," Works Progress Administration, Federal Writers' Project, A124, folder: "Illinois Religion," Library of Congress; George Lane and Algirmantas Keyzs, *Chicago Churches and Synagogues: An Architectural Pilgrimage* (Chicago: Loyola University Press, 1981), 78–79.

33. "The Worlds Largest Church," *Afro-American*, 9 January 1926.

34. Drake and Cayton, *Black Metropolis*, 63–64; P. J. Stackhouse, *Chicago and the Baptists* (Chicago: University of Chicago Press, 1933), 200–207.

35. "Facts and Figures: Olivet Baptist Church," pamphlet, Carter G. Woodson Papers, Library of Congress; "History of Olivet Baptist Church," Olivet Baptist Church, 1992 (document in possession of author); S. Mattie Fisher, "Olivet as a Christian Center," *Missions* 10 (March 1919): 199–202; "The Worlds Largest Church."

36. "The Largest Protestant Church in America," *Pittsburgh Courier*, 27 July 1929; Stackhouse, *Chicago and the Baptists*, 200–207.

37. Milton C. Sernett, *Bound for the Promised Land: African American Religion and the Great Migration* (Durham, N.C.: Duke University, 1997), 160.

38. "The Royal Prayer Band, Pentecostal, Interview," Federal Writers' Project, box 185, folder: "All Nations Pentecostal Assembly," Illinois Historical Library, Springfield.

39. Fisher, "History of Olivet," 52–57; "Razing of Old Olivet Baptist Church Prompts a Probe of Its History," *Chicago Defender*, 18 October 1941.

40. "Monumental Baptist Church" and "Liberty Baptist Church," Illinois Writers' Project, box 18, Carter G. Woodson Regional Branch, Chicago Public Library; Sernett, *Bound for the Promised Land* 160.

41. "Indiana Methodist Church," Illinois Writers' Project, box 18, Carter G. Woodson Regional Branch, Chicago Public Library.

42. "St. Edmund's Episcopal Church," Illinois Writers' Project, box 18, Carter G. Woodson Regional Branch, Chicago Public Library.

43. Lincoln and Mamiya, *The Black Church*, 159; E. Franklin Frazier, *The Negro Church in America*, (New York: Schocken, 1974), 83; Willard Gatewood,

Aristocrats of Color, 275; W. E. B. Du Bois, *The Negro Church* (Atlanta: Atlanta University Press, 1903), 139.

44. Farm Security Administration—Office of War Information Photograph Collection, Library of Congress; "History of the Church of St. Edmund," Samuel J. Martin Papers, box 1, folder 3-1, Schomburg Center for Research in African American Culture, New York; Samuel J. Martin, Jr., telephone interview with author, Princeton University, 23 March 2003; Annette Martin Craighead, telephone interview with author, Princeton University, 28 March 2003.

45. Kimberley L. Phillips, *AlabamaNorth: African-American Migrants, Community, and Working-Class Activism in Cleveland, 1915–1945* (Urbana: University of Illinois Press, 1999), 166.

46. St. Clair Drake, "Churches and Voluntary Associations in the Chicago Negro Community," (Report of Official Project 465-54-3-386, conducted under the auspices of the Works Progress Administration, (Chicago, December 1940), 6–7.

47. "And Churches," Illinois Writers' Project Files, "Negro in Illinois," box 45, folder 1,Vivian Harsh Collection, Carter G. Woodson Regional Branch, Chicago Public Library.

48. Although religion served as a primary theme in the fiction and nonfiction writing of James Baldwin, the literature that discusses Baldwin's ideas about religion remains small. See Shirley S. Allen, "Religious Symbolism and Psychic Reality in Baldwin's *Go Tell It on the Mountain*," *CLA Journal* 19 (1975): 175–199; Barbara K. Olsen, "Come to Jesus Stuff in James Baldwin's *Go Tell It on the Mountain* and 'The Amen Corner,'" *African American Review* 31 (Summer 1997): 295–301; Clarence E. Hardy III, *James Baldwin's God: Sex, Hope and Crisis in Black Holiness Culture* (Knoxville: University of Tennessee Press, 2003).

49. James Baldwin, *Go Tell It on the Mountain* (reprint, New York: Dell Publishing, 1981), 50.

50. "Exodus to Freedom," *Chicago Tribune*, 12 February 1995; Arna Bontemps and Jack Conroy, *Anyplace but Here* (New York: Hill and Wang, 1966), 166.

51. Arthur E. Paris, *Black Pentecostalism: Southern Religion in an Urban World* (Amherst: University of Massachusetts Press, 1982), vi.

52. Drake and Cayton, *Black Metropolis*, 671.

53. Ibid., 632.

54. "Negro Religious Bodies in Chicago, Store Fronts 1938," St. Clair Drake Papers, box 57, Schomburg Center for Research in Black Culture, New York.

55. Drake and Cayton, *Black Metropolis*, 632–638; Frazier, *The Negro Church in America*, 58.

56. Drake and Cayton, *Black Metropolis*, 614–635.

57. Marsha Natalie Taylor, "'Shouting': The Dance of the Black Church" (Ph.D. diss., Case Western Reserve University, 1997); Drake and Cayton, *Black Metropolis*, 639.

58. Miles Mark Fisher, "Negro Churches in Illinois: A Fragmentary History with Emphasis on Chicago," *Journal of the Illinois State Historical Society* 61 (Autumn 1963): 557.

59. Fisher, "Negro Churches in Illinois," 560; Fisher, " History of Olivet Baptist," 40–42; "Some Noted Leaders: Chicago Clergymen who Preach to Colored Congregations," *Chicago Tribune*, 19 November 1893; William J. Simmons, *Men of Mark: Eminent, Progressive, and Rising* (New York: Arno, 1968), 252–256. Podd

was somewhat of a prodigy. He took the mantle at Olivet in his mid twenties after having been schooled in England. Given to "fainting spells," he was also not at all healthy and was known to drink. He was forced to relocate to Florida for his health in 1886. He died there of consumption at the age of 31.

60. "Grace Presbyterian Church," Works Progress Administration, Federal Writers' Project Files, container A125, Library of Congress; "Celebrate the Journey," guide to the Grace Presbyterian Church collection, Chicago Historical Society.

61. William E. Montgomery, *Under Their Own Vine and Fig Tree: The African-American Church in the South, 1865–1900* (Baton Rouge: Louisiana State University Press, 1993), 253–306; Paul Harvey, *Redeeming the South: Religious Cultures and Racial Identities among Southern Baptists, 1865–1925* (Chapel Hill: University of North Carolina Press, 1997), 108. Stephanie M. H. Camp, "The Pleasure of Resistance: Enslaved Women and Body Politics in the Plantation South, 1830–1861," *Journal of Southern History* 68 (August 2002), 535.

62. W. E. B. Du Bois, *The Souls of Black Folk* (New York: New American Library, 1969), 211; Nell Irvin Painter, *Exodusters: Black Migration to Kansas after Reconstruction* (reprint, New York: Norton, 1992), 14.

63. Myrta L. Avary, *Dixie after the War: An Exposition of the Social Conditions Existing in the South during the Twelve Years Succeeding the Fall of Richmond* (reprint, New York, 1969), 203–205; Philip Bruce, *The Plantation Negro as a Freedman: Observations on His Character, Condition, and Prospects in Virginia* (New York: G.P. Putnam's Sons, 1889), 106–107; quote by Cordelia Anderson Jackson found in Paul Harvey, *Redeeming the South*, 108.

64. Albert J. Raboteau, *Slave Religion: The 'Invisible Institution' in the Antebellum South* (New York: Oxford University Press, 1978); Winthrop S. Hudson, *Religion in America: An Historical Account of the Development of American Religious Life*, 2nd ed. (New York: Charles Scribner's Sons, 1973), 342–345; Sydney E. Ahlstrom, *A Religious History of the American People*, vol. 2 (New York: Image, 1975), 287–291; Vinson Synan, *The Holiness Pentecostal Tradition: Charismatic Movements in the Twentieth Century* (Grand Rapids, Mich.: Eerdman's, 1997), 1–21.

65. Dee E. Andrews, *The Methodists and Revolutionary America, 1760–1800: The Shaping of an Evangelical Culture* (Princeton, N.J.: Princeton University Press, 2000).

66. Allan Coppedge, "Entire Sanctification in Early American Methodism, 1812–1835," *Wesleyan Theological Journal* 13 (Spring 1978), 34–50; Timothy L. Smith, "Righteousness and Hope: Christian Holiness and the Millennial Vision in America, 1800–1900," *American Quarterly* 31 (Spring 1979), 21–45.

67. Christine Leigh Heyrman, *Southern Cross: The Beginnings of the Bible Belt* (Chapel Hill: University of North Carolina Press, 1997), 218–220; Albert J. Raboteau, *A Fire in the Bones: Reflections on African American Religious History* (Boston: Beacon, 1995), 152–157; Cheryl J. Sanders, *Saints in Exile: The Holiness-Pentecostal Experience in African American Religion and Culture* (New York: Oxford University Press, 1996).

68. Synan, *Holiness Pentecostal Tradition*, 108–112.

69. Charles D. Killian, "Bishop Daniel A. Payne: An Apostle of Wesley," *Methodist History* 24 (1986): 107–119; James T. Campbell, *Songs of Zion: The African Methodist Episcopal Church in the Unites States and South Africa* (Chapel Hill: University of North Carolina Press, 1998), 38–43.

70. H. T. Kealing, "A Race Rich in Spiritual Content," *Southern Workman* (January 1904); quote found in Harvey, *Redeeming the South*, 108.

71. Drake and Cayton, *Black Metropolis*, 672.

72. Drake, "Churches and Voluntary Associations," 234. The assertion that the earth is flat is reminiscent of the celebrated sermon by the nineteenth-century African American preacher John Jasper, "The Sun Do Move." Hiley H. Hill, "Negro Storefront Churches." (M.A. thesis, Howard University, 1947), 10.

73. Strong, "Social Types in the Negro Community of Chicago: An Example of the Social Type Method," (Ph. D. diss., University of Chicago, 1940), 210; "The Church of God in Christ—Elder Roberts 40th and State Street," Federal Writers' Project Files, box 184, Illinois Historical Library, Springfield, Ill.; Frances Kostarelos, *Feeling the Spirit: Faith and Hope in an Evangelical Black Storefront Church* (Columbia: University of South Carolina Press, 1995), 3; "The Church of God, 4338 Prairie Avenue," Federal Writers' Project, box 186, Illinois Historical Library, Springfield.

74. *Chicago Defender*, 2 November 1935. Unfortunately, a book Elder Smith referred to that recorded her charitable distributions has not been found. A sampling from the book, however, was recorded in Herbert Smith's University of Chicago master's thesis. See Herbert M. Smith, "Three Negro Preachers" (M.A. thesis, University of Chicago, 1935), 17, 18; "Little Lucy" Collier, granddaughter of Elder Lucy Smith, interview with author, Chicago, 2 December 1996; "General Survey," Federal Writers' Project Files, box 185, Illinois State Historical Library, Springfield; Smith, "Three Negro Preachers," 19. *Chicago Defender*, 2 November 1935. Elder Smith's editorial would seem to contradict the claim by Arnold Hirsch that "opposition to the project came only from realtors and others outside the black community." At least some within the black community did oppose the building of the Ida B. Wells Homes and wrote the *Chicago Defender* to express that opposition. See Arnold R. Hirsch, *Making the Second Ghetto: Race and Housing in Chicago, 1940–1960* (Chicago: University of Chicago Press, 1998), 11.

75. Richard Wright, *12 Million Black Voices* (reprint, New York: Thunder's Mouth, 1988), 134.

76. "Social Stratification: Interview with Mrs. Fitzgerald," Federal Writers' Project, box 185, folder: "COGIC, copy 2 edited," Illinois Historical Library, Springfield.

77. Bontemps and Conroy, *Anyplace but Here*, 173–174.

78. Scott, "Additional Letters," 454–455, 457, 463.

79. "Interview with Mrs. G. W. Neighbors," St. Clair Drake Papers, box 57, folder: "Olivet Baptist Church," Schomburg Center for Research in Black Culture, New York.

80. Drake and Cayton, *Black Metropolis*, 675.

81. Ibid., 650–652.

82. "Interview with Mrs. Mattie Ford," Federal Writers' Project Files, box 185, folder: COGIC, copy 2 edited, Illinois Historical Library, Springfield.

83. St. Clair Drake, "Churches and Voluntary Associations," 198; Drake and Cayton, *Black Metropolis*, 632, 634; Hiley H. Hill, "Negro Storefront Churches," 7. See also Vattel E. Daniel, "Ritual and Stratification in Chicago Negro Churches," *American Sociological Review* 7 (June 1932); Vattel E. Daniel, "Ritual in Chicago's South Side Churches for Negroes" (Ph.D. diss., University of Chicago, 1940), 13; Evans Edgar

Crawford, "The Leadership Role of the Urban Negro Minister" (Ph.D. diss., Boston University, 1957), 59.

84. "Religious Enthusiasts," *Chicago Defender*, 10 September 1921; Benjamin E. Mays and Joseph W. Nicholson, *The Negro's Church* (1933; reprint, New York: Arno, 1969), 17, 220, 59; Ira de A. Reid, "Let Us Prey," *Opportunity* 4 (September 1926): 274–278; Drake and Cayton, *Black Metropolis*, 415, 420.

85. *Chicago Defender*, 31 March 1917.

86. "Sunlight Church of the Sabbath" (7 February 1938), St. Clair Drake Papers, box 57, Schomburg Center for Research in Black Culture, New York.

87. Timuel Black, telephone interview with author, Princeton University, 20 March 2003.

88. "First Church of Deliverance Spiritualist," Works Progress Administration, Federal Writers' Project Files, container A124, Library of Congress.

89. Sukie de la Croix, telephone, interview with author, Princeton University, September 20, 2002; Sukie de la Croix, "Chicago Whispers: A Very Personal Gay and Lesbian History," *Outlines*, 8 December 1999.

90. "General Survey," Federal Writers' Project Files, box 185, Illinois State Historical Library, Springfield.

91. *Chicago Defender*, 19 November 1921, 28 November 1936, 1 March 1941, 18 October 1941, 20 December 1941, 25 July 1942; Johnson, "These Colored United States: Chicago," 928.

92. For a discussion of migrant clubs, see Grossman, *Land of Hope*, 96–97.

93. Strong, "Social Types," 219.

94. Drake and Cayton, *Black Metropolis*, 629.

95. Samuel Strong, "Social Types," 206–207; Lincoln and Mamiya, *The Black Church*, 293.

CHAPTER 3

1. Carol Marks, *Farewell—We're Good and Gone: The Great Black Migration* (Bloomington: Indiana University Press, 1989), 1; Ira Katznelson, *Black Men in White Cities: Race, Politics, and Migration in the United States, 1900–1930, and Britain, 1948–1968* (New York: Oxford University Press, 1973), 32; Ray Stannard Baker, "The Negro Goes North," *World's Work* 34 (July 1917): 315; August Meier, *Negro Thought in America, 1880–1915* (Ann Arbor: University of Michigan Press, 1966), 170.

2. Julie Saville, The *Work of Reconstruction: From Slave to Wage Laborer in South Carolina, 1860–1870* (New York: Cambridge University Press, 1994); Eric Foner, *Nothing but Freedom: Emancipation and Its Legacy* (Baton Rouge: Louisiana State University Press, 1983), 6; Rebecca J. Scott, "Defining the Boundaries of Freedom in the World of Cane: Cuba, Brazil, and Louisiana after Emancipation," *American Historical Review* 99 (February 1994): 70–102. I would like to thank Dylan Penningroth for this important insight and for leading me to these sources.

3. The best and most comprehensive studies of the transitory nature of the Reconstruction are W. E. B. Du Bois's *Black Reconstruction in America: 1860–1880* (New York: Atheneum, 1985) and Eric Foner's *Reconstruction: America's Unfinished*

Revolution, 1863–1877 (New York: Harper and Row, 1988). See also Paul Moreno, "Racial Classifications and Reconstruction Legislation," *Journal of Southern History* 61 (May 1995), 271–304.

4. St. Clair Drake and Horace Cayton, *Black Metropolis: A Study of Negro Life in a Northern City* (reprint, Chicago: University of Chicago Press, 1993), 677–678.

5. "Grace Presbyterian Church," Works Progress Administration, Federal Writers' Project, container A125, folder: "Illinois Religion," Library of Congress; "Atty. Marshall Pleads to Help 'Newcomers,'" *Chicago Defender*, 20 October 1917.

6. *Chicago Defender*, 4 August 1917; "The Old Timer and the New Comer," *Chicago Whip*, 20 September 1919.

7. "The Negro Goes to Church," *Opportunity* (March 1929): 91.

8. Reverdy C. Ransom, *The Pilgrimage of Harriet Ransom's Son*, 109–111; Allan Spear, *Black Chicago: The Making of a Negro Ghetto, 1890–1920* (Chicago: University of Chicago Press, 1967), 95; *Inter-Ocean*, 29 July 1900; Terrell Dale Goddard, "The Black Social Gospel in Chicago, 1896–1906: The Ministries of Reverdy C. Ransom and Richard R. Wright, Jr.," *Journal of Negro History* 84 (Summer 1999), 227–246; David Wills, "Reverdy C. Ransom: The Making of an A. M. E. Bishop," in Randall K. Burkett and Richard Newman, eds., *Black Apostles: Afro-American Clergy Confront the Twentieth Century*, (Boston: n.p., 1978), 181–212; Calvin S. Morris, *Reverdy C. Ransom: Black Advocate of the Social Gospel* (Lanham, Md.: University Press of America, 1990); "Reverend R. C. Ransom, B.D.," *Christian Recorder*, 1 January 1898; "Rev. R. C. Ransom: The Pastor of Bethel A. M. E. Church, Chicago—A Model," *Freeman*, 27 January 1900.

9. *Chicago Daily Tribune*, 8 February 1908.

10. Alice T. Anderson, ed., *From Ocean to Ocean, 1920: Record of the Work of the Woman's American Baptist Home Mission Society* (Chicago: n.p., 1920), 189–191.

11. "New Negro Goes to Church," *Opportunity* (March 1929): 91; James Grossman, *Land of Hope: Chicago, Black Southerners and the Great Migration* (Chicago: University of Chicago Press, 1989), 156; S. Mattie Fisher, "Olivet as a Christian Center," *Missions* 10 (March 1919): 199–202; Milton C. Sernett, *Bound for the Promised Land: African American Religion and the Great Migration* (Durham, N.C.: Duke University Press,) 119; Alice T. Anderson, ed., *Ocean to Ocean, 1918–1919: A Record of the Work of the Women's American Baptist Home Mission Society* (Chicago: n.p., 1919), 189–191.

12. Lillian B. Horace, *Crowned with Glory and Honor: The Life of Rev. Lacey Kirk Williams* (Hicksville, N.Y.: Exposition, 1978), 148; Drake and Cayton, *Black Metropolis*, 652.

13. The most definitive study of the race riot of 1919 remains William M. Tuttle, Jr., *Race Riot: Chicago in the Red Summer of 1919*. See also C. K. Doreski, "From News to History: Robert Abbott and Carl Sandburg Read the 1919 Chicago Riot," *African American Review* 26 (1992): 637–660.

14. Anderson, ed., *Ocean to Ocean, 1919–1920*: 62–64; Alice T. Anderson, ed., *From Ocean to Ocean: Including Forty-Seventh Annual Report of the Woman's American Baptist Home Mission Society, The Story of the Year, 1923–1924* (New York: n.p., 1924), 73; Miriam Davis, ed., *From Ocean to Ocean: Including the Fiftieth Annual Report of the Woman's American Baptist Home Mission Society, The Story of the Year, 1926–1927* (New York: n.p., 1927), 198.

15. "To Members of the Race Coming from the South," *Chicago Defender*, 21 March 1917; Fisher, "Olivet as a Christian Center," 199.

16. Grossman, *Land of Hope*, 69–77; Alan D. Desantis, "Selling the American Dream: The *Chicago Defender* and the Great Migration of 1915–1919" (Ph.D. diss., Indiana University, 1993); *Soldiers without Swords: The Black Press*," (Stanley Nelson, 1999), film.

17. "Facts and Figures: Olivet Baptist Church," Carter G. Woodson Papers, Library of Congress; *Chicago Daily News*, 12 July 1929; Sernett, *Bound for the Promised Land*, 157; "And Churches," Illinois Writers' Project, box 45, folder 1, Vivian Harsh Collection, Carter G. Woodson Regional Branch, Chicago Public Library.

18. "Blackwell Memorial African Methodist Episcopal Zion Church," Works Progress Administration, Federal Writer's Project Files, container A124, folder: "Illinois Religion," Library of Congress; "Greater Walters African Methodist Episcopal Zion Church," Works Progress Administration, Federal Writers' Project Files, container A124, folder: "Illinois Religion," Library of Congress.

19. Drake and Cayton, *Black Metropolis*, 677.

20. "The Good Shepherd Congregational Church in Chicago," *Negro History Bulletin* 3 (October 1930); Arvarh E. Strickland, *History of the Chicago Urban League* (Urbana: University of Illinois Press, 1966), 34; Harold Kingsley, *The Negro in Chicago: A Spiritual Interpretation of an Economic Problem* (Chicago: Chicago Congregational Missionary and Extension Society, 1933), 12.

21. "News in the Making at the Parkway Community House, 1944–1945," box 3, Horace Cayton Papers, Vivian Harsh Collection, Carter G. Woodson Regional Branch, Chicago Public Library. "The People's Forum: Black Metropolis—A Challenge to Chicago, 1946," Horace Cayton Papers, box 42, Vivian Harsh Collection, Carter G. Woodson Regional Branch, Chicago Public Library.

22. "NAACP New Release," NAACP Papers, box C45, folder: "Chicago, IL., 1946," Library of Congress; Michel Fabre, *The Unfinished Quest of Richard Wright*, trans. Isabel Barzum, 2nd ed. (Urbana: University of Illinois Press, 1993), 131; Richard S. Hobbs, *The Cayton Legacy: An African American Family* (Pullman: Washington State University Press, 2002), 116–119; Vanita Marian Vactor, "A History of the Chicago Federal Theater Project Negro Unit: 1935–1939," (Ph.D. diss., New York University, 1999).

23. William E. Hatcher, *John Jasper: The Unmatched Negro Philosopher and Preacher* (New York: Fleming H. Revel, 1908); Leslie Catherine Sanders, ed., *The Collected Works of Langston Hughes*, vol. 5 (Columbia: University of Missouri Press, 2002), 591, 647–648.

24. Judith L. Stephens, "Anti-Lynch Plays by African American Women: Race, Gender, and Social Protest in American Drama," *African American Review* 26 (1992): 329–339; Elwood Pratt Williams, "An Examination of Protagonists in Selected Federal Theatre Project Plays as a Reflection of New Deal Society and Politics" (Ph.D. diss., Kent State University, 1984); Annette T. Rubinstein, "The Radical American Theatre of the Thirties," *Science and Society* 50 (1986): 300–320; E. Quita Craig, *Black Drama of the Federal Theater Era: Beyond the Formal Horizons* (Amherst: University of Massachusetts Press, 1980); Malcolm Goldstein, *The Political Stage: American Drama and Theater of the Great Depression* (New York: Oxford University Press, 1974).

25. "News in the Making at the Parkway Community House, 1944–1945," Horace Cayton Papers.

26. Richard Wright, "The Negro and Parkway Community House" (1941), Horace Cayton Papers, box 12, folder: "Parkway Statement," Vivian Harsh Collection, Carter G. Woodson Regional Branch, Chicago Public Library.

27. "Yes, This Is PCH," box 42, folder 1942, Horace Cayton Papers, Vivian Harsh Collection, Carter G. Woodson Regional Branch, Chicago Public Library; Wright, "The Negro and Parkway Community House," Horace Cayton Richard Wright, "They Are Refugees from a Southern Folk Culture," box 42, folder 1942, Horace Cayton Papers, Vivian Harsh Collection, Carter G. Woodson Regional Branch, Chicago Public Library.

28. Davis, ed., *From Ocean to Ocean*, 188.

29. Helen C. Harris, "The Negro Church on the South Side in Chicago: How It Meets the Problems of the Need for Charity," box 142, folder 5, Ernest Burgess Papers, University of Chicago Special Collections; "Elder Lucy Smith Rallies to the Poor," *Chicago Defender*, 31 December 1938; "Little Lucy" Collier, granddaughter of Elder Lucy Smith, interview with author, Chicago, 2 December 1996. The Colored Methodist Episcopal Church did not become the Christian Methodist Episcopal Church until 1954.

30. Harris, "The Negro Church on the South Side in Chicago, Ernest Burgess Papers.

31. Clark A. Chambers, "Women in the Creation of the Profession of Social Work," *Social Service Review* (March 1986): 1–33; Daniel J. Walkowitz, "The Making of a Feminine Professional Identity: Social Workers in the 1920s," *American Historical Review* 94 (October 1990): 1051–1075; Louise DeKoven Bowen, *The Colored People of Chicago: An Investigation Made for the Juvenile Protective Association* (Chicago: Rogers and Hall, 1913), 21.

32. Harris, "The Negro Church on the South Side of Chicago," Ernest Burgess Papers; Randall K. Burkett, "The Baptist Church in the Years of Crisis: J. C. Austin and Pilgrim Baptist Church, 1926–1950," in Paul Boyer, ed., *African American Christianity* (Berkeley: University of California Press, 1994), 139.

33. U.S. Census (fifteenth), 1930, Newberry Library, Chicago; Anderson, ed., *From Ocean to Ocean, 1920*, 190.

34. Although W. E. B. Du Bois proposed the idea of a National Negro Business League in 1899, it was Washington who formed the organization, infusing it with the notions of practical education and economic selfsufficiency espoused in his "Atlanta Speech" of 1895. The league became immensely popular in Chicago and throughout the country. By 1915 there existed six hundred local leagues, and membership estimates ranged from five thousand to fourty thousand. Throughout the life of the league, it was the "organizational center of Negro conservatism," and its pundits never wavered from the cardinal doctrine of African American self-help, asserting that blacks "must steadily become more interdependent and at the same time more self-respecting and more self-sustaining." See Louis R. Harlan, "Booker T. Washington and the National Negro Business League," in William G. Shade and Roy C. Herrenkohl, eds., *Seven on Black: Reflections on the Negro Experience in America* (Philadelphia: Lippincott, 1969), 73–91; Roscoe C. Simmons, "What Has the Negro Business League Accomplished?" *Colored American* 5 August

1905; William A. Aery, "Business Makes Men, Especially if the Men Are Negroes," *Survey* 35 (September 1915).

35. "A.B.C. Launches Plan to Give Local Pastors a Trip Abroad," *Chicago Defender*, 12 June 1926; "Pastors Speak at Bethesda Day Meeting of Business Folks Club," *Chicago Defender*, 24 October 1925; "A.B.C. Urges Race to Spend Money with Our Own Merchants," *Chicago Defender*, 20 December 1925.

36. Charles S. Johnson, "These Colored United States, Chicago: Mecca of the Migrant Mob," *Messenger* (December 1923): 5; "A.B.C. Launches Plan to Give Local Pastors a Trip Abroad," *Chicago Defender*, 12 June 1926; "The Future of Negro Business," *Messenger* (November 1923): 878; Drake and Cayton, *Black Metropolis*, 428.

37. Drake and Cayton, *Black Metropolis*, 438; Karla F. C. Holloway, *Passed On: African American Mourning Stories* (Durham, N.C.: Duke University Press, 2002), 20–22, 37.

38. The A. A. Rayner Funeral Parlor handled the body of Emmett Till in 1955, bringing international attention to the organization, as well as to Roberts Temple Church of God in Christ, where the funeral was held. Donna Raynor, interview with author, 27 July 1998, Newberry Library, Chicago; *Chicago Defender*, 5 April 1941; 10 September 1955.

39. "Rev. J. C. Austin at the Exposition of Negro Business" (4 April 1938), St. Clair Drake Papers, box 57, Schomburg Center for Research in Black Culture, New York (emphasis in original).

40. "Excerpt from Sermon of Rev. Austin" (10 April 1938), St. Clair Drake Papers, box 57, Schomburg Center for Research in Black Culture, New York.

41. Drake and Cayton, *Black Metropolis*, 438.

42. Ibid., 440.

43. Ibid., 443.

44. Ibid., 453.

45. E. Franklin Frazier, *The Negro Family in Chicago* (Chicago: University of Chicago Press, 1932); *Black Bourgeoisie* (New York: Macmillan, 1957), 129.

46. Frazier, *Black Bourgeoisie*, 132–139; Anthony M. Platt, "Between Scorn and Longing: Frazier's Black Bourgeoisie," in James E. Teele, ed., *E. Franklin Frazier and Black Bourgeoisie* (Columbia: University of Missouri Press, 2002), 71–84; Martin Kilson, "The Black Bourgeoisie Revisited: From E. Franklin Frazier to the Present," *Dissent* 30 (1983): 85–96; Bart Landry, "A Reinterpretation of the Writings of Frazier on the Black Middle Class," *Social Problems* 26 (1978): 211–222; Dale R. Vlasek, "Economics and Intergration: The Economic Thought of E. Franklin Frazier," *American Studies* 20 (1979): 23–40.

47. Kingsley, *The Negro in Chicago*, 4–5; "Good Shepherd Congregational Church," Illinois Writers' Project, box 18, Carter G. Woodson Regional Branch, Chicago Public Library.

48. "Church of God in Christ," Works Progress Administration, Federal Writers' Project Files, box 184, Illinois Historical Library, Springfield.

49. Benjamin E. Mays and Joseph W. Nicholson, *The Negro's Church* (New York: Institute for Social and Religious Research, 1933), 18; Drake and Cayton, *Black Metropolis*, 415.

50. "Carter Temple Boasts Only Complete 'Junior Church,'" *Chicago Defender*, 28 November 1925; "Bishop Carter Widens Field of C.M.E. Church Activities," *Chicago Defender*, 28 November 1925.

51. *Chicago City Directory*, 1923, Harold Washington Branch, Chicago Public Library; *Chicago Defender*, 16 April 1921; *Chicago Defender*, 29 September 1923; *Chicago Defender*, 6 June 1925; *Chicago Defender*, 24 July 1926.

52. Coolidge made this remark at the American Society of Newspaper Editors Convention in Washington, D.C. He is usually quoted as having said, "the business of America is business."

53. Paul A. Carter, *The Decline and Revival of the Social Gospel: Social and Political Liberalism in American Churches, 1920–1940* (New York: Archon, 1971), 94; Sydney Ahlstrom, *A Religious History of the American People* (New York: Image, 1975), 387, 385, 392; Robert T. Handy, "The American Religious Depression, 1925–1935," *Church History* 29 (March 1960): 3–16; William Leach, *Land of Desire: Merchants, Power, and the Rise of a New American Culture* (New York: Vintage, 1994), 217.

54. Ahlstrom, *Religious History*, 383.

55. Bruce Barton, *The Man Nobody Knows: A Discovery of Jesus* (Indianapolis: Bobbs-Merrill, 1925).

56. James A. Nuechterlein, "Bruce Barton and the Business Ethos of the 1920s," *South Atlantic Quarterly* 76 (Summer 1977): 303; Leo P. Ribuffo, "Jesus Christ as Business Statesman: Bruce Barton and the Selling of Corporate Capitalism," *American Quarterly* 33 (Summer 1981): 206–231.

57. Ribuffo, "Jesus Christ as Business Statesman," 220.

58. Ibid., 206; James M. Ferreira, "Only Yesterday and the Two Christs of the Twenties," *South Atlantic Quarterly* 80 (Winter 1981): 80.

59. "More Business in Religion is Church Slogan," *Chicago Defender*, 28 November 1925.

60. Kingsley, *Negro in Chicago*, 3.

CHAPTER 4

1. St. Clair Drake and Horace Cayton, *Black Metropolis: A Study of Negro Life in a Northern City* (reprint, Chicago: University of Chicago Press, 1993), 416.

2. The historiography of black preaching and homiletics is growing, yet there remains much work to be done to assist our understanding of the cultural and social importance of this aspect of the African American religious tradition. Some of the most helpful works include Henry H. Mitchell, *Black Preaching* (New York: J. B. Lippincott, 1970); Jon Michael Spencer, *Sacred Symphony: The Chanted Sermon of the Black Preacher* (New York: Greenwood, 1987); Evans E. Crawford, *The Hum: Call and Response in African American Preaching* (Nashville, Tenn.: Abingdon, 1995); Gerald L. Davis, *I Got the Word in Me and I Can Sing, You Know* (Philadelphia: University of Pennsylvania Press), 1985; *The Sacred Art: Preaching and Theology in the African American Tradition* (Valley Forge, Pa.: Judson, 1995); Frank A. Thomas, *They Like to Never Quit Praising God: The Role of Celebration in Preaching* (Cleveland: United Church Press), 1997; and Cleophus J. LaRue, *The Heart of Black Preaching* (Louisville, Ky.: Westminster John Knox, 2000).

3. William E. Hatcher, *John Jasper: The Unmatched Negro Philosopher and Preacher* (New York: Fleming H. Revell, 1908), 9; Works Progress Administration in Virginia, *The Negro in Virginia* (Winston-Salem, N.C.: John F. Blair, 1994), 276–277;

William E. Montgomery, *Under Their Own Vine and Fig Tree: The African American Church in the South, 1865–1900* (Baton Rouge: Louisiana State University Press, 1993), 309–310.

4. Daniel Wolff, *You Send Me: The Life and Times of Sam Cooke* (New York: William Morrow, 1995), 20; Evelyn Brooks Higginbotham, "Rethinking Vernacular Culture: Black Religion and Race Records in the 1920s and 1930s," in Wahneema Lubiano ed., *The House that Race Built* (New York: Vintage, 1998), 166–167; Michael W. Harris, *The Rise of Gospel Blues: The Music of Thomas Andrew Dorsey in the Urban Church* (New York: Oxford University Press, 1992), 156; Paul Oliver, *Songsters and Saints: Vocal Traditions on Race Records* (New York: Cambridge University Press, 1984), 140.

5. Okeh Records/Document Records. During the 1930s, Gates turned his attention to the economic crisis and produced a number of sermons that addressed it directly: "These Hard Times Are Tight Like That;" "Pray for Better Times to Come;" "President Roosevelt Is Everybody's Friend;" and "No Bread Lines in Heaven" (Document Records, 1930–1934).

6. W. E. B. Du Bois, *The Souls of Black Folk*, (reprint, New York: New American Library, 1903), 211.

7. "Should a Minister be Educated," *Chicago Defender*, 27 January 1917; "The Uneducated Preacher," *Chicago Defender*, 23 August 1924; David Rice Hedgley, "The Attitude of Negro Pastors in Chicago toward Christian Education" (M.A. thesis, University of Chicago, 1935). Evans Edgar Crawford found in his 1957 study that as much as 75 percent of black Baptist ministers in Chicago were without theological training, a percentage which had remained unchanged in 25 years. See Crawford, "The Leadership Role of the Urban Negro Minister" (Ph.D. diss., Boston University, 1957), 82.

8. Fisher, "History of the Olivet Baptist Church of Chicago" (M.A. thesis, University of Chicago, 1922), 58 and 40, respectively.

9. Drake and Cayton, "Bronzeville," *Holiday* (May 1962): 130; *Black Metropolis*, 673.

10. Robert Lee Sutherland, "An Analysis of Negro Churches in Chicago" (Ph.D. diss., University of Chicago, 1930), 126.

11. Fisher, "History of Olivet Baptist," 89; *Chicago Daily News*, 12 July 1929.

12. In 1930 W. E. B. Du Bois commissioned Clarence Darrow to write an article to be published in *Crisis* on "Religion among Negroes" which would be a "straight from the shoulder article criticizing the ideas and antics and ideals of the American Negro." Darrow complied two years later with a piece that asserted the overwhelming religiosity of black Americans. Black religion worked against reason, was overly emotional, and was fundamentally anti-intellectual, he argued. While he understood why the daily struggles of African Americans would lead them to this type of "self hypnotism," it remained the greatest hindrance to their social progress. "Their [African Americans] slow and painful struggle for greater opportunities," he concluded "would be made easier if they were less religious." See W. E. B. Du Bois Papers, reel 33, frame 15, Library of Congress; Clarence Darrow, "Religion and the Negro," W. E. B. Du Bois Papers, reel 35, frames 1264–1266, Library of Congress.

13. Sutherland, "Analysis of Negro Churches," 98.

14. Ibid., 98.

15. *Chicago Defender*, 14 April 1956; *Chicago Defender*, 13 November 1915.

16. Drake and Cayton, *Black Metropolis*, 674.

17. Sutherland, "Analysis of Negro Churches," 94.

18. Drake and Cayton, *Black Metropolis*, 678, 676; Mark 12:13–17 (NIV).

19. Tocqueville, *Democracy in America*, vol. 2, 142; Sutherland, "Analysis of Negro Churches," 126; Drake and Cayton, *Black Metropolis*, 674.

20. Du Bois, *Souls of Black Folk*, 212.

21. Vattel Elbert Daniel, "Ritual in Chicago's South Side Churches for Negroes" (Ph.D. diss., University of Chicago, 1940), 134.

22. *Black Metropolis*, 674; Sutherland, "Analysis of Negro Churches," 126.

23. Sutherland, "Analysis of Negro Churches," 126.

24. Daniel, "Ritual in Chicago's South Side Churches," 131–132.

25. Mellonee V. Burnim, "The Black Gospel Music Tradition: A Complex of Ideology, Aesthetic, and Behavior," in Irene Jackson-Brown, ed., *More than Dancing: Essays on Afro-American Music and Musicians*, (Westport, Conn.: Greenwood, 1985), 149; Mellonee V. Burnim and Portia K. Maultsby, "From Backwoods to City Streets: The Afro-American Musical Journey," in Geneva Gay and Willie L. Baber, eds., *Expressively Black: The Cultural Basis of Ethnic Identity* (New York: Praeger, 1987), 109–136.

26. *Chicago Defender*, 2 February 1919.

27. Fenton Johnson, "Negroes in Illinois (Music)," Works Progress Administration, Federal Writers' Project Files, container A876, Library of Congress; *Chicago Defender*, 18 March 1916.

28. "The Chicago Choral Study Club," Illinois Writers' Project Files, box 50, "Music and Art" file, Vivian Harsh Collection, Carter G. Woodson regional Library, Chicago; Johnson, "Negroes in Illinois (Music)"; "The Negro in Music in Chicago," *InterOcean*, 24 May 1908.

29. E. Deutsch and O. Winkfield, "Music (Chicago South Side)," Works Progress Administration, Federal Writers' Project Files, container A876, Library of Congress; Louise Henry, "A History of Negro Music and Musicians in Chicago," Federal Writers' Project Files, box 201, folder: "Negro Music and Musicians," Illinois Historical Library, Springfield. Ellistine Perkins Holly, "Black Concert Music in Chicago, 1890 to the 1930s," *Black Music Research Journal* 10 (Spring 1990): 146.

30. "Divas and Divans," Illinois Writers' Project Files," box 17, folder: "The Negro in Illinois, Vivian Harsh Collection, Carter G. Woodson Regional Branch, Chicago Public Library.

31. Deutsch and Winkfield, "Music (Chicago South Side)."

32. *Chicago Defender*, 10 May 1910. Thanks to Alexander Rehding for this insight into the use of Wagner's *Rienzi*.

33. Lawrence W. Levine, *Black Culture, Black Consciousness: Afro-American Folk Thought from Slavery to Freedom* (New York: Oxford University Press, 1978), 180.

34. Eileen Southern, *The Music of Black Americans: A History*, 2nd ed. (New York: W.W. Norton, 1983), 449, 451; Gwen Ihnat and John Russick, "That's Good News! Chicago and the Birth of Gospel Music," *Chicago History* 28 (2000): 22–37.

35. Ironically, the song was apparently an adaptation of a Negro spiritual by the same name. Lyrics printed in "A Pamphlet of the Glorious Church of the Air" (1936), Lucy Collier Papers, Vivian Harsh Collection, Carter Woodson Regional Branch, Chicago Public Library. See also Edward Boatner, *The Story of the Spirituals: 30 Spirituals and Their Origins* (Dayton, Ohio: McAfee Music, 1973), 6–11.

36. Irene Viola Jackson, "Afro-American Gospel Music and Its Social Setting with Special Attention to Roberta Martin" (Ph.D. diss., Wesleyan University, 1974); M. J. Rinderer, "The Gospel Music Mothers," *Daughters of Sarah* 17 (1991): 14–18; Cheryl A. Kirk-Duggan, *Justified, Sanctified, and Redeemed: Blessed Expectation in Black Women's Blues and Gospels* (Maryknoll, N.Y.: Orbis, 1997); Horace Boyer, "Roberta Martin," in W. Wiley Hitchcock, ed., *The New Grove Dictionary of American Music*, vol. 4 (London: Macmillan, 1986); Bernice Johnson Reagan, ed., *We'll Understand It Better By and By* (Washington, D.C.: Smithsonian Institution Press, 1992).

37. John Lovell, Jr., "The Social Implications of the Negro Spiritual," *Journal of Negro Education* 8 (October 1939): 634–643; "Reflections on the Origins of the Negro Spiritual," *Negro American Literature Forum* 3 (Autumn 1969): 91–97; LeRoy Moore, Jr., "The Spiritual: Soul of Black Religion," *American Quarterly* 23 (December 1971): 658–676; James H. Cone, *The Spirituals and the Blues* (New York: Orbis, 1992).

38. Norman W. Spaulding, "The History of Black Oriented Radio in Chicago, 1929–1963" (Ph.D. diss., University of Illinois, Champagne-Urbana, 1981), 141; Edward Boatner and Rudolf Schramm, "Freedom Suite: Rise and Shine" (Hammond Music, 1966); Michael Harris, *Rise of Gospel Blues: The Music of Thomas Andrew Dorsey in the Urban Church* (New York: Oxford University Press, 1992), 198, 158.

39. Burnim, "Black Gospel Music Tradition," 150; Levine, *Black Culture, Black Consciousness*, 183; Harris, *Gospel Blues*, 201.

40. Spaulding, "History of Black Oriented Radio," 2; Steven Kaplan, "Gospel Man: Thomas Dorsey," *Horizon* 25 (1982): 16–19; Timothy Michael Kalil, "The Role of the Great Migration of African Americans in Chicago in the Development of Traditional Black Gospel Piano by Thomas A. Dorsey, circa 1930" (Ph.D. diss., Kent State University, 1993).

41. Harris, *Gospel Blues*, 209.

42. Remarking about the significance of Austin's encounter with Dorsey and black Gospel, Michael Harris wrote, "Only an old-line preacher and church of the stature of Austin and Pilgrim could have imparted respect to gospel blues' notoriety. From this perspective, the February 1932 meeting between Dorsey and Austin marked a turning point in the emergence of gospel blues in old-line churches." See Harris, *Gospel Blues*, 200.

43. Austin's statement further claimed, "we have here now, hundreds who are suffering intensely, many of whom have money but cannot get accommodations. The good ones from the South are being made to suffer with the bad because of many unreasonable things committed by the thoughtless. I know this will eventually work against all of us in the North, thus I am sparing no time in trying to meet the issue." "Attitude Northern Negroes—1916," Carter G. Woodson Collection, Library of Congress.

44. Harris, *Gospel Blues*, 196.

45. Ibid., 196.

46. "Echoes of Glory," *Chicago Tribune*, 29 March 1998; Randall K. Burkett, "The Baptist Church in the Years of Crisis: J. C. Austin and Pilgrim Baptist Church, 1926–1950," in Paul Boyer, ed., *African American Christianity* (Berkeley: University of California Press, 1994), 134–158.

47. Jerma Jackson, "Testifying at the Cross: Thomas Andrew Dorsey, Sister Rosetta Tharpe, and the Politics of African American Sacred and Secular Music" (Ph.D. diss., Rutgers University, 1995).

48. "Interview with Mrs. Leola (Ware) Hartwell" (8 February 1938), St. Clair Drake Papers, box 57, Schomburg Center for Research in Black Culture, New York.

49. Harris, *Gospel Blues*, 201.

50. "Sunlight Church of the Sabbath," St. Clair Drake Papers, box 57, Schomburg Center for Research in Black Culture, New York.

51. Harris, *Gospel Blues*, 198–199, (emphasis in original).

52. Ibid., 201, 198, and 197, respectively.

53. Boatner wrote more than two hundred spirituals in his lifetime. He also produced musicals, plays, and at least one novel. Ironically, his son, Sonny Stitt (Edward H. Boatner, Jr.) went on to become a jazz great who played the tenor and baritone sax. See "Biography," Edward H. Boatner Papers, Schomburg Center for Research in African American Culture, New York.

54. Harris, *Gospel Blues*, 201.

55. Farah Jasmine Griffin, *Who Set You Flowin'? The African American Migration Narrative* (New York: Oxford University Press, 1995), 61.

56. Roger Randolph House III, "'Keys to the Highway': William 'Big Bill' Broonzy and the Chicago Blues in the Era of the Great Migration" (Ph.D. diss., Boston University, 1999).

57. Cheryl J. Sanders, *Saints in Exile: The Holiness-Pentecostal Experience in African American Religion and Culture* (New York: Oxford University Press, 1996); Cheryl Townsend Gilkes, *If It Wasn't for the Women: Black Women's Experience and Womanist Culture in Church and Community* (Maryknoll, N.Y.: Orbis, 2001), 78; Zora Neale Hurston, *The Sanctified Church* (Berkeley, Calif.: Turtle, 1981).

58. *Guitar Evangelists, 1928–1951*, Document Records, DOCD-5101, 1992; *Gospel Classics—Vol. 2*, Document Records, DOCD-5313, 1994; Paul Oliver, *Songsters and Saints: Vocal Traditions on Race Records* (New York: Cambridge University Press, 1984), 93–94.

59. *Gospel Classics—Vol. 2*, Document Records.

60. Spaulding, "History of Black Oriented Radio," 1.

61. Brenda Dervin and Bradley S. Greenberg, *Use of Mass Media by the Urban Poor: Findings of Three Research Projects with an Annotated Bibliography* (New York: Praeger, 1970); Roi Ottley, *The Lonely Warrior: The Life and Times of Robert S. Abbott* (Chicago: H. Regnery, 1955).

62. Spaulding, "History of Black Oriented Radio," 143; Drake and Cayton, *Black Metropolis*, 522.

63. Derek Valillent, "Sounds of Whiteness: Local Radio, Racial Formation, and Public Culture in Chicago, 1921–1935," *American Quarterly* 4 (March 2002): 38–39; William Barlow, *Voice Over: The Making of Black Radio* (Philadelphia: Temple University Press, 1999), 96; "Biographical Sketch of Jack L. Cooper,"

Biographical Files, Chicago Historical Society; "Meet Jack L. Cooper: 'Dynamo of Radio,'" *Chicago Defender*, 5 March 1949.

64. Although, as Lawrence Levine has claimed, a budding sense of folk community developed in America during the 1930s by way of such popular broadcasts as those by Father Coughlin, Huey Long, and FDR, African Americans worried that radio depictions of blacks were restricted to degrading images and exaggerated stereotypes. In 1931, the *Pittsburgh Courier* went so far as to launch a drive to remove *Amos 'N' Andy* from the airwaves. The drive was unsuccessful. See Lawrence W. Levine, "The Folklore of Industrial Society: Popular Culture and Its Audiences," *American Historical Review* 97 (December 1992): 1393; Margaret T. McFadden, "America's Boy Friend Who Can't Get a Date: Gender, Race, and the Cultural Work of the Jack Benny Program, 1932–1946," *Journal of American History* 80 (June 1993): 132; Melvin Patrick Ely, *The Adventures of Amos 'N' Andy: A Social History of an American Phenomenon* (New York: Free Press, 1991), 173–186; J. Fred MacDonald, *Don't Touch That Dial!* (Chicago: Nelson and Hall, 1980), 332–334.

65. Cooper's commitment to the *Search for Missing Persons Program* was reflected in a letter dated 9th February 1941 in which a recent migrant sought Cooper's cooperation in finding her son. Cooper simply replied, "we do not charge for this important service." See Jack L. Cooper Papers, box 1, folder 3, Chicago Historical Society.

66. Spaulding, "History of Black Oriented Radio," 79.

67. "Biographical Sketch of Jack L. Cooper," 1.

68. Higginbotham, "Rethinking Vernacular Culture," 167; "World's Greatest Spiritual!" *Chicago Defender*, 20 June 1925.

69. Spaulding, "History of Black Oriented Radio," 102.

70. "Little Lucy" Collier, interview with author, Chicago 5 November 1996; *Chicago Defender*, 31 December 1938; Robert Lucas, "All Nations Pentecostal Church: Divine Healing Service," Illinois Writers' Project, box 182, folder 36, Illinois Historical Library, Springfield.

71. Jack L. Cooper Papers, box 1, folder: "Correspondence of Jack L. Cooper"; box 2, folder: "Program Schedules, Feb. 1956 to Jan. 1958," Chicago Historical Society.

72. Jack L. Cooper Papers, box 1, folder: "Correspondence of Jack L. Cooper."

73. Letters dated 28 December 1949 and 24 January 1949, Jack L. Cooper Papers, box 1, folder 2, Chicago Historical Society.

74. Spaulding, "History of Black Oriented Radio," 102; Barlow, *Voice Over*, 98–103; Tona J. Hangen, *Redeeming the Dial: Radio, Religion, and Popular Culture in America* (Chapel Hill: University of North Carolina Press, 2002), 23–25.

75. Higginbotham, "Rethinking Vernacular Culture," 163.

Chapter 5

1. W. E. B. Du Bois, *The Souls of Black Folk* (reprint, New York: New American Library, 1903), 217.

2. Manning Marable, *Black Leadership* (New York: Columbia University Press, 1998), 59; David Levering Lewis, *W. E. B. Du Bois: Biography of a Race, 1868–1919*

(New York: Henry Holt, 1993), 65–66; "The Negro Church," *Crisis*, May 1912.

3. U.S. Bureau of the Census, *Religious Bodies: 1906* (Washington, D.C.: Government Printing Office, 1910); C. Eric Lincoln and Lawrence H. Mamiya, *The Black Church in the African American Experience* (Durham, N.C.: Duke University Press, 1990), 53; James T. Campbell, *Songs of Zion: The African Methodist Episcopal Church in the United States and South Africa* (Chapel Hill: University of North Carolina Press, 1998), 32. Other AME institutions include Morris Brown (1881), Atlanta, Georgia; Allen (1870), Columbia, South Carolina; Paul Quinn (1881), Waco, Texas; Shorter Junior College (1886), North Little Rock, Arkansas; and Edward Waters (1901), Jacksonville, Florida.

4. "Quinn Chapel," Federal Writers' Project, container A876, Library of Congress; "Quinn Chapel A.M.E. Church, 1847–1967," Archives of Inspired Partnerships, Chicago (document in possession of author).

5. "New Bethel African Methodist Episcopal," Illinois Writers' Project, box 18, Carter G. Woodson Regional Branch, Chicago Public Library; Albert Barnett, "Pioneer House of Worship Faces a Glorious Future," *Chicago Defender*, 14 April 1956; "The Work of the Churches," *Chicago Defender*, 13 November 1915.

6. Milton C. Sernett, "If Not Moses, Then Joshua: African American Methodists and the Great Migration of 1916–1918," 1–2 (unpublished paper in possession of author); Clarence Walker, *A Rock in a Weary Land: The African Methodist Episcopal Church during the Civil War and Reconstruction* (Baton Rouge: Louisiana State University Press, 1982), 51; Wesley J. Gaines, *African Methodism in the South: Or Twenty Five Years of Freedom* (Atlanta Franklin, 1890), x, 302, 300–301.

7. Sernett, "If Not Moses," 1–2; "Address of the Council of Bishops, A.M.E. Church," *Christian Recorder*, 16 August 1917; "Bishops in Council Urge Action," *Christian Recorder*, 8 March 1917; "Report of the Bishop's Council, A.M.E. Church," quoted in Emmett Scott, *Negro Migration during the War* (reprint, New York: Arno, 1969), 145–146; J. W. Ranking, "The Active Missionary Role," *Christian Recorder*, 26 July 1917.

8. Robert Gregg, *Sparks from the Anvil of Oppression: Philadelphia's African Methodists and Southern Migrants, 1890–1940* (Philadelphia: Temple University Press, 1993), 173.

9. Carter G. Woodson, *A Century of Negro Migration* (Washington, D.C.: Associated Press, 1918), 187.

10. Sernett, "If Not Moses," 14, 2; "Bishops in Council Urge Action," *Christian Recorder*, 8 March 1917; "Bishops Council Discuss Negro Migration North," *Southern Christian Advocate*, 1 March 1917.

11. *Christian Recorder*, 3 May 1917; "Advises Migration of Negroes North," *Christian Recorder*, 16 July 1917; Sernett, "If Not Moses," 21; R. R. Downs, "How We Should Deal with Our People Who Are Migrating from the South," *Voice of Missions*, June 1917; R. R. Wright, *The Bishops of the African Methodist Episcopal Church* (Nashville, Tenn.: AME Sunday School Union, 1963), 214; George A. Singleton, *The Romance of African Methodism: A Study of the African Methodist Episcopal Church* (New York: Exposition, 1952), 127.

12. The most concise history of the efforts of black Methodists to unify has been written by Dennis Dickerson. Dickerson recounted the attempts made by black Methodists to attain "organic union" between 1918 and 1932, arguing that

opponents of the efforts feared union would "work against their particular denominational interests and destroy their historical identity." See Dennis Dickerson, "Black Ecumenicism: Efforts to Establish a United Methodist Episcopal Church, 1918–1932," *Church History* 52 (December 1983): 479–491.

13. "A Great Meeting: Impressive Scene—Church Problems Discussed—Issue Address on Migration—Plan for Organic Union—Commissions Appointed—Large Attendance of Official and Visiting Clergymen," *Star of Zion*, 28 February 1918.

14. *Star of Zion*, 19 July 1917; Wright, Jr., *Bishops of the AME*, 147.

15. Winthrop S. Hudson, *Religion in America* (New York: Charles Scribner's Sons, 1965), 292; Martin Marty, *Modern American Religion*, vol. 1, *The Irony of It All, 1893–1919* (Chicago: University of Chicago Press, 1986), 151; S.S. Acquaviva, *The Decline of the Sacred in Industrial Society*, trans. Patricia Lipscomb (New York: Harper and Row, 1979), 136; Josiah Strong, *Our Country* (reprint, Cambridge, Mass.: Harvard University Press, 1963), 171–178.

16. Sernett, "If Not Moses," 3; Levi J. Coppin, "The Thorn in the Flesh . . . What's the Remedy?" *Church Review* 26 (January 1910): 263–266; David W. Wills, "Aspects of Social Thought in the African Methodist Episcopal Church, 1884–1910" (Ph.D. diss., Harvard University, 1975), 233.

17. Sernett, "If Not Moses," 5; Booker T. Washington, "Rural Negro and the South," and James Grossman, *Land of Hope: Chicago, Black Southerners and the Great Migration* (Chicago: University of Chicago Press, 1989), 59; *Star of Zion*, 19 July 1917.

18. Sernett, "If Not Moses," 5; Grossman, *Land of Hope*, 57. On the Country Life Movement, see L. H. Bailey, *The Country Life Movement in the United States* (New York: Macmillan, 1920), and William L. Bowers *The Country Life Movement in America, 1900–1920* (Port Washington, N.Y.: Kennikat, 1924) 15; Benjamin F. Hubert, "The Country Life Movement for Negroes," *Rural America* 7 (May 1929); Mervin Swanson, "The Country Life Movement and the American Churches," *Church History* 46 (September 1977): 358–373, and various essays in Carl C. Taylor, *Rural Life in the United States* (Westport, Conn.: Greenwood Press Publishers; New York: Knopf, 1949).

19. Sernett, "If Not Moses," 5; "Negroes Are Advised to Stay South," *Montgomery Advertiser*, 11 December 1916; "Ministers Try to Help Whites Keep Laborers South," *Chicago Defender*, 19 August 1916; *Charlotte Observer*, 24 October 1916.

20. "Colored Pastors Lament the Spread of Negro Exodus," *Birmingham Herald*, 21 April 1917; Grossman, *Land of Hope*, 94.

21. C. T. Shaffer, "Shall the Negro Leave the South?" *AME Church Concern*, 20 October 1903.

22. *Christian Recorder*, 1 February 1917; Emmett J. Scott, "Additional letters of Negro Migrants of 1916–1918," *Journal of Negro History* 4 (October 1919): 415, 434–437, 440, 444; Shaffer, "Shall the Negro Leave."

23. "A History of Allen Temple," Illinois Writers' Project, folder: "The Negro In Illinois," box 18, Carter G. Woodson Regional Library, Chicago; "20th Century Churches—Interviews," Illinois Writers' Project, folder: "The Negro in Illinois," box 18, Carter G. Woodson Regional Library, Chicago; "Migration Era Churches" and "The History of Coppin AME Church," Illinois Writers' Project,

folder: "The Negro in Illinois," box 18, Carter G. Woodson Regional Library, Chicago; *Chicago Defender*, 1 August 1942; "Coppin AME," Federal Writers' Project, container A125, folder: "Illinois Religion," Library of Congress.

24. Allan Spear, *Black Chicago: The Making of a Negro Ghetto, 1890–1920* (Chicago: University of Chicago Press, 1967), 178; Bishop Levi J. Coppin, *Unwritten History* (Philadelphia: AME Book Concern, 1919), 341–343; St. Clair Drake, "Churches and Voluntary Associations in the Negro Community" (Report of Official Project 456-54-3-386 (3), conducted under the auspices of the Works Progress Administration, Chicago; December 1940), 147.

25. "Methodism's New Bishop," *Chicago Whip*, 24 April 1920.

26. Timuel Black, telephone interview with author, Princeton University, March 18, 2003.

27. Campbell, *Songs of Zion*, 41–43.

28. Vattel Elbert Daniel, "Ritual in Chicago's South Side Churches for Negroes" (Ph.D. diss., University of Chicago, 1940), 134; Campbell, *Songs of Zion*, 39; Sernett, "If Not Moses," 31; Robert S. Gregg, "The Earnest Pastor's Heated Term: Robert J. Williams at 'Mother' Bethel, 1916–1920," *Pennsylvania Magazine of History and Biography* 113 (1989): 67–88; Gregg, "Sparts from the Anvil," 176–180.

29. St. Clair Drake and Horace Cayton, *Black Metropolis : A Study of Negro Life in a Northern City* (New York: Harcourt, Brace, 1945), 673–675.

30. Federal Writers' Project, container A125, folder "Illinois Religion," Library of Congress; Spear, *Black Chicago*, 178.

31. "Institutional African Methodist Church," Federal Writers' Project, container A125, folder "Illinois Religion," Library of Congress; Reverdy Ransom, *The Pilgrimage of Harriet Ransom's Son* (reprint, Nashville, Tenn.: Sunday School Union, 1949), 88; Spear, *Black Chicago*, 96.

32. Joseph A. Logsdon, "The Rev. Archibald J. Carey and the Negro in Chicago Politics" (M.A. thesis, University of Chicago, 1961), 17–18.

33. Charles R. Branham, "The Transformation of Black Political Leadership in Chicago, 1864–1942 (Ph.D. diss., University of Chicago, 1981)," 180.

34. Ibid., 180; Chicago Commission on Race Relations, *The Negro in Chicago: A Study of Race Relations and a Race Riot* (Chicago: University of Chicago Press, 1922), 147–148; Coppin, *Unwritten History*, 340–341.

35. Logsdon, "Rev. Archibald J. Carey," 62.

36. Logsdon, "Rev. Archibald J. Carey," 17–18.

37. "Dr. Archibald J. Carey," *Half Century Magazine* (September 1919)?; "Is the Methodist Transfer System a Good or a Bad Thing?" *AME Church Review* 23, no. 1 (July 1906): 40; Logsdon, "Rev. Archibald J. Carey," 17.

38. Richard R. Wright, Jr., *Encyclopedia of African Methodism* (Philadelphia: Book Concern of the AME, 1947), 310–311; June O. Patton, "'And the Truth Shall Make You Free': Richard Robert Wright, Sr., Black Intellectual and Iconoclast, 1877–1897," *Journal of Negro History* 81 (Winter-Autumn, 1996): 17–30; Elizabeth Ross Haynes, *The Black Boy of Atlanta* (Boston: House of Edinboro, 1952); Reverdy Ransom, "AME Churches Tell of Conditions," *Christian Recorder*, 14 December 1916; Richard R. Wright, Jr., "The Industrial Condition of the Negro in Chicago" (B.D. thesis, University of Chicago, 1901), 11.

39. "Trinity Mission," Illinois Writers' Project, folder: "Negro in Illinois," box 18, Carter G. Woodson Regional Library, Chicago; Wright, *Bishops of the AME*, 303; R. R. Wright, Jr., "The Migration of Negroes to the North," *Annals of the American Academy of Political and Social Science* 27 (May 1906): 108.

40. Wright, "The Migration of Negroes," 97; R. R. Wright, Jr., "Social Work and Social Science," *Charities* 30 (November 1907): 88; R. R. Wright, Jr. "Negro in Times of Industrial Unrest," *Charities* 15 (October 7, 1905): 69–73; R. R. Wright, Jr., "Industrial Condition," 23; Sernett, "If Not Moses," 14.

41. Sernett, "If Not Moses," 8; "Should the Negroes Come North?" *Christian Recorder*, 31 August 1916; *Christian Recorder*, 9 November 1916.

42. Reverdy Ransom, "AME Churches Tell of Conditions," *Christian Recorder*, 14 December 1916.

43. J. W. Rankin, "The Active Missionary Role," *Christian Recorder*, 26 July 1917. See also Milton C. Sernett, *Bound for The Promised Land: African American Religion and the Great Migration* (Durham, N.C.: Duke University Press, 1998).

44. Sernett, "If Not Moses," 34–35; U.S. Bureau of the Census, *Religious Bodies: 1926.*

45. "Bethel Church Split . . .: Dr. Cook Severs Connection with A.M.E. Conference," *Chicago Defender*, 9 October 1920; "Rebellion [Splits Bethel Church]: Removal of Dr. Cook Defied," *Chicago Whip*, 9 October 1920.

46. *Chicago Defender*, 9 October 1920; "Metropolitan Community Church," Illinois Writers' Project, box 18, Carter G. Woodson Regional Branch, Chicago Public Library.

47. Stephen Angell, "The Controversy over Women's Ministry in the AME Church during the 1880s: The Case of Sarah Ann Hughes," in Judith Weisenfeld and Richard Newman, eds., *This Far by Faith: Readings in African-American Women's Religious Biography* (New York: Routledge, 1996): 101–103; *Christian Recorder*, June 5, 1884; J. H. A. Johnson, "Female Preachers," *AME Church Review* (October 1884): 102–105.

48. Literature on the Community Church Movement remains slim. Volumes written in the earliest decades of the movement remain the authoritative ones. See Henry E. Jackson, *A Community Church* (New York: Houghton Mifflin, 1919); Albert Clay Zumbrunnen, *The Community Church: A Probable Method of Approach and Bases for Denominational Unity* (Chicago: University of Chicago Press, 1922); John Haynes Holmes, *New Churches for Old* (New York: Dodd Mead, 1922); David R. Piper, *Community Churches: The Community Church Movement* (Chicago: Willet, Clark and Colby, 1928); J. Ralph Shotwell, *Unity without Conformity: The Community Church Movement*, 2nd ed. (Frankfort, Ill.: Community Church Press, 2000).

49. Zumbrunnen, *Community Church*, 1.

50. Martin Marty, *Modern American Religion*, vol. 2, *The Noise of Conflict, 1919–1941* (Chicago: University of Chicago Press, 1986), 15; Piper, *Community Churches*, 27.

51. Piper, *Community Churches*, 47; Zumbrunnen, *Community Church*, 76.

52. Zumbrunnen, *Community Church*, 78; Piper, *Community Churches*, 10.

53. Piper, *Community Churches*, 8.

54. "The Unrest in the Church," *Chicago Defender*, 12 January 1924.

55. "A History of Metropolitan Community Church, 1920–1995," 75th Church Anniversary Bulletin, Inspired Partnerships Archives, Chicago; A. Williams and E. Jennings, "Nineteenth Century Churches Chicago," Illinois Writers' Project, folder: "The Negro in Illinois," box 18, Carter G. Woodson Regional Branch, Chicago Public Library; "Calendar of the *Chicago Defender* News, October 17, 1924," from Frederic H. Robb, *The Negro in Chicago, 1779 to 1927* (Chicago: Washington Intercollegiate Club of Chicago, 1927).

56. "History of Metropolitan Community Church," 75th Church Anniversary Bulletin; *Chicago Defender*, 4 December 1920; "Dedicated a Sanctuary: Services at the New Forty-First Street Presbyterian Church," *Chicago Tribune*, 22 December 1890.

57. *Chicago Defender*, 12 January 1924.

58. "The Metropolitan Community Center: The People's Church," Federal Writers' Project, container A124, folder: "Illinois Religion," Library of Congress; "Metropolitan Community Church," Illinois Writers' Project.

59. "St. Mary's Church," *Chicago Defender*, 31 March 1923; "Dr. J. R. Harvey Organizes the Cosmopolitan Community Center," *Chicago Defender*, 29 September 1923.

60. "History of Metropolitan Community Church," 75th Church Anniversary Bulletin.

61. Zumbrunnen, *Community Church*, 76.

62. "Is the Methodist Transfer System a Good or a Bad Thing?" 39.

63. It is also likely that Lucas was separated from his wife and having some marital difficulties. They lived at separate addresses and she did not appear at the formal inquest held the day after the incident. The *Chicago Defender* sought to interview her about her husband's death. She refused. "War Looms Up in the Methodist Churches Here," *Chicago Whip*, 5 November 1927; "Jumps from Third Floor of Hospital," *Chicago Defender*, 29 May 1926; "Bishop Sees Dr. Lucas as Martyr-Hero," *Chicago Defender*, 5 June 1926; "Pastors Attack Bishop Carey in Lucas Affair," *Chicago Defender*, 12 June 1926.

64. Historian Carol Marks is the first to ever attempt a critique of the photo, suggesting that the manner of their dress was "not typical of the region." She infers by this that the family was relatively well off. However, the family worked as sharecroppers on the Hodges farm and were not likely to be wealthy. The dispute they had with J. Hodges was about money Hodges insisted the family owed him. See Carol Marks, *Farewell—We're Good and Gone: The Great Black Migration* (Bloomington: Indiana University Press, 1989), 5.

65. The ordeal of the Arthur family was a major news story in the summer of 1920. Newspapers all across the nation picked up the story and ran it for several weeks. As executive director of the NAACP, James Weldon Johnson made sure of that. In addition to pressuring newspapers to print the story, Johnson informed black churches and numerous civic organizations about it. Many of these became exasperated with Johnson, who refused to reveal his source, an "eyewitness" to the events of July 6, 1920. It was a local doctor, who urged Johnson to maintain his anonymity less he be harmed by fellow residents. "Running North: A Family History," *Chicago Tribune*, 2 February 1998; NAACP Files, "Sub-file—Lynching, Paris, Tex. July–Oct, 1920," box C369, Library of Congress; *New York Times*, 7 July 1920; *The Shreveport Times*, 7 July 1920; *Texas Statesman*, 8 July 1920; *Texas Freeman*, 4 September 1920; "How Arthur Boys Were Lynched and Three Sisters Raped," *New York Age*, 4 September 1920.

66. *Chicago Defender*, 25 September 1926.

67. *Chicago Defender*, 12 January 1924; *Chicago Defender*, 25 September 1926.

68. *Chicago Defender*, 25 September 1926; U.S. Bureau of the Census, *Census of Religious Bodies*, 1936 (Washington, D.C: Government Printing Office, 1940); Drake and Cayton, *Black Metropolis*, 414; Robert Lee Sutherland, "An Analysis of Negro Churches in Chicago" (Ph.D. diss., University of Chicago, 1930), 15.

69. "Edict by Pastor of Hyde Park Church Starts Row," *Chicago Defender*, 7 February 1925.

70. Drake and Cayton, *Black Metropolis*, 423.

71. "AME Church Needs New Blood," *Chicago Defender*, 7 March 1936; "'African Methodism in Need of a Reformation' Says Conference Leader," *Chicago Defender*, 7 March 1936.

72. Sernett, "If Not Moses," 35.

CHAPTER 6

1. Joanne J. Meyerwitz, *Women Adrift: Independent Wage Earners in Chicago, 1880–1930* (Chicago: University of Chicago Press, 1988), 23.

2. Gwendolyn Brooks, *Maud Martha* (New York: Harper and Row, 1953), 63–64.

3. Richard Wright, *American Hunger* (reprint, New York: Harper and Row, 1977), 3. See also Malin Levon Walther, "Re-Wrighting Native Son: Gwendolyn Brook's Domestic Aesthetic in Maud Martha," *Tulsa Studies in Women's Literature* 13 (Spring 1994): 143–145; You-Me Park and Gayle Wald, "Native Daughter in the Promised Land: Gender, Race, and the Question of Separate Spheres," *American Literature* 70 (September 1998): 623–625.

4. Evelyn Brooks Higginbotham, *Righteous Discontent: The Women's Movement in the Black Baptist Church, 1880–1920* (Cambridge, Mass.: Harvard University Press, 1993); Cheryl Townsend Gilkes, *If It Wasn't for the Women: Black Women's Experience and Womanist Culture in Church and Community* (Maryknoll, N.Y.: Orbis, 2001); Bettye Collier-Thomas, *Daughters of Thunder: Black Women Preachers and Their Sermons, 1850–1979* (San Francisco: Jossey-Bass, 1997); Vashti M. McKenzie, *Not without a Struggle: Leadership Development for African American Women in Ministry* (Cleveland: United Church Publishers, 1996); Teressa Hoover, "Black Women and the Churches: Triple Jeopardy," in Gayraud Wilmore and James Cone, eds., *Black Theology: A Documentary History* (Maryknoll, N.Y.: Orbis, 1979); Nancy J. Fairley, "Men Have the Church, Us Have the Conference: Decreasing Sexist and Assimilationist Policies in the Church," *New York Folklore* 18 (1992): 161–177; Allison Calhoun-Brown, "No Respect of Persons? Religion, Churches and Gender Issues in the African American Community," *Women and Politics* 20 (1999): 27–44; Jualynne E. Dodson, "Power and Surrogate Leadership: Black Women and Organized Religion," *Sage* 5 (1988): 37–42; Delores C. Carpenter, "Black Women in Religious Institutions: A Historical Survey from Slavery to the 1960s," *Journal of Religious Thought* 46, (1989–90): 7–27.

5. "Faith Healer: Chicago's Lucy Smith Claims to Have Cured 200,000 by Spiritual Healing," *Ebony* (January 1950).

6. "Bring the whole tithe into the storehouse, that there may be food in my house. Test me in this says the Lord Almighty, and see if I will not throw open the floodgates

of heaven and pour out so much blessing that you will not have room enough for it," Malachi 3:10 (RSV).

7. Samuel Strong, "Social Types in the Negro Community of Chicago: An Example of the Social Type Method" (Ph.D. diss., University of Chicago, 1940), 206.

8. Herbert M. Smith, "Three Negro Preachers" (M.A. thesis, University of Chicago, 1935), 12; St. Clair Drake and Horace Cayton, *Black Metropolis: A Study of Negro Life in a Northern City* (reprint, New York: Harper and Row, 1962), 643.

9. Samuel Strong, "Social Types," 273.

10. "Return of a Birth" certificate, Washington, D.C., 13 January 1891; Twelfth Census of the United States, 1900, Library of Congress. The midwife who delivered Mary Evans listed her as male. Although the official certificate was never corrected, presumably some accounting had to be made for the mistake at some point during Evans's lifetime. Any transaction in her life requiring this documentation—such as acquiring a passport, for example—would have drawn attention to the discrepancy. The alternative interpretation as to why Evans was listed as male on her birth certificate is more daunting, and outside of further evidence, will be left to speculation.

11. "Cosmopolitan Community Church," Federal Writers' Project Files, container A124, folder: "Illinois Religion," Library of Congress; *Proceedings of the Eighty-Ninth Annual Session of the Indiana Conference of the African Methodist Episcopal Church* (Nashville, TN.: AME Sunday School Union, 1927), 52.

12. Caroll Hibler, "Historical Encyclopedia of Chicago Women Project Entry Assignment: Reverend Mary G. Evans Informant Interview Summary," 7 (interview transcripts in possession of author and used by permission).

13. Strong, "Social Types," 398.

14. Zilpha Elaw maintained, for example, that "no ambition of mine, but the special appointment of God, [has] put me into the ministry, and therefore I had no option in the matter." Jerena Lee, who was given to dreams and visions, declared that she had "distinctly heard" God tell her to "Go Preach the Gospel!" She, too, insisted that examples of women in the Bible supported a woman's right to preach, even black women. "Did not Mary, a woman, preach the Gospel?" she asked. See Catherine A. Brekus, *Strangers and Pilgrims Female Preaching in America, 1740–1845* (Chapel Hill: University of North Carolina Press, 1998), 185, 200; Zilpha Elaw, "Memoirs of the Life, Religious Experiences, Ministerial Travels, and Labors of Mrs. Zilpha Elaw," in William L. Andrews, ed., *Sisters of the Spirit: Three Black Women's Autobiographies of the Nineteenth Century* (Bloomington: Indiana University Press, 1986), 82, 136; Jarenq Lee, *Religious Experiences and Journal of Mrs. Jarena Lee: A Preachin Woman* (reprint, Nashville, Tenn.: AMEC Sunday School Union/Legacy Publishers, 1991), 18.

15. Brekus, *Strangers and Pilgrims*, 134; James A. Handy, *Scraps of African Methodist Episcopal History* (Philadelphia: A.M.E. Book Concern, 1901), 345; L. L. Berry, *A Century of Missions of the African Methodist Episcopal Church* (New York: Gutenberg, 1942), 39; Jeane B. Williams, "Loose the Woman, and Let Her Go! Pennsylvania's African American Women Preachers," *Pennsylvania Heritage* 21 (Winter 1996): 5.

16. "God's Saintly Servant," *Now!* 6 January 1962.

17. Hibler, "Historical Encyclopedia Assignment," 16, 24.

18. "Muscular Christianity" was the religious aspect of a broader cultural movement known as the "cult of masculinity," which lasted into the late 1920s. The

first religious organization to express the masculinist claims of this movement was the Men in Religion Forward Movement, with the motto, "More men for religion, more religion for men." Gail Bederman, "The Women Have Had Charge of the Church Work Long Enough: The Men and Religion Forward Movement of 1911–1912 and the Masculinization of Middle-Class Protestantism," *American Quarterly* 41 (1989): 432–465; Michael S. Kimmel, "The Contemporary 'Crisis' of Masculinity in Historical Perspective," in Harry Brod, ed., *The Making of Masculinities: The New Men's Studies* (Boston: Allen and Unwin, 1987), 121–154; Joe L. Dubbert, "Progressivism and the Masculinity Crisis," in Elizabeth H. Pleck and Joseph H. Pleck, *The American Man* (Englewood Cliffs, N.J.: Prentice Hall, 1980), 303–320; Donald E. Hall, ed., *Muscular Christianity: Embodying the Victorian Age* (New York: Cambridge University Press, 1994).

19. "God's Saintly Servant," *Now!* 6 January 1962.

20. Strong, "Social Types," 206–207; "Sunday Service," Federal Writers' Project files, box 185, Illinois State Historical Library, Springfield.

21. Elaine J. Lawless, "Writing the Body in the Pulpit: Female-Sexed Texts," *Journal of American Folklore*, 107 (Winter 1994), 56.

22. "Mrs. Williams (Pastor of the Royal Prayer Band)," Federal Writers' Project Records, box 185, folder: "All Nations Assembly," Illinois State Historical Library, Springfield.

23. The equation of women with flesh and men with spirit has been a theological construct since the middle ages. Caroline Walker Bynam has written that "women theologians in the later Middle Ages saw woman as the symbol of humanity, where humanity was understood as physicality." See Carolyn Walker Bynam, "'And Woman His Humanity': Female Imagery in the Religious Writing of the Later Middle Ages," in Carolyn Walker Bynam, Steven Harrell, and Paula Richman, eds., *Gender and Religion: On the Complexity of Symbols* (Boston: Beacon, 1986).

24. Brekus, *Strangers and Pilgrims*, 80–97.

25. Caroll A. Hibler, "Evans, Mary Green," in Rima Lunin Schultz and Adele Hast, *Women Building Chicago 1790–1990: A Biographical Dictionary* (Bloomington: Indiana University Press, 2001), 250–251; Fifteenth Census of the United States: 1930, Newberry Library, Chicago; Caroll Hibler, "Historical Encyclopedia Assignment," 2, 14; Carol Hibler, interview by author, Harry S. Truman College, Chicago, IL., December 1996.

26. Alice Walker, *In Search of Our Mother's Garden: Womanist Prose* (New York: Harcourt Brace and Jovanovich, 1983), xi.

27. Carol Smith-Rosenberg, "The Female World of Love and Ritual: Relations between Women in Nineteenth Century America," *Signs* 1 (1975): 1–30; John Demilio and Estelle B. Freedman, *Intimate Matters: A History of Sexuality in America* (New York: Harper and Row, 1988), 192.

28. Jean McMahon Humez, ed., *Gifts of Power: The Writings of Rebecca Jackson, Black Visionary, Shaker Eldress* (University of Massachusetts Press, 1981), 9, 17.

29. Caroll Hibler, "Historical Encyclopedia Assignment," 10; "In Testimony of the Faith of the Reverend Mary G. Evans, D.D.," Marjorie Stewart Joyner Papers, Vivian G. Harsh Collection, Carter G. Woodson Regional Branch, Chicago Public Library; "Cosmopolitan Community Church," Federal Writers' Project Files, container A125, folder: "Illinois Religion," Library of Congress.

30. I realize that for historians the use of photographs raises some interesting epistemological questions, or as Nell Irvin Painter would say, questions regarding "ways of knowing and being known." But in light of the fact that Evans left relatively few written records of her ministry and none (that I've discovered) of her personal life, I think these photos are a viable means by which to understand her. They are a "text" of her life in the way that the abundance of church records that she did leave are as well. See Nell Irvin Painter, "Representing Truth: Sojourner Truth's Knowing and Becoming Known," *Journal of American History* 81 (September 1994): 461–492.

31. "Church 'Amens' Stop; Too Much Truth Is Told: Bobbed Haired Evangelist Rips into the Hypocrisy of So-called Christians," *Chicago Defender*, 2 December 1922.

32. "All Nations Pentecostal Church," Federal Writers' Project Files, box 182, folder 36, Illinois State Historical Library, Springfield.

33. Drake and Cayton, *Black Metropolis*, 645.

34. Strong, "Social Types," 394.

35. The 1920 census has William Smith living in the same residence with his wife at the time. They had a son Henry who was born in Illinois in 1912, two years after Lucy Smith came to the city. Her husband, then, would have followed her to Chicago within a year or so. U.S. Census, vol. 23, E.D. 96, sheet 7, line 23, Newberry Library, Chicago.

36. William Smith obituary (1938), Lucy Smith Collier Papers, Vivian Harsh Collection, Carter G. Woodson Regional Branch, Chicago Public Library; Strong, "Social Types," 396.

37. This aspect of Pentecostalism has shown to be especially pronounced in international contexts. See Cecelia Loreto Mariz and Maria Das Dores Campos Machado, "Pentecostalism and Women in Brazil," in Edward L. Cleary and Hannah W. West-Cambino, eds., *Power, Politics, and Pentecostalism in Latin America* (Boulder, Colo.: Westview, 1997).

38. Smith, "Three Negro Preachers," 11; Fifteenth Census of the United States, 1930, Newberry Library, Chicago.

39. Brekus, *Strangers and Pilgrims*, 272. See also Elaw, "Memoirs."

40. James T. Campbell, *Songs of Zion: The African Methodist Episcopal Church in the United States and South Africa* (Chapel Hill: University of North Carolina Press, 1998), 45; Brekus, *Strangers and Pilgrims*, 179; Jarena Lee, *Religious Experiences*, 22, 8, 14.

41. Brekus, *Strangers and Pilgrims*, 259. See also Williams, "Loose the Woman, 4–9.

42. The phrase "sisters of the spirit" is from William L. Andrews.

43. C. Eric Lincoln and Lawrence Mamiya, *The Black Church in the African American Experience* (Durham, N.C.: Duke University Press, 1990), 287–288.

44. Miles Mark Fisher, "Organized Religion and the Cults," *Crisis* 44 (January 1937), 10; Lincoln and Mamiya, *Black Church in African American Experience*, 307.

45. See *Latter Rain Evangel* (October 1908), 3; *Latter Rain Evangel* (August 1913), 2; Rosemary Gooden, ed., *Faith Cures and Answers to Prayer: Mrs. Edward Mix* (Syracuse, N.Y.: Syracuse University Press, 2001).

46. The term "Latter Rain" has long been used as an alternative way to describe the early Pentecostal movement. Early Pentecostals interpreted the outpouring of

the Holy Spirit at Azusa as the promised "latter rain" in Joel 2:23. It is not to be confused with the Latter Rain Movement of the late 1940s centered on the faith healing ministry of William Branham. W. C. Stevens, *The Latter Rain* (New York: Alliance, 1907); D. Wesley Myland, *The Latter Rain Covenant and Pentecostal Power in Three Early Pentecostal Tracks* (New York: Garland, 1985); Richard Riss, "The New Order of the Latter Rain," *Assemblies of God Heritage* 7 (Fall 1987); "The Latter Rain Movement of 1948," *Pneuma* 4 (Spring 1982).

47. "General Principles of the All Nations Pentecostal Church," Lucy Smith Collier Papers, Vivian Harsh Collection, Carter G. Woodson Regional Branch, Chicago Public Library.

48. The two principal All Nations Pentecostal churches in Nebraska and Alabama were also under the leadership of women, Elder Jessie Cayson and Sister Green-field, respectively. "General Principles"; *Chicago Defender*, 22 August 1936; "Little Lucy" Smith Collier, interview with author, Chicago, 30 October 1999.

49. Brekus, *Strangers and Pilgrims*, 295–296; David W. Wills, "Womanhood and Domesticity in the AME Tradition: The Influence of Daniel Payne," in David W. Wills and Richard Newman, eds., *Black Apostles at Home and Abroad* (Boston: G. K. Hill, 1982), 140–142.

50. *Proceedings of the Eighty-Ninth Annual Session of the Indiana Conference of the African Methodist Episcopal Church* (Nashville, Tenn.: AME Sunday School Union, 1927), 9, 13.

51. I consider Elder Lucy Smith's autobiography to be of dubious origin, not because I do not believe it to be authentic, but because it is not clear that Elder Smith could actually read and write proficiently enough to produce such a work. This being the case, it is not clear who assisted her and for what purpose. One edition of the biography (there are two) appears as an appendix to Samuel Strong's 1940 dissertation and was titled, "From the Farm to the Pulpit." See Strong, "Social Types," 397.

52. "The Biography of Lucy Smith," Lucy Collier Papers, Vivian Harsh Collection, Carter G. Woodson Regional Branch, Chicago Public library.

53. Unfortunately, a book Elder Smith referred to that recorded her charitable distributions has not been found. A sampling from the book, however, was recorded in Herbert Smith's "Three Negro Preachers," pages 17 and 18. "Little Lucy" Collier, Granddaughter of Elder Lucy Smith, interview with author, Chicago, 2 December 1996; "General Survey," Federal Writers' Project Files, box 185, Illinois State Historical Library, Springfield; Herbert Smith, "Three Negro Preachers," 19.

54. When asked, Lucy Collier denied that her grandmother would have ever allowed any of her members to play policy, and the words seems to have been edited to a degree by Samuel Strong, but the sentiment expressed seems consistent with philosophies of Elder Lucy Smith. Also, there had always been claims that church members played policy. In fact, one policy station owner insisted in the late 1930s that "every policy station in the city of Chicago would have to close up if it were not supported by church people." Collier interview, 2 December 1996; "All Nations Pentecostal Church," Federal Writers' Project Files, box 182, folder 36, Illinois State Historical Library, Springfield; Drake and Cayton, *Black Metropolis*, 492; Strong, "Social Types," 270.

55. Strong, "Social Types," 270; "General Survey," Federal Writers' Project Files, box 185, Illinois State Historical Library, Springfield.

56. Strong, "Social Types," 5; Caroll Hibler, "Historical Encyclopedia Assignment," 7; *Chicago Defender*, 2 December 1922.

57. "In Testimony of the Faith of Mary G. Evans," pamphlet found in the Marjorie Stewart Joyner papers, dated 4 November 1949, Vivian Harsh Collection, Carter G. Woodson Regional Branch, Chicago Public Library.

58. "Churches District 40," Federal Writers' Project, container A125, folder: "Illinois Religion," Library of Congress; "Cosmopolitan Community Church," Federal Writers' Project, container A125, folder: "Illinois Religion," Library of Congress.

59. Caroll Hibler, "Historical Encyclopedia Assignment," 7.

60. *Proceedings of the Eighty-Ninth Annual Session*, 52; "Annual Report of Cosmopolitan Community Church, January 1st, 1964 through December 31st, 1964," Marjorie Stewart Joyner Papers, Carter G. Woodson Regional Branch, Chicago Public Library; *Chicago Defender*, 31 October 1936; Benjamin E. Mays and Joseph W. Nicholson, *The Negro's Church*, (1933; reprint, New York: Arno, 1969), 18; Drake and Cayton, *Black Metropolis*, 415.

61. Lizabeth Cohen, *Making a New Deal: Industrial Workers in Chicago, 1919–1939* (New York: Cambridge University Press, 1990), 249.

62. "God's Saintly Servant," *Now!* 6 January 1962.

63. Caroll Hibler, "Historical Encyclopedia Assignment, 12, 16, 20; "Officer's Council Cosmopolitan Church, November 6, 1940," Marjorie Stewart Joyner Papers, Carter G. Woodson Regional Branch, Chicago Public Library.

64. *Chicago Defender*, 30 January 1943; "God's Saintly Servant," *Now!* 6 January 1962; "Chicago Churches Active in NAACP Membership Drive," NAACP Papers, box C44, folder: "Chicago, IL., 1942," Library of Congress; Christopher Robert Reed, *The Chicago NAACP and the Rise of Black Professional Leadership, 1910–1966* (Bloomington: Indiana University Press, 1997), 117; "Cosmopolitan Community Church," Federal Writers' Project, container A124, folder: "Illinois Religion," Library of Congress.

65. "God's Saintly Servant," *Now!* 6 January 1962.

66. This is why Lizabeth Cohen's depiction of Cosmopolitan as a "revivalist" church is understandable, but not entirely accurate. See Cohen, *Making a New Deal*, 226.

67. Evans was actually in two serious accidents in her life, the first taking place sometime in the late 1930s and the other in 1941. According the *Chicago Defender*, Mary Evans was pinned in an overturned bus she and Cosmopolitan members were riding in Tennessee on the way to a preaching engagement. Although a crowbar was needed to free her, she was not hurt. See *Chicago Defender*, 30 August 1941; Caroll Hibler, "Historical Encyclopedia Assignment," 2; Strong, "Social Types," 273.

68. Strong, "Social Types," 273.

69. "Pastor Delivers Ash Day Sermon," *Chicago Defender*, 25 February 1950.

70. "Cosmopolitan Community Church," Federal Writers' Project, container A125, folder: "Illinois Religion," Library of Congress.

71. "History of the Cosmopolitan Community Church," document found in the Marjorie Stewart Joyner Papers, Carter G. Woodson Regional Branch, Chicago Public Library.

72. "Ibid., Strong, "Social Types," 273–274; "Cosmopolitan Community Church," Federal Writers' Project.

73. The definitive works on Aimee Semple McPherson are Aimee Semple McPherson, *The Story of My Life* (Waco, Tex.: Word, 1973); Nancy Barr Mavity, *Sister Aimee* (New York: Doubleday, Doran, 1931); Daniel Mark Epstein, *Sister Aimee: The Life of Aimee Semple McPherson* (New York: Harcourt Brace Jovanovich, 1993); and Edith W. Blumhofer, *Aimee Semple McPherson: Everybody's Sister* (Grand Rapids, Mich.: Eeardmans, 1993).

74. "Churches to Hear Actress Now Evangel," *Chicago Defender*, 28 November 1936; Miles Mark Fisher, "Organized Religion and the Cults," 44 *Crisis* (January 1937): 10; *Chicago Defender*, 1 March 1941; 29 November 1941; 25 July 1942.

75. Federal Writers' Project Files, box 187, folder: "Negro Materials," Illinois State Historical Library, Springfield; Strong, "Social Types," 270, 274.

76. Smith, "Three Negro Preachers," 10

77. "Tour—Lucy Smith's Pentecostal Church," Federal Writers' Project Files, box 182, folder 36, Illinois Historical Library, Springfield.

78. "All Nations Pentecostal Church," Federal Writers' Project Files, box 182, folder 36, Illinois State Historical Library, Springfield; "Interview with Elder Lucy Smith," Federal Writers' Project Files, Illinois State Historical Library, Springfield.

79. "All Nations Pentecostal Church Sunday Night Broadcast," Federal Writers' Project Files, box 182, folder 36, Illinois State Historical Library, Springfield; "Interview with Elder Lucy Smith," Federal Writers' Project Files, box 182, folder 36, Illinois State Historical Library, Springfield; Strong, "Social Types," 270.

80. "All Nations Pentecostal Church," Federal Writers' Project Files, box 182, folder 36, Illinois State Historical Library, Springfield; "All Nations Pentecostal Church, Divine Healing," "All Nations Pentecostal Church Healing Service," and "All Nations Pentecostal Church Healing Service," Federal Writers' Project Files, box 182, folder 36, Illinois State Historical Library, Springfield.

81. Strong, "Social Types," 269; Smith, "Three Negro Preachers," 17.

82. The reference is from the Old Testament text: "These I will bring to my holy mountain and give them joy in my house of prayer. Their burnt offerings and sacrifices will be accepted on my alter; for my house will be called a house of prayer for all nations." Isaiah 56:7 (RSV).

83. "Healing Service," Federal Writers' Project Files, box 182, folder 36, Illinois State Historical Library, Springfield; Smith, "Three Negro Preachers," 14, 18; "Divine Healing Service," Federal Writers' Project Files, box 182, folder 36, Illinois State Historical Library, Springfield; "All Nations Pentecostal Church," Federal Writers' Project Files, box 182, folder 36, Illinois State Historical Library, Springfield, Illinois.

84. Smith, "Three Negro Preachers," 11; "General Survey" and "All Nations Pentecostal Church Healing Service," Federal Writers' Project Files, box 182, folder 36, Illinois State Historical Library, Springfield.

85. "All Nations Pentecostal Church Healing Service," Federal Writers' Project Files, box 182, folder 36, Illinois State Historical Library, Springfield.

86. "General Survey," Federal Writer's Project Files, box 185, Illinois State Historical Library, Springfield.

87. "General Survey," Federal Writers' Project Files, box 185, Illinois State Historical Library, Springfield; Allan Spear, *Black Chicago: The Making of a Negro*

Ghetto, 1890–1920 (Chicago: University of Chicago Press, 1967), 176; Strong, "Social Types," 269.

88. "Little Lucy" Smith Collier, interview with author, 26 October 1999; "Interview with Elder Lucy Smith" and "General Survey," Federal Writers' Project Files, box 185, Illinois State Historical Library, Springfield; Smith, "Three Negro Preachers," 11.

89. "Cosmopolitan Community Church," Federal Writers' Project, container A125, folder: "Illinois Religion," Library of Congress.

90. Caroll Hibler, "Historical Encyclopedia Assignment," 25.

91. Smith, "Three Negro Preachers," 19; Fisher, "Organized Religion and the Cults," *Crisis* 44 (January 1937): 9.

92. Spear, *Black Chicago*, 176; Drake and Cayton, *Black Metropolis*, 643.

93. Strong, "Social Types," 206–207.

94. Collier interview, 2 December 1996; *Chicago Defender*, 31 July 1937.

95. *Chicago Defender*, 21 August 1937; 10 June 1939; 25 May 1940.

96. "Little Lucy" Smith Collier concurred. Regarding Chicago area ministers, she insisted, "my grandmother had communication with all of them." Smith, "Three Negro Preachers," 18; Collier interview, 2 December 1996.

97. Norman W. Spaulding, "History of Black Oriented Radio in Chicago, 1926–1963," (Ph.D. diss., University of Illinois, Champaign-Urbana, 1981), 101; Claude Barnett Papers, reel 48/1072, Chicago Historical Society; *Chicago Defender*, 15 June 1935; 21 June 1952; 12 March 1955.

98. Spaulding, "History of Black Oriented Radio," 101; "Famed Chicago Radio Pastor, Elder Lucy Smith, Dies," Claude Barnett Papers, reel 48/1072, Chicago Historical Society.

99. Spaulding, "History of Black Oriented Radio," 43; "Cultural Rise of Negroes in Chicago Shown," *Chicago Daily News*, 22 June 1936; Brenda Dervin and Bradley S. Greenberg, *Use of Mass Media by the Urban Poor* (New York: Preager, 1970).

100. "Elder Lucy Smith Rallies to Poor," *Chicago Defender*, 31 December 1938; Collier interview, 2 December 1996.

101. "General Survey," Federal Writers' Project Files, box 185, Illinois State Historical Library, Springfield; Earl Calloway, interview with author, Chicago Defender Library, 29 October 1998.

102. Claude A. Barnett Papers, reel 48/1072, Chicago Historical Society; Strong, "Social Types," 269; Collier interview, 2 December 1996.

103. "All Nations Pentecostal Church" and "The Langley Avenue All Nations Pentecostal Church," Federal Writers' Project Files, box 182, folder 36, Illinois State Historical Library, Springfield; Smith, "Three Negro Preachers," 15; "Tour—Lucy Smith's Pentecostal Church," Federal Writers' Project Files, box 182, folder 36, Illinois State Historical Library, Springfield; James Weldon Johnson, ed., *The Book of American Negro Poetry* (New York: Harcourt, Brace and Company, 1922), 145; Arna Bontempts, ed., *American Negro Poetry* (New York: Hill and Wang, 1963), 59; Paul Breman, ed., *The Daily Grind/Fenton Johnson* (London: Paul Breman, 1994).

104. Strong, "Social Types," 269.

Conclusion

1. "Chicago's Largest in History," *Chicago Defender*, 28 June 1952; *Chicago Herald American*, 25 June 1952.

2. The fire at his funeral set off a flurry of speculation about Williams's moral character. Many, including Powell, viewed the fire as divine retribution for the murder of Edward D. Pierson. Pierson, who had been auditor of the NBC, had found some discrepancies in NBC records regarding the misappropriation of funds and was on his way to report them to Williams in mid-April 1930. He never made it. His bullet-riddled body was found in the Muscatatuck River in Scottsburg, Indiana, a day after he was killed. Although several NBC officials were indicted for murder, no one was brought to trial. Williams was never able to disassociate himself completely from the incident, and it became a part of his legacy. *New York Age*, 30 November 1940; Claude A. Barnett Papers, box 385, folder 5, Chicago Historical Society; Randall K. Burkett, "The Baptist Church in the Years of Crisis: J. C. Austin and Pilgrim Baptist Church, 1926–1950," in Paul Boyer, ed., *African American Christianity* (Berkeley: University of California Press, 1994), 142; "Baptists Lead Drive to Solve Slaying," *Chicago Defender*, 3 May 1930.

3. *Chicago Herald American*, 25 June 1952.

4. Farah Jasmin Griffin argues that Richard Wright explored the psyche of black southern migrants more than any other writer. Most of his works can be described as treatments of the confrontation of southerners with urban existence. In these narratives, however, black women migrants in particular are viewed to be ill-equiped emotionally and psychologically to face city life. According to Wright, as Griffin states, "few of them acquire the necessary critical consciousness to resist the negative effects of urbanization." See Farah Jasmin Griffin, *"Who Set You Flowin'?" The African American Migration Narrative* (New York: Oxford University Press, 1995), 69.

5. *Chicago Tribune*, 13 January 1929.

6. Drake and Cayton, *Black Metropolis*, 416.

7. "The Cosmopolitan Community Church," Federal Writers' Project Files, box 187, Illinois Historical Library, Springfield, IL.

8. Sukie de la Croix, telephone interview with author, Princeton University, September 20, 2002, Sukie de la Croix, "Chicago Whispers: A Very Personal Gay and Lesbian History," *Outlines*, 8 December 1999; Pearly Mae, "Black Pearls," *Outlines*, 8 February 1999.

9. E. Patrick Johnson makes a similar argument. He states: "In their attempt to be closer to God and to express their sexuality, black gay men transgressively unite body and soul by moving from the prescribed 'place' of the black church into the ambiguous 'space' of the gay nightclub." Johnson, however, understands the liberation of the body and spirit (of churchgoing homosexuals) to take place not in the church but in the nightclub. It is the "space" of true liberation in a way the church is not. He continues: "Thus the notion of feeling the spirit in the dark engenders a celebration of the black gay body as well as a communion with the Holy Ghost. Precisely because the black gay and Christian body are highlighted in performance, the veil of darkness dividing body from soul in the 'place' of the black church is lifted in the darkened 'space' of the gay nightclub." See E. Patrick Johnson,

"Feeling the Spirit in the Dark: Expanding Notions of the Sacred in the African American Gay Community," in Delroy Constantine-Simms, ed., *The Greatest Taboo: Homosexuality in Black Communities* (Los Angeles: Alyson, 2000), 89.

10. George Chauncey, *Gay New York: Gender, Urban Culture, and the Making of the Gay Male World, 1890–1940* (New York: Basic, 1994).

11. Tim Retzloff, "'Seer or Queer?' Postwar Fascination with Detroit's Prophet Jones," *Gay and Lesbian Quarterly* 8 (2002): 286. For a discussion of homophobia in African American culture, see Constantine-Simms, ed., *Greatest Taboo*.

12. "First Church of Deliverance Spiritualist," Works Progress Administration, Federal Writers' Project Files, container A-124, Library of Congress.

13. Bernice Johnson Reagon, "Kenneth Morris: I'll Be a Servant for the Lord," in Bernice Johnson Reagon, ed., *We'll Understand It Better By and By* (Washington, D.C.: Smithsonian Institution Press, 1992), 329–341.

14. "First Church of Deliverance (Spiritual): Interview with Rev. Cobbs," Federal Writers Project Files, box 187, folder: "First Church of Deliverance [ed. Copy 1]," Illinois Historical Library, Springfield.

15. Laurraine Goreau, *Just Mahalia Baby* (Waco, Tex. Word, 1975), 116–117; Anthony Heilbut, *The Gospel Sound: Good News and Bad Times* (New York: Simon and Schuster, 1971), 96–97.

16. Louis Armstrong was able to persuade Jackson to perform a duet with him in a jazz festival in 1958.

17. Ralph Ellison, *Going to the Territory* (New York: Random House, 1988), 133; St. Clair Drake, "Churches and Voluntary Associations in the Chicago Negro Community," report of Official Project 465-54-3-386, conducted under the auspices of the Works Progress Administration (December 1940), 6–7.

Index

Page references followed by *fig* indicate an illustration or photograph; followed by a *t* indicates a table.

A. A. Rayner Funeral Home, 86
Abbott, Mrs. Robert S., 43
Abbott, Robert S., 7, 21, 37, 85, 187
ABC (Associated Business Club of
   Chicago), 85
Acquaviva, S. S., 124
active construction, 3
Addams, Jane, 74, 192
Adler, Dankmar, 46
African American Catholic churches, 20. *See
   also* black Protestant churches
African American Christianity. *See* black
   religion
African American women pastors: *Chicago
   Defender* on street preaching by, 67; cul-
   ture of opposition to, 154–55; exchange
   between, 177–78; long tradition of,
   153–54; rising number of, 67; role in
   developing new sacred order, 11–12,
   149–50; specter of sex/sexual impropriety
   as subtext to, 161–62; strategies to deflect
   attention away from their gender by,
   155–56. *See also* Evans, Rev. Mary G.;
   female sacred order; new sacred order;
   Smith, Elder Lucy
African Methodist Episcopal Church. *See*
   AME (African Methodist Episcopal
   Church)
agency, 3, 186–87
Ahlstrom, Sydney, 13
"Ain't That Good News" (Collier), 102–3
Alexander, Rev. F. A., 67
Ali, Noble Drew, 20
Allen, Richard, 118, 119, 128
All Nations Pentecostal Church: charitable
   distribution program of, 61; demonstrative worship services of, 152, 173; epi-
   logue on, 192; faith healing practice of,
   169–70, 171–73, 183; female sacred order
   of, 11, 12; financial debt of, 167; founding
   of, 163, 164; "The Glorious Church of
   the Air" (Smith broadcast) as showcase

for, 11, 61, 115, 117, 150, 151, 178–79,
   181; gospel music used during services of,
   179; interracial worship practiced of, 174;
   membership of, 170, 174–75, 180;
   "mother church" role of, 150; South Side
   map showing, 42*fig*; "trophy room" of,
   171, 172*fig*. *See also* Pentecostal churches
All Negro Hour (Cooper radio show), 113
AME (African Methodist Episcopal
   Church): adaptation of worship styles to
   attract southern migrants, 129–30; addressing material conditions of black
   Chicagoans, 130–31; anxiety regarding
   urbanization/migration by, 124–27;
   Bethel AME Church, 98, 101, 102, 129,
   134–35, 138, 192; centralized structure
   of, 119–20; challenges of northern migration faced by, 120–24; circular on
   "migrating people" sent out by, 121–22;
   Community Church Movement rebellion
   against, 11, 128, 135–38; concerns regarding ill treatment of southern migrants by, 122–23; continued ambivalence
   toward migration by, 133–34; failure to
   respond to needs of black southern migrants by, 184; female pastors of, 163–66;
   full ordination of women instituted
   (1948) by, 154; Hyde Park AME, 144–46;
   Institutional African Methodist Episcopal
   (AME), 74, 130–31, 132; laity reform organization and petition to, 142–44; large
   membership of, 44; people claiming
   membership (1938) to, 144–45*t*; process
   of ecclesiastical decentralization among
   Chicago's, 120–21; Quinn Chapel AME,
   36, 44, 57, 102, 119, 129–30, 140, 192;
   seven churches in Chicago domination,
   119; slow growth in northern, 127–28;
   Trinity Mission of, 128, 132. *See also*
   Methodist churches
AME General Conference (St. Louis,
   1920), 134

CPSIA information can be obtained
at www.ICGtesting.com
Printed in the USA
BVOW02s0011070117

472900BV00002B/56/P